An Environmental
Proposal for Ethics

Studies in Social and Political Philosophy

General Editor: James P. Sterba, University of Notre Dame

An Environmental Proposal for Ethics

The Principle of Integrity

Laura Westra

Rowman & Littlefield Publishers, Inc.

ROWMAN & LITTLEFIELD PUBLISHERS, INC.

Published in the United States of America
by Rowman & Littlefield Publishers, Inc.
4720 Boston Way, Lanham, Maryland 20706

3 Henrietta Street, London WC2E 8LU England

British Cataloging in Publication Information Available

Library of Congress Cataloging-in-Publication Data

Westra, Laura.
An environmental proposal for ethics : the principle
of integrity / Laura Westra.
p.   cm. — (Studies in social & political philosophy)
Includes index.
1. Environmental ethics.   2. Ecological integrity.
I. Title.   II. Series.
GE42.W48   1994
179'.1—dc20   93–45335 CIP

ISBN 0–8476–7894–6 (cloth : alk. paper)
ISBN 0–8476–7895–4 (pbk. : alk. paper)

Printed in the United States of America

 TM The paper used in this publication meets the minimum requirements of
American National Standard for Information Sciences—Permanence of
Paper for Printed Library Materials, ANSI Z39.48–1984.

For Henry Regier

Contents

Foreword

by Holmes Rolston III

In perhaps the most seminal insight launching environmental ethics in the twentieth century, Aldo Leopold concludes his "Land Ethic" exclaiming, "A thing is right when it tends to preserve the integrity, stability, and beauty of the biotic community. It is wrong when it tends otherwise."[1] Those memorable words remarkably blend facts and values, biology and ethics, because whether or not an ecosystem is stable and integrated is, first, a matter of descriptive fact, if also, secondly, a matter of evaluation and prescription. We do not wish our communities to be disintegrated, unstable, or ugly.

Leopold's hope for integrity has, in ensuing years, even become the law of the land, with legislation sometimes employing that very phrase, sometimes using related concepts such as environmental quality, land health, and resource sustainability, not only in the United States but in Canada and elsewhere. In this perspective the National Forest Management Act, the Wilderness Acts, national parks legislation, and legislation about clean water and air, old-growth forests, acid rain, pesticide and herbicide pollution, overuse of fertilizers, loss of wetlands, soil conservation, fire policy, ecosystem management—all these, if we put them under one umbrella idea, are about the integrity of the environment.

But what is integrity? Can we be more precise about both the descriptive and the evaluative components of the term? Nor is integrity simply a biological term; in fact the term has as its primary context descriptions and evaluations of human character, and, by extension, judgments about human societies, institutions, and cultures. Like health, integrity conveys the idea of wholeness and of unbroken functioning. Integrity further has a moral dimension: there is dignity and personal

---

1. Aldo Leopold, *A Sand County Almanac* (New York: Oxford University Press, 1949, 1968), 224–25.

worth; we praise those who achieve it. Actually, though we all value integrity and health, both terms are a little strange applied to ecosystems. We say that a friend or a business has integrity; seldom do we say this of rivers, even though, as we learn below, the U.S. Congress has mandated the "biological integrity of the nation's waters."

Perhaps we cannot be rigorous about integrity; the idea is soft, visionary, rhetorical, politically and emotionally correct, but philosophically and biologically suspect because it cannot be made operational. Integrity can mean anything you choose it to mean; it has begun to slip around as soon as we start to think about it. But we use many broadly paradigmatic concepts to conserve values: justice, freedom, love, democracy, rights, tolerance, or privacy. Diversity and complexity, even nature and culture, are slippery words. All these are system-wide words, symbols that orient us—they are open concepts, not subject to calculus, but that does not mean they are sloppy and under no logical control. They give general directions and what we believe about them shapes our present and our future.

Then too, with biological integrity as the governing concept, perhaps we can, at the strategic level, often be more specific. For we can find thresholds—a level of so many parts per million of a toxic substance above which fish cannot any longer live in the river; or a carrying capacity of so many elk on a winter range, beyond which the range will not recover in the following summer. We can identify the introduced, feral, or exotic species that are disrupting the normal ecosystem patterns. We can measure soil loss, erosion rates, sedimentation, endangered species losses and recovery rates, and set ourselves some limits of acceptable change.

Biological integrity will, we hope, characterize natural ecosystems, though that might not always be so. Here Leopold's "stability," in the short range a value world, can become more problematic in longer ranges. Ecosystemic integrity is historical, not something static; it is dynamic and ongoing. From time to time, even natural systems have had their integrities upset (when volcanoes exploded, or tsunamis destroyed them), and integrity then had to re-evolve. Integrity in ecosystems includes the capacity to evolve. Stability, and nothing more, would squelch this creativity. On a big enough scale, ecology meets evolution. Or, perhaps we should say, the evolution going on all the time becomes evident.

Still, we find that natural systems are, on the whole, as evolutionary and ecological theory both teach, places of adapted fit with many species integrated into long persisting relationships, life perpetually sustained and renewed. There is cycling and re-cycling of energy and materials. The member organisms are flourishing as interrelated fits in their niches. The system is spontaneously self-organizing in the fundamental processes of climate, hydrology, speciation, photosynthesis, and trophic pyramids. There is resistance to, and resilience after, perturbation. So we characteristically find that the original system had its integrity, and presume that such integrity, in place or restored, will continue dynamically into the future. But we do not always and everywhere want entirely natural ecosystems, and nothing more. If there is to be any culture at all, especially a modern culture, we want to transform wild nature into rebuilt environments over most of our landscape. After all, Leopold was urging a land ethic for farmers in Wisconsin, as well as urging the preservation of pristine wilderness. A flourishing culture requires revamping much of wild nature. Perhaps now what we value in culture has sometimes to be traded against what we value in nature, that is, biological integrity must be compromised for cultural integrity. However, if this goes too far, then the natural system can become degraded or even collapse; culture depends on agriculture, and ecosystems, and hydrology, and meterology. We still want land health, even when pristine integrity has been compromised in order to support various forms of cultural integrity.

We soon realize that Leopold's vision is seminal but that his aphoristic maxim needs extended treatment. The most important such examination yet to appear is Laura Westra's fine analysis which here lies before the reader. She moves systematically through the significance, and the subtleties, of integrity—its philosophical, legal, biological (both organismic and ecosystemic), cultural, and ethical senses. She presses steadily toward making the principle of integrity operational, both in policy and in personal practice, both in vision of what ought to be and in realistic proposal of what can be.

Earth, from here onward, will become increasingly a managed planet. If humans wish a society with integrity, such management, for the foreseeable future, continues to require integrity and health in ecosystems, keeping them stable in the midst of historical change. Further, if humans wish optimal values conserved on Earth, such management ought to conserve appropriate biological integrity forever. Westra's analysis points us forward for a new century, even a new millennium.

Holmes Rolston III
Department of Philosophy
Colorado State University

Preface

This book is written in support of practical action on behalf of the environment. Books of practical philosophy, such as those directed at ethics in health care, business, the professions, or policy-making, start with implicit or explicit adherence to well-entrenched and accepted moral principles, and then proceed to use these to deal with novel or difficult problems. But I chose a different path.

Proceeding in the opposite direction, this work starts with practical, existing binational legislation, specifically with the Great Lakes Water Quality Agreement (GLWQA) of 1978 (ratified 1988), which introduces a new goal of public policy: the call to "restore integrity" to the Great Lakes Basin Ecosystem. Working "backwards" from there, I raise a question about this policy goal. What does "integrity" mean, in the environmental sense in which it is used? Further, once its meaning is clarified, another question arises: Is there an existing traditional moral doctrine that can support both the ideal it indicates and the obligation that ideal engenders?

The answer to the first question has proved to be extremely difficult. Even now, after several years of grappling with the "concept of integrity," and of intensive interaction with scientists and philosophers, and although I have written over sixty pages about "integrity," the concept still remains elusive. Like other rich ultimate values such as "happiness," "health," "freedom," or "justice," it seems that the more one studies and analyzes it, the more facets the concept exhibits and the more complexity one discovers within it. Yet, unlike "health," "happiness," "freedom," and "justice" valued from time immemorial, the concept of integrity (at least in its environmental connotations) represents a *new* "ultimate" value. Thus the answer to the second question is no. Even if "integrity" can be shown to be a value, it is one which does not rest on only moral doctrine presently used in philosophical discourse.

This indisputable fact has led me to believe (a) that integrity was placed in official legislation *precisely* because it interjected a totally new note in the discourse of environmental concern, rather than being some modification of a presently existing concept; and (b) that "integrity" represents a value important and basic enough to support a new moral principle. Hence, the unusual combination of a new regulatory ideal, undefined and unanalyzed in the literature, and a notion I believed was well worthy of study and attention, gave rise to my determination to use it as foundational in a new moral principle.

If notoriously "centrist," middle-of-the-road policy makers, felt impelled to break new (conceptual) grounds in providing regulations and legislation to address the acute and accumulating environmental threats that face us, then it seemed incumbent upon philosophers to follow suit, that is, to take up the gauntlet and respond to the challenge of an ideal that was new and an obligation presently not supported by existing moral theory. I attempt here to analyze this ideal and to show that it can support an obligation through a new theory. That this was a worthwhile project seemed obvious: not only did it represent an attractive and stimulating goal of research, but also it seemed to suggest a moral obligation in itself. In the face of unprecedented environmental threats of global import, anything that can help to support and defend the goal of restoring "integrity," represents a call to the philosopher to use her expertise in a collaborative, constructive way.

Moreover, if the goal of restoring "integrity" is a worthwhile one, and if it indicates means of stopping the present drive to possible extinction, then those who can (and who care) should indeed work it into a theory that might suggest a new way to be moral today. Hence, this book is meant to be both intensely practical in its ultimate aim and its starting point, supporting the goal of present legislation and showing it represents not only law, but also, quite convincingly, morality. But in its practical aim, which combines analysis with advocacy, it is also intensely theoretical.

Inspired as it is by the work of Aldo Leopold and Arne Naess, the principle of integrity supports holism, and can be broadly classified as a form of deep ecology. But both Leopold and Naess, although highly respected, are not used in mainstream environmental policy, except for the recent adoption of certain aspects of Leopold's thought in Forestry Professional codes. Nor are they widely used in present environmental philosophical debate. Both are judged to be somewhat vague, or not defensible through tight philosophical argument. They represent noble goals, to be sure, but neither is capable of issuing and supporting a universal obligation, based as they are on imperfect science and less than convincing argument.

On the other hand, some of the most important insights in today's environmental debate come precisely from the work of Leopold and Naess, whatever the status of the arguments that support those insights. Hence, the recognition of the importance of "integrity" as a new goal and vision, perhaps the *only* one capable of changing the present downhill slide to a more optimistic scenario, immediately suggested the need for the present work. The lack of respect accorded to holistic and "deep ecology" theories in general, also suggested a specific agenda: a much more carefully argued, less experiential and phenomenological approach had to be chosen. My sympathy for phenomenology only shows itself in the opening sections of Chapter One, in its reworking of Hans Jonas's call to "responsibility." I have also tried to treat responsibility itself in a more analytical mode, inspired by Donald Scherer's *Upstream/Downstream*.

After justifying the whole enterprise by showing "integrity" as capable to heed that "call," Chapter Two focuses directly on the concept of integrity, and views it from a number of perspectives, in order to show its value, and more its possible status as the "ultimate value," as this book proposes. In Chapter Three, the newly established value is used in the formulation of a principle intended to provide an obligation which supersedes those of all other present interhuman moral doctrines. The principle proposes that, just as all individual and group interests need to start with the preservation of their existence, so too all our moral doctrines prescribing appropriate principles for human interaction, should be preceded by a principle aimed at preserving life in general, in and through ecosystems. The possible objection that sometimes human interest in life preservation is not primary, as it is not in the case of the presence of great pain, and indignity in terminal patients requesting euthanasia, is not appropriate within this context, although it clearly represents a factual exception to the general position supported here.

The priority of life-support systems suggests also that the anthropocentric–nonanthropocentric distinction no longer operates at this level. Humans are part of the biota and their life-support system is thus primary; this position appears to be equally acceptable whether or not one's main concern is with humankind. The principle defends and supports only the "strong rights" (to life) of humans in an unequivocal manner; for other human (weaker) rights, the principle can only operate as a limiting condition, rather than suggest further principles and priorities for human interaction. For instance, it is perfectly correct from the moral standpoint, to continue even with the present thrust to more and more individual rights and freedoms, *provided* that the common life-support system is not at stake. If it should be, then the latter retains primacy.

The "principle of integrity" here proposed is already embodied in at least one nation, in the Dutch concept of the existing "superministry." In essence its function is to permit or condemn any business/economic/policy decision from the standpoint of its possible environmental impact, *before* it is even considered from any other point of view. The freedom-loving Dutch people are generally not supportive of tight government regulations or control over citizens' activities. Hence, they envision this as a necessary but temporary measure, until such time as the values implicit in the measure become internalized by individuals, and their society no longer needs regulations and enforcement to follow an obviously prudential and moral rule.

In order to support and facilitate the internalizing and appropriation of such moral rules, a defensible theory should be articulated. Similarly, to use such concepts as "justice," or "liberty," or the "common good" is now part of general, nonphilosophical discourse. But each of these concepts has been analyzed, discussed, and incorporated in moral theories in various ways in the last 2,000 years, thus the concepts *can* be logically defended, whether or not the general public or the politicians who use the terms have clearly in mind the step-by-step arguments deployed in support of the concepts used, or the doctrine that incorporates them. However, while the politician can (and does) speak of the common "good," or of the ideal of "freedom" or human rights, without the need to cite Aristotle, John Stuart Mill, John Rawls, or Immanuel Kant, the philosopher cannot, at least within her own discipline. The moral philosopher, on the other hand, cannot legislate the "good," but must answer both questions coherently: (1) what is the "good" or ultimate value? and (2) why should I do it?

In essence, the imposition of an enforceable regulatory system such as that of the government of the Netherlands or even a regulatory one such as the GLWQA (or, for that matter, the Clean Air Act or the Clean Water Act, both of which use similar language), are clearly paternalistic measures. Their aim is to protect us from harm until we all (including the powerful interest groups that influence public policy at this time) can autonomously and freely protect ourselves. Moral theory, after all, presupposes that rational individuals can be persuaded by reason: thus the present work hopes to provide reasons for autonomous ecological choices.

Both Leopold's and Naess's great foundational work moved very quickly ahead from observations and statement of goals, to practical recommendations. Their recommendations are, on the whole, excellent, fully appropriate as activity recommended and permitted under the principle of integrity. By contrast, in these pages, I spend much time in a careful construction of a theory based upon *the value of integrity*. Part One (Chapters One to Four) starts with the philosophical and practical reasons for undertaking the "project of integrity" (in Chapter One). Chapter Two is entirely devoted to one issue, the examination of integrity as a value, from a number of different standpoints, leading to a summary of all aspects that combine to make it an ultimate value. In Chapter Three, the value of integrity is used as the basis for the principle of integrity (PI), and the proposed new moral imperative. Chapter Four concludes the theory of integrity as it defends the principle against attacks on holistic positions in general, as well as specific objections that can be raised against the principle itself. Both in this chapter and in parts of Chapter Two, the Aristotelian roots of integrity's value are disclosed. Aristotelian thought provides the unifying philosophy supporting integrity, but those who are not familiar with Aristotle, may safely leave the portions dealing with his thought aside, and simply take the argument as it stands, apart from my effort to disclose its historical background.

Part Two moves from theory to practice, as it lays the ground for rendering the principle operational. Chapter Five moves from "principles to policy," as it considers the implications of the principle for human society in general. Chapter Six considers specific consequences of the adoption of the principle for individuals and groups. Part A deals with both individuals and political (group) implications, from the city to the global level; Part B traces the connection between the principle and animal ethics; Part C deals with some particular concerns of human "culture" in the world, mainly agriculture and Third World considerations.

The main concern of this work has been to establish a theoretical position that can be held consistently in support of the laws and regulations that employ the notion in practical applications. The concept is both new and interdisciplinary, hence the theory based upon the concept of integrity has required much philosophical work, and I am extremely grateful to those who have helped me by stringent but constructive critiques of the argument, and provided various objections which I was forced to confront; my thanks primarily to Holmes Rolston III and Kristin Shrader-Frechette for their thorough and painstaking critiques of earlier drafts of the manuscript and their invaluable comments and help. Thanks are also due to John Rist, Mark Sagoff, and Peter Miller.

The analysis of integrity itself in all its aspects, led me to those scientists who have worked with and used the ecosystem approach and integrity, coming to it through their own discipline. I must express my greatest thanks to Henry Regier, Director of the Institute for Environmental Studies, to whom this book is dedicated, for his endless patience and help in turning around a scientific illiterate, surely one of the hardest teaching assignments of his career, and primarily, for being the first to raise the question of "integrity" in my mind, and the first to permit me to pursue it through an ongoing philosophical dialogue with him initiated in 1986. I am also grateful to scientists James Kay, Robert Ulanowicz, Don DeAngelis, Robert O'Neill, David Pimentel, Margaret Mellon, Tom Lacher, Wes Jackson, O. W. Barnett, Larry Stowell, Kira Bowen, Bert de Vries, Brad Marden, Jere A. Brittain, and many others with whom I have interacted through conferences and programs of the American Association for the Advancement of Science (AAAS), the Entomological Society of America, the Society for Conservation Biology, the American Phytopathological Association, and the Society for Environmental Toxicologists and Chemists.

I am particularly grateful to the Social Sciences and Humanities Research Council (Canada), which generously supported the "integrity project" for 1992–93 when the major portion of the scientific research was undertaken, and which is presently supporting the rest of the project through 1995.

No doubt, the heavily interdisciplinary thrust of many parts of the book (primarily Chapter Two), will leave many dissatisfied: the philosopher will feel there is too much practical and theoretical science; the scientists, that there is far too much philosophy. This is to be expected in interdisciplinary work, where one needs to start by understanding each other's language and concerns, before any dialogue can be initiated. In the interest of efficiency and the time constraints, I could not pursue in depth an understanding of each discipline with which I needed to interact: not only did I not have the time, I also lack the appropriate scientific background. So I resorted to the next best plan: I threw myself at the mercy of scientists who donated their time and expertise to point out my mistakes and misunderstandings within my reading of their disciplines, and directed me to appropriate sources to learn more. Without their gracious help (see list above) this work could not have been done.

But I also considered carefully my position. I came to the issue of integrity not only as a philosopher, but also as a concerned citizen, not as a scientific expert. Before I could either endorse or reject the mandates put before me, I needed to understand them, and I fully accepted the responsibility to seek this understanding within my own limitations. However I did not feel it incumbent upon me to acquire degrees in scientific disciplines: the time and concern I brought to the issue were already far in excess of those of the average voter. Hence problems and errors no doubt remain in my scientific understanding of the issues, and for these I apologize. Some of these I outline here as requiring ongoing research, another problem that is normally not present in purely philosophical works. The research and interdisciplinary dialogue here reflect the science and "facts" of 1993 science. Hence many points, including the carefully worked out "definition of integrity" in Chapter Two will need continued fine-tuning, through dialogue with appropriate scientists.

The principle is meant to provide specific practical guidelines for policy, and I have already used it in a number of issues (in professional codes of ethics, agriculture, business), approached from the standpoint of a commitment to integrity. The full range of the principle, however, will only be appreciated when it is "tested." (Don De Angelis promised to keep our definition, to which he contributed, in mind when working on the restoration of the Everglades.) When possible I have discussed practical applications. Some of these tentative applications can be seen in the *Journal of Social Philosophy, Environmental Values,* and *Business Ethics Quarterly,* in all of which I refer at some point to the principle outlined here. On the other hand, parts of Chapter Three and Chapter Six have appeared already, in *Epistemologia* (1989) and *Environmental Ethics* (1989), respectively.

In conclusion, a special word of thanks to Gay Christofides, who helped to remove my "Italian accent" from the manuscript, and to Lucy Brown, Pat Jolie, and Diane Dupuis from the University of Windsor Word Processing Center, whose professional expertise made order out of my typing chaos. Most of all, thanks are due to my husband, Peter, who supported me patiently through the book's lengthy gestation and birth.

Part One

The Theory of Integrity

1

A New Ethic

". . . it's only ours to borrow, let's save some for
tomorrow, keep it and pass it on down. . . ."

(From "Pass It On Down," by
Alabama, Earthday 1990) © 1990
Maypop Music

Introduction

The fate of life on earth depends on our ability to moderate our quest
for power over our environment and the indiscriminate exercise of this
power. The changed circumstances of our life on earth have led to an
urgent need for an altered consciousness. The problem is being increasingly addressed within the scientific community,[1] both as a major societal problem and as an accumulation of separate but interwoven
worries about specifics: global warming, deforestation, soil erosion,
pollution, and toxic waste disposal. It is recognized that many concepts which once carried favorable connotations have now acquired a
sinister meaning: "growth," "newness," "technological discoveries," a
"high standard of living," have all been shown to possess a clear down-
side and to have dangerous connotations. These, and other such expressions of self-satisfied, technologically sophisticated, and acquisitive
modernity, have been indicted as both undesirable and unenlightened.
At the very least, Northern–Western attitudes, values, and lifestyles to
which they belong, have been disclosed to be shallow, in two main
senses: (1) they reflect a poor understanding of the reality of environmental interdependence; and (2) they demonstrate a lack of moral

3

sensitivity and an unrealistic lack of awareness of the developed world's responsibility to others.

Among many philosophical works addressing the true reach of this shallowness, a particularly apt and useful one is Donald Scherer's recent collection of essays, *Upstream/Downstream*.[2] Its main theme is that in some sense we are all "upstream" dwellers; yet we are all also equally "downstream": we both affect and are affected by other people through activities which do not take into consideration that environmental effects are global, and hence transcend spatial and temporal boundaries. A problem arises because of ". . . the ability of technologically driven action to outstrip human powers of foresight, thereby challenging standards of responsibility."[3] This conclusion indicates the need for a moral approach different in kind from present moral doctrines. Scherer lists seven areas within which "traditional human norms often fail in upstream/downstream environments": (1) lack of "reciprocity" or one-way causation; (2) lack of relational symmetry; (3) specialization of roles; (4) the increased importance of thresholds; (5) the emergence of social constraints, required by (a) anonymity, (b) "traditionally" broad conceptions of liberty, and (c) correspondingly narrow definitions of harm, with the added complexity of the international dimensions of all these difficulties; (6) ignorance (primarily of the consequences of activities) at various levels; and (7) difficulty in assigning responsibility. There are, in addition, the interactions among all these.[4]

All Scherer's points are valid, and they illustrate that even within the limitation of an anthropocentric point of view, traditional moral theories are insufficient even to account for our responsibility to others within our own species. Hard as this conclusion is to accept in the context of present day emphasis on a value theory that is largely contractarian and strongly individualistic, it may still not go far enough. In the next chapters, in which "integrity" is analyzed from a number of standpoints, I will argue that it is necessary to move radically beyond traditional moral doctrine by altering the range of our moral constituency to include moral "patients."[5]

The legal and normative goal of "restoring integrity"[6] is as we will see, a holistic one that depends upon an "ecosystem approach" which embraces all parts of the biota, including humans, without setting them apart. This goal demands "upstream/downstream" considerations of the sort that Scherer suggests, but goes beyond them. In the final analysis, if human "good," human "rights and interests,"or even human "justice" are to be the only arbiters of what defines moral action, then human definitions of these terms will retain ultimate power. And even enlightened humans may tend to define the "good" or any of the other "ultimates" in nonsustainable, unecological terms.

At a recent "Pollution Prevention" meeting at Traverse City, Michigan,[7] a number of highly placed officials and industry leaders, including the head of the U.S. Environmental Protection Agency and Canada's Minister of the Environment, clearly showed the difficulty of transcending what amounts to a schizophrenic position. The mandate of binational legislation is to "restore integrity"; in the area of pollution control, it means that "zero discharge" is the goal. However, the officials' interpretation of that goal was "reduction of pollution while improving the economy" and while "fostering development," an obvious impossibility. I am reminded of Carlo Goldoni's famous comedy, *The Servant of Two Masters*: you cannot serve two "primary" goals simultaneously. Only one can be primary, if the term is to mean anything at all, and "development" needs to be specified and qualified for a society already living beyond ecological limits.

Democracy, the emphasis on individual choices, and the reality of uneven power among competing interests, all conspire to ensure that while goals remain purely humanistic, decisions implementing a holistic, ecosystemic goal will not be made. Even the existence of committed grassroots groups, other environmentally concerned movements, institutions, and citizens, is not sufficient to ensure that the present worldview and power structure will be transformed in time to make a difference. It is a formidable task.

Therefore, the recognition of "upstream/downstream" relations has a great impact on current value theory. Morality, makes an important contribution, but is insufficient, in itself, to bring about the required changes quickly enough, though it may represent a contributing factor. Even scientific sources point out where the core problem is: in the moral poverty of the anthropocentric position. The August 16, 1991, issue of *Science* was entirely devoted to "Biodiversity," and contains several important articles, including one by M. E. Soulé. It calls for a changed worldview and changed moral consciousness, concluding that anthropocentrism, is one of the major obstacles to environmentally favorable policies: "Anthropocentrism. Many conservationists argue that current cultural values are antithetical to effective conservation policies, and that a new ethic or a revolutionary change in human consciousness is necessary before significant progress is made."[8]

It is in this spirit that the present work was undertaken. Rather than attempting to formulate yet another "environmental ethic," I will suggest that the "principle of integrity," is an imperative which must be obeyed *before* other human moral considerations are taken into account. Just as life is presupposed before moral choice can be effected by humans, so too, the *basis* for all life is a holistic value, prior to all other values that can be discussed. This principle is proposed as a moral imperative, rather than simply a prudential consideration. However, before such a radical change can be accepted, the argument must be laid out in several steps. First of all, the place of human beings in the global context needs to be examined. A holistic rather than an aggregate goal implies a "good" beyond that of contractarian choices. Secondly, the value of this chosen "good," that is "integrity," must be analyzed from many angles, in order to establish its viability for that role. After all, when defending a "good" such as "happiness" in order to show that it is indeed an ultimate value for humans, little or no argument is necessary. "Integrity" in the ecosystemic sense is, however, not such an obvious candidate for the role of "ultimate good." It is not sufficient to point out the problems which it is meant to resolve, or the desirable consequences that might follow upon its adoption. What is required is a defining analysis, in order to show its strength as an "ultimate value," and hence its capacity to serve as a basis for a binding obligation. These tasks will be addressed in turn.

I will start by addressing the first question, that of a revised understanding of the place of human beings, by appealing to the work of Hans Jonas and his call to "responsibility." His main point, that radically changed circumstances require a radically changed ethic, hints at the further requirement of a different understanding not only *for* humans but also *of* humans, which is my main contention in this section. (Note: Although I will use alternative expressions, in the interest of textual fidelity, I will refer to "man" whenever I am citing or paraphrasing Jonas and others who use that term.)

Jonas argues that the nature of human action has changed and that the prevailing ideology of the age, the "scientific view of nature,"[9] is no longer acceptable for a viable ethic, if it ever was. All previous ethics, he claims, were flawed in regard to our main problem, that of the future. In brief, all previous ethics (a) treated the nonhuman world as ethically neutral and the human *techne* connected with the world in the same vein; (b) were anthropocentric; (c) considered man's essential being as unchanging with the result that the mutual impact of man/techne was not explored; (d) and viewed all "ends" of man as "proximate," both temporally and geographically.[10] Present circumstances demand a changed worldview. Once we realize that when we interact with the nonhuman world we are—at the same time—affecting not only specific human beings but, a fortiori, humanity as such, the claim of ethical neutrality can no longer be sustained. The main change which Jonas perceives is in the import of human power. However, great power need not be condemned as such, I think, unless it is coupled with self-serving, controlling arrogance, the *hubris* of earlier times. The great power of a saint, or of Jesus, for instance, is not in conflict with traditional ethics. Yet as far as we are concerned, up to now there has been, as David Ehrenfeld puts it, an "assumption of omnipotence" which has served as the basis for the "arrogance of Humanism."[11] Ehrenfeld suggests that we need to moderate both our arrogance and our belief that if only we dissect, analyze, and fund one problem enough, the "solution" will be found, and all will be well. In this Ehrenfeld takes a position opposite to that of Jonas, claiming that the very assumption that "we can create a world fit for future generations to live in" is an "odd conceit, considering that we have taken a world which was perfectly fit for humans (often beautiful, though often unpleasant and harsh) and turned it into a world that either by rational or emotional criteria is unfit (opulent for some, stressful, inhuman and lacking peace for nearly all, and offering multiple threats of vast and terrible destruction)."[12] He traces the problem of humanism and its arrogance to Plato's "facts" abstracted and "situation free." When reality is reduced, for the sake of convenience and ease of study, to a model, we obtain an "illusion of power and control which is not substantiated when we return to reality with our 'solution.'"[13] If we find Ehrenfeld's argument convincing, and agree substantially with his plea for the recognition of and reduction of arrogance, must we then abandon Jonas's position as overly optimistic? Is Jonas committed to an unjustified meiorism, even though it is different from that suggested by previous ethics and world views? His optimism is coupled with the suggestion of a new role of "stewardship" for humankind, in which nature is viewed as having diffuse "rights" and intrinsic value, based on the "dignity of ends" it possesses.

Was it the limited reach and scope of previous ethical systems that prevented human beings from reassessing their own nature and that of nature itself? If raised consciousness and an increased awareness of the pressing problems we are now facing can be used to lead us to a new ethic, maybe our uninspiring past performance can be transcended and a better future can be made possible after all. In that case, our main task is to reexamine human beings in their interrelationship with nature, by reassessing the implications of their power and freedom in the context of our new circumstances.

If human actions and roles within the world have undergone a substantial change, then human nature and our understanding of it must have been affected as well. Such sweeping changes as those indicated by Jonas and Ehrenfeld cannot be unilateral, and a metaphysical reassessment of the nature of humankind appears in order: if previous ethics are no longer adequate, there must be aspects of the human "good," *ergon*, or virtue, which also need reassessing.[14] It will be our task to consider these inadequate aspects, specifically those underdeveloped or ignored areas of human nature which the present environmental problems force us to reconsider.

Many environmental philosophers have suggested the necessity for a changed consciousness, while others emphasize the dual role of technology affecting the human environment and the humans that employ it at one and the same time. Martin Heidegger is especially well known for having raised "The Question Concerning Technology." And even in his earlier work, *Being and Time*, Heidegger does not view the "nature of man" as something that is either static or essential. He speaks of Da-sein (being-present), as the better way of understanding humankind. Perhaps Da-sein's existential rhythm could be viewed as primarily possibilities, active choices, limited only by the "thrownness" and the diachronic and synchronic aspects of our historicity. Da-sein as "being-present" is no doubt to be understood differently when the presencing is to a radically changed epoch. J. Kockelmans, too, has emphasized the "strange process of appropriation: man is delivered over to Being and Being is appropriated to the essence of man," as part of the changes brought about by the "Essence of Technicity."[15] The changes of understanding required are based on "meditative thinking," resolutely espoused in place of the prevailing "merely calculative form of thinking." This is no easy task.[16]

Therefore present environmental problems require not only a new ethic, but also a deepened ontological or metaphysical grasp of human beings, *who* they are and *where* they are. Because ecosystemic wholes are "prior to their component species," the atomistic, divisive metaphysical systems of the past are no longer sufficient. J. Baird Callicott, for instance, cites Arne Naess's claim that ecology revives "the metaphysical doctrine of internal relations":[17] if our ability to think rationally and to conceptualize has evolved from our interaction with our *whole* environment, when we allow it to become depleted we risk a corresponding depletion of the mental capacities of human beings, "as lacking a rich and complex natural environment to support—as correspondent, analogue, and stimulus—a rich and complex intelligence. . . ."[18] Holmes Rolston further emphasizes the lack of "clear demarcation" between one's self and the environment, as he meditates on a lake's shore:

The waters of the North Inlet are part of my circulatory system, and the more literally we take this truth the more nearly we understand it. I incarnate the solar energies that flow through the lake. No one is free living. . . . Bios is intrinsically symbiosis.[19]

Thus not only does nature have, as Jonas puts it, a "dignity of ends," but more to the point for the metaphysics required and implied by the new ethic, its ends are also our ends.

A New Understanding of Human Beings

What about the changed, enriched, philosophical understanding of human beings? This new understanding is both physical and metaphysical, an "ought" brought about and prescribed by a clearer, deeper understanding of the "is" that we face and we are. What are the characteristics of human beings in the age of environmental crisis? I will list and discuss five primary aspects, as requirements for the new ethic, then outline some of the secondary aspects that follow from the primary ones.

The *first characteristic* will require a return to a metaphysical, rather than mathematical/scientific mode of thinking, such as the one Jonas and K. Schmitz, for instance, discuss. Jonas further calls for the abandonment of the "two dogmas": "There is no Metaphysical truth" and "No path leads from an Is to an Ought." The first supports the change required by the "first characteristic." "Being" and its scientific description and analysis are not value free as has been assumed and that, therefore, the present emphasis on the "scientific model" as the measure of all things is insufficient and fraught with logical difficulties.[20] It is this scientific model which is the basis for the requirement of an impossible "scientific proof" of metaphysical truths.

Our attempts at understanding the nature of things, when openly undertaken, force us to reach beyond ethics into metaphysics.[21] The mathematical/scientific way of thinking provides a model which is based on an atomistic, materialistic view of the universe and a coherency theory of truth. What is required instead, is the understanding of the self not as primarily individualistic, but as relational in line with the primacy of ecosystemic wholes. On the question of the subject matter of ethics G. E. Moore too, at an earlier time acknowledges that ". . . the grossest errors will be committed in such comparison (i.e., the relative values of various goods) if it is assumed that whenever two things form a whole, the value of that whole is merely the sum of the values of those two things."[22] The metaphysical holism to which we must return can be traced back to Heraclitus and Plotinus among others.

The Greek understanding of the cosmos as one living, breathing organism is not a quaint, archaic notion our enlightened age should forget. Instead it is a source of the understanding of human beings as parts of a living, primary reality.

The *second characteristic* emphasizes the kinship between human beings and other, nonhuman entities, because of shared aspects—two of which—purposiveness and intelligibility, I will discuss. Not only ecosystems and species demand recognition, but also individual entities, because they possess in turn characteristics which we respect and value in ourselves. This leads to the abandonment of speciesism while retaining respect for individuals. It also brings out a possible objection to the first characteristic. This approach helps us transcend the individualistic, divisive thrust of most ethical doctrines, and is in line with the thought of such major environmentalists as Aldo Leopold, for instance, who defines right conduct as that which "tends to preserve the ecological stability, *integrity*, and beauty of biotic communities, and wrong as it tends otherwise," that is as it tends to destroy or disrupt ecological process.[23] On the other hand one may respond that this ethic gives no place to the good of individual organisms, other than when that good contributes to the well-being of the whole.[24] One way out of this dilemma rests precisely on kinship and intrinsic relations. Kinship may be based on "purposiveness": Jonas argues convincingly for the existence of causally powerful "subjective ends" of nonhuman natural entities and defends the existence of both efficient and final ends in nature, by expanding the notion of "purpose," across reality.[25] Yet the "value" or superior status claimed by humans is based on more than "purposes," but most criteria of "value" or "good" are based entirely on human judgments.

An alternative criterion of living the life of one's own species to the best of one's ability is a criterion of "good" that does not single out human beings, unless we define "good" in human terms, thus begging the question.[26] Kinship may also be based on a better understanding of "rationality." "Rationality" of both means and ends, if conceived only in the human context, is unfair when used as a universal standard. If it is understood in both its active and its passive senses it can maintain the connotation of high value it exhibited from Greek times, without implying "human only" limits. The passive sense may be found in the "intelligibility" of all natural entities, singly and as wholes.[27] Aside from being composed of naturally organized wholes and entities, everything in nature is governed by universal laws. These laws may not all be known at this or at any other time, but they appear to be, in principle, knowable, that is, such that they can be grasped by reason. They are in a word, rational, which "accounts for their capacity of disclosure, i.e., intelligibility and truth."[28] This can form the basis for respect: "their 'truth' is a value in itself before it is a value for us."[29]

The *third characteristic* of human beings that needs reemphasizing is man's relation to time. Human beings now need to be future-oriented, whereas no previous, traditional doctrine put such emphasis on time. Emphasis was on unchanging eternal value, so that time appeared to have little importance. Jonas sees the obligation to ensure that "there ought to be through all future time such a world for human habitation" as being grounded in a categorical imperative.[30] This is radically different from the previous ethics of contemporaneity and proximity. For Heidegger also, man's being-in-the-world entailed a futural stance: the quest for a "hero" was not undertaken blindly or carelessly, but rather, carefully and with an understanding of those aspects of tradition which were worth passing on, from the present. He says: "Only an entity which, in its Being is essentially futural so that it is free for its death and can let itself be thrown back upon its factical there, by shattering itself against death. . . ."; moreover, "Repeating is handing down explicitly."[31] Both aspects, that of being "futural," and that of "having been" are necessary components of choosing a possibility worth handing down. Thus both Jonas and Heidegger view the aspect of temporality, as a major requirement grounding the responsibility engendered by the age needs, to be a major, essential characteristic of humankind.

The *fourth characteristic* lies in the essential finitude of human beings. One of the Heidegger passages cited gives a prominent role to *death* as required to establish man's futural stance. Death, understood as the possibility of global and species death, plays a fundamental role in Jonas's "heuristic of fear," the basis for his new "ethic of responsibility." Human beings have always been aware of their limits; for instance, the importance of fame and glory in Greek poetry and tragedy attest to the need of human beings to transcend their own death by "living on," in a favorable light, in the thoughts of their descendants. The "heuristic of fear," on the other hand, does not extol any present individual by extending his "life" through continuing fame, but instead submerges the individuality of present choices, by submitting them to the survival of humankind as such. The individual is deeply aware of the "summum malum," the very real possibility of the complete annihilation of the human race, in comparison with which the significance even of our own demise pales.

The question is, why is this so? Jonas suggests that we find the "summum malum" easier to grasp than the "summum bonum," because "this is the way we are."[32] I see it as a basic instinctive drive to self-preservation not only as individuals, but also as a species, one which we share with all other living things. This point seems to drive us back to the "universal" aspects of past ethics that Jonas casts as the insufficient reference to "static natures." It is insufficient because it is not only ourselves, or some other individual human being that we are driven to preserve, but also, through the species, the very "Idea of Man." It is humankind as such that represents the telos of our responsibility, as it is that which manifests "the true horizon of our futurity"[33] in a reconciliation of universality and temporality as one common goal. We therefore bear an "ontological responsibility" for the idea of man, which is such that it demands "the presence of its embodiment in the world."[34]

Finally, what is the main and final characteristic of the ontological idea of humankind? The *fifth characteristic*, and perhaps the most important, both ethically and metaphysically, is that of Freedom. It is the understanding of both the depth of and the limits of our freedom that gives meaning to the new ethic. We are indeed free to choose, at least initially, whatever path we prefer; whatever action or technology. If our action affects anything else at all, as action subsumed under "moral agency" is apt to do, its consequences can be studied throughout and—within certain limits—perhaps even predicted, but they cannot be decided upon on our own. Our limits, like it or not, are the limits of humankind as a species, one among many in the natural world which we can affect, even destroy, but never change essentially, in its basic laws. Jonas says:

> Granted that we can take our own evolution in hand, it will slip from that hand by the very pulse it has received from it; and here more than anywhere else applies the adage that we are free at the first step, but slaves at the second and all further ones.[35]

The history of philosophy abounds with examples where human beings are perceived as ideally "free," but only within the context of their status as human beings, variously defined.[36] Heidegger too ascribes a cardinal role to "freedom" in his ontology; "Freedom, understood as letting beings be, is the fulfillment and consummation of the essence of truth in the sense of disclosure of beings."[37]

Freedom, as we normally think of it, is related primarily to us, to the subject who wants to be free from impediments and free to pursue his own choices. Heidegger immediately moves the emphasis to the other: I am free when I let others be, thus manifesting care (Sorge), interest, and concern, in order to understand what they truly are and allow them to be just that. I discussed in detail the role of this free-ing, truth-engendering concern elsewhere, also in regard to environ-mental concerns and the right of the future to be.[38] What is important for our purpose is the connection between truth and freedom. As it serves to emphasize the essential aspect of freedom for human beings true freedom reflects the necessity of recognizing the place and role of humans in the Universe from both a physical and a metaphysical standpoint. This grounds our obligation to say, through our actions, an emphatic "yes" to life, thus recognizing explicitly the categorical imperative to foster life. The kind of "freedom" which would destroy all life, and with it the very "idea of man," is not truly "freedom," and our natural concern for self-preservation, both individual and spe-cies-oriented, constitutes clear support for this distinction.

"Care" and "Trust"

If we accept both "care" and "responsibility" for a community ex-tending both in space and time, the role of "Shepherd of Being"[39] appears appropriate. Such a role demands that we accept a position of "trusteeship" vis-à-vis all future life. In general our obligation to pre-serve our heritage is expressed in political and legal documents which reflect custom, religious beliefs, and cultural norms: our natural heri-tage may be viewed in the same light. The new responsibility to our-selves and to future generations can be well served in practice by simply restating the problem and our obligations in the light of an "intergenerational trust."[40]

Edith Brown Weiss, an environmental lawyer, suggests that such a trust can be analyzed in the light of charitable trust law, already ex-isting and accepted in most countries. If this mode of reasoning is adopted, we need no specific people as targets of our goodwill or bearers of rights. Our position is that of beneficiaries vis-à-vis past generations, and fiduciaries in regard to future ones. What could be viewed as the purpose of a "planetary trust?" Weiss suggests three subpurposes: to sustain life-support systems of the planet; to sustain ecological processes and environmental conditions necessary for the survival of the human species; and to sustain a healthy and decent environment. These purposes are "consistent with those permitted un-der domestic charitable law."[41] It is important to understand what is, in general, required of trustees. Let us look at the terminology in-volved: "The 'corpus' or 'res' of a trust refers to the capital or prop-erty held under that trust, as distinguished from the income required therefrom."[42] This definition suggests possible requirements for the administration of the trust, and is particularly apt when natural entities are under consideration: any appropriate and allowable uses must not "diminish the capital."

The responsibility argued for in Part One needs a recognized enriched metaphysical basis if the philosophical dimensions of human beings are to be better understood. The five characteristics suggested in order to move toward this understanding are (1) a return to a metaphysical mode of thinking and an understanding of human beings as part of a valuable whole (see also Chapter Five); (2) an understanding of human beings as individuals belonging to one species among many, all of which, in turn, share certain characteristics, such as purposiveness and intelligibility (see Chapter Six and Chapter Five); (3) the essential temporality of humankind, and its intrinsic relationship to past, present, and future; (4) the essential finitude of human beings, manifested through the impact of the consideration of individual death and—even more—through the "heuristic of fear," which brings into question the survival of the species and the very "Idea of Man"; and finally, (5) freedom, as a value both human and transcendent, method and goal, and as "truth": intrinsically, essentially what a human being ought to be.

What follows from the understanding of human beings in the light of these characteristics, is a stronger basis for the quest for Jonas's new ethic of responsibility, and a better justification of that enterprise. This multifaceted understanding also fosters a further acceptance of an extended sense of community and suggests the necessity for "care" and for a position of trusteeship with regard to future generations. Both primary and secondary characteristics here ascribed to humankind, help us to acknowledge a better metaphysical basis for an ethic for the age, which goes beyond an environmental ethic.

To speak of an "environmental ethic" is to think in terms of applied philosophy, that is, as one of the many practical applications possible of **existing** ethical systems. On the other hand, as Callicott says:

> . . . it may be understood to be an exploration of alternative moral and even metaphysical principles, forced upon philosophy by the magnitude and recalcitrance of these problems.[43]

It is in this spirit that the present work was undertaken, to discover ethical principles which are based on a nonanthropocentric value theory. In such a theory, as we shall see, conservation and preservation coincide, rather than manifesting opposing viewpoints. The explicit task of the "principle of integrity" is to restore harmony, so that we might say with John Seed, "alienation subsides."[44] Perhaps through such a deepened understanding of the nature of humankind, we might be permitted to heed Ehrenfeld's warnings about unjustified and unproven optimism, and yet find some hope in a changed mind-set, as Jonas advocates, through the "principle of integrity" I suggest.

The Role of the Philosopher and Sagoff's Proposal

Against this background, two questions need to be raised: (1) is there anything that a philosopher can contribute to the solution of these problems? And, if the answer is affirmative, (2) does the concept of "integrity" help to develop an understanding of the goals and aims we need to espouse, as well as the best route to their implementation? I propose an affirmative answer to both questions. There is an abundance of literature attesting to the fact that environmental problems are not exclusively, or even primarily, technological or scientific questions, and it will not be necessary to repeat the insights on this topic of such thinkers as Kristin Shrader-Frechette or A. MacIntyre, to mention but two of the most prominent ones.[45] On the other hand, the recent work by Mark Sagoff, *The Economy of the Earth*, needs special mention. While most others argue that the citizen and the ethicist ought to have a place in policy-making when the questions raised affect the public interest, Sagoff adds that a special role is to be played by the economist, a role unlike the dominant one which he normally plays. Beyond the existence of rules of morality and logical consistency, which are often disregarded in Risk/Cost/Benefit Analyses, Sagoff suggests the existence of a "national idea," a vision, one might say, which goes beyond the satisfaction of preferences in the market place, but supports some values the implementation of which is the goal of the government, as the representative of the public.

He argues convincingly that there is a strong difference between individual preferences and desirable social values, and that since the latter cannot be collapsed within the ambit of the former, a tally of preferences as indicated by market trends and results will not necessarily yield desirable policy options.[46] It is noteworthy that these theories are unfolded against a background of problems arising from toxics and radioactive waste buried (but not forgotten) in a disposal site in Lewiston, New York (near the site of the Lake Ontario Ordnance Works).[47] The experience of local citizens, their terror in the face of the mounting number of leukemia cases in children, and their demand for explanations and solutions are all briefly detailed and discussed as Sagoff concludes:

> . . . the residents of Lewiston asked for an explanation, justice and truth, and they were told their wants would be taken care of. They demanded to know the reasons for what was continually happening to them. They were offered a personalized response instead.[48]

When officials offered "estimates" of their willingness to pay for safety," and cost-benefit analyses coupled with talk of "tradeoffs," residents were angry, not impressed, just as they had been when their legitimate anxiety for their lives and those of their children were deemed "irrational."[49]

What was, and always is, at stake in this case and those like it, is the unrecognized difference between consumer and citizen, between market preferences and those values to which economic considerations do not apply.

The function of social policy makers, Sagoff argues, is to conform to what we *are*, the values that represent "our [U.S.] national goals and aspirations." In fact, the government, through the requirements of the Clean Water Act and the Clean Air Act (or of any Environmental Protection Act in Canada) does not suggest or even permit a "rebalancing" of its goals by the criteria of "economic theory"; therefore, the role of administration is *not* to translate value-affirming policies into market values:

> The principal purposes of legislative action are to weigh and affirm social values and to define and enforce the right and duties of the member of the society through representative democracy.[50]

For instance, Sagoff argues that "this is right" or "I believe this because" are not equivalent to "I want this" and "this is what I prefer" as the analyst supposes. Thus, "segregation is a national curse, and if we are willing to pay for it, that does not make it better, but only makes us worse. Similarly the case for or against abortion rights must stand on its merits, it cannot be priced at the margin."[51] In the same manner, environmental values embodying safety and justice for all citizens, are not "negotiable" or amenable to economic calculation. It is for that reason that we must regain a deontological perspective in which the claim that something is true is an objective one, and not to be sought in and through market preferences; like "love" and other deeply meaningful things, environmental values are moral and aesthetic. "These things"—Sagoff says—"have a *dignity* rather than a price."[52] Citizens of the United States (and Canada) have deeply held and cherished values and beliefs. Their demands with regard to ecology provide an "independent obligation (to) government(s) to preserve individuals' share and to protect public safety and health."[53]

Now, if we find Sagoff's argument convincing, we, as philosophers, need to reenter the field of policy-making, perhaps not as Platonic philosopher kings or queens but, at the very least, as part of a team composed of scientists and policy makers. Both conceptual analysis and ethical discussion are within our province and both can only benefit from dialogue cooperation which is interdisciplinary.

The Project of Integrity

Sagoff's analysis strongly defends ethical input into policy-making; in turn I propose that "integrity" can provide a new and better basis of a philosophical defense of environmental obligation. The increasing presence of the concept in legal regulations and mandate, suggests that there is minimally, a corresponding political support for integrity. Its value, even in its undefined and specified state, is and has been sufficiently attractive to different groups, to prompt them to use it to recommend a changed approach to the environment.

Given the difficulties of bringing about a change of beliefs and priorities in an urgent, crisis situation, "integrity" appears a value well worth exploring. But in order to gain from its use and defense, we need first of all to establish its value. Only when that is accomplished, will it be possible to make use of the concept in a principle expressing the obligation of a new moral position. Hence the first portion of this work, analyzing "integrity" from various standpoints, will be primarily exploratory, and the following chapters (Chapter Three and Chapter Four) will be mainly theoretical, presenting the "principle of integrity" (PI) in the former, and possible objections and responses, in the latter.

The remaining chapters will make the principle operational. The principle and its possible individual and social implications will be discussed in Chapter Five, and a discussion of the political implications of its adoption will follow, in Chapter Six. In Chapter Seven, the practical consequences of the adoption of PI will be considered, in relation to our interaction with animals and to nonpristine ecosystems within human "culture."

Notes

1. *Science* 253 (16 August 1991): 709–824, includes an editorial on "Pressing Biodiversity," the theme of the whole issue; articles by M. E. Soulé, T. L. Erwin, H. J. Morowitz, and D. Jablonski; also a long article, "Biodiversity Studies" in "Science and Policy," by P. R. Ehrlich and E. O. Wilson, 758–61.

2. Donald Scherer, ed., *Upstream/Downstream, Issues in Environmental Ethics* (Philadelphia: Temple University Press, 1990).

3. Ibid., "Introduction," 5.

4. Ibid., "Molding of Noms and Environments," 20–22.

5. Donald VandeVeer, *People, Penguins & Plastic Trees* (Belmont: Wadsworth Publishing, 1986).

6. See Chapter 2, section (f), this volume.

7. On September 30, 1991 a meeting of the International Joint Commission took place in Traverse City, Michigan, in conjunction with a conference on "Pollution Prevention" jointly sponsored by the U.S. Environmental Protection Agency (Chicago) and Environment Canada.

8. M. E. Soulé, "Conservation: Tactics for a Constant Crisis," in *Science*, E. 253: 744–49.

9. Hans Jonas, *The Imperative of Responsibility* (Chicago: University of Chicago Press, 1984), 8. As was noted, the scientific community itself is revising its reductionistic stance and is no longer united in one position; for instance, the impact of chaos theory is making itself felt. See Chapter Two, this volume, for a discussion of its relation to "integrity."

10. Ibid., 4.

11. David Ehrenfeld, *The Arrogance of Humanism* (New York: Oxford University Press, 1978), 141–43.

12. Ibid., 143–44.

13. Ibid., 148–51.

14. Kenneth Schmitz, "Metaphysics: Radical, Comprehensive, Determinate Discourse," *Review of Metaphysics* 39 (June 1986): 691.

15. J. Kockelmans, *On the Truth of Being* (Bloomington: Indiana University Press, 1984), 239.

16. Ibid., 243; Schmitz, 677.

17. J. Baird Callicott, "The Metaphysical Implications of Ecology," *Environmental Ethics* 8, no. 4 (Winter 1986): 311–12.

18. Ibid., 312.

19. Holmes Rolston, "Lake Solitude: The Individual Wilderness," *Main Currents of Modern Thought* 31 (1975): 122.

20. These points are discussed in detail in Kristin Shrader-Frechette, *Science Policy, Ethics and Economic Methodology* (Dordrecht, The Netherlands: O. Reidel Publishing, 1985), 32–64; cp. also A. MacIntyre, "Utilitarianism and Cost-Benefit Analysis: An Essay on the Relevance of Moral Philosophy to Bureaucratic Theory" in O. Scherer and T. Attig, eds., *Ethics and the Environment* (Englewood Cliffs, N.J.: Prentice-Hall, 1983), 139–51; see also R.

Rosen, *Life Itself* (New York: Columbia University Press, 1991), especially his discussion of "Hard Science-Soft Science," 2–7; and 34–38, discussion of "Physics."

21. Jonas, 8.

22. G. E. Moore *Principia Ethica* (Cambridge, U.K.: Cambridge University Press, 1971), 36.

23. Aldo Leopold, *A Sand County Almanac and Sketches Here and There* (New York: Oxford University Press, 1949), defends this viewpoint.

24. Paul Taylor, *Respect for Nature* (Princeton, N.J.: Princeton University Press, 1986), 118.

25. Jonas, 51–75; cp. also 75.

26. Taylor, 130–31.

27. K. Schmitz, "Natural Value," *Review of Metaphysics* 28, No. 1 (September 1984): 3–16.

28. Ibid., 15.

29. Ibid.

30. Jonas, 10.

31. Martin Heidegger, *Being and Time*, John MacQuarrie and Edward Robinson, Jr., eds. (New York: Harper and Row, 1962), 437 (para. 336).

32. Jonas, 27.

33. Ibid., 122.

34. Ibid., 43.

35. Ibid., 32.

36. V. Cilento, "Libertà Divina e Discorso Temerario," in *Saggi su Pilotino* U. Mursia and C. Milano, 1973; 97–122.

37. Martin Heidegger, "On the Essence of Truth," in *Basic Writings* (New York: Harper and Row, 1977), 29; cp. Heidegger, *Being and Time*, 227, cp. 235–241.

38. Laura Westra, "Let it Be: Heidegger and Future Generations," *Environmental Ethics* 7 (Winter 1985): 341–50.

39. M. Heidegger, "Letter on Humanism," in *Basic Writings*, 196.

40. Edith Brown Weiss, "The Planetary Trust: Conservation and Intergenerational Equity," *Ecology Law Quarterly* 11, No. 4 (1984): 500; cp. also n. 21.

41. Ibid., citing *Black's Law Dictionary*, 310, 1172, 5th ed., 1979.

42. Ibid., 511; cp. nn. 80, 81, and 83.

43. J. Baird Callicott, "Non-Anthropocentric Value Theory and Environmental Ethics," *American Philosophy Quarterly* 21 (1984): 299.

44. John Seed, "Anthropocentrism," Appendix E, in Bill Devall and George Sessions, *Deep Ecology: Living as if Nature Mattered* (Salt Lake City, Nev.: Peregrin Smith Books, 1985), 243.

45. These points are discussed in detail in Shrader-Frechette, *Science Policy* 32-64; cp. also MacIntyre, "Utilitarianism," 139–51.

46. Mark Sagoff, *The Economy of the Earth* (Cambridge: Cambridge University Press, 1989), 24.

47. Ibid., 46.

48. Ibid., 47.
49. Ibid., 46.
50. Ibid., 29.
51. Ibid., 45.
52. Ibid., 69.
53. Ibid., 115.

2

On Integrity

Introduction

Professor Henry Regier, Director of the Institute for Environmental Studies, University of Toronto, has written:

> The Ecological Committee of the International Joint Commission's Science Advisory Board and the Board of Technical Experts of the Great Lakes Fishery Commission convened a workshop on "Ecosystem Integrity in the Context of Surprise," at Burlington, Ontario on June 14–16, 1988. The intent was to discover conceptual and practical meaning in the language of the U.S./Canada Water Quality Agreement (GLWQA) of 1978, as revised in 1987, and specifically in the statement: "The purpose of the Parties is to restore and maintain the chemical, physical and biological integrity of the waters of the Great Lakes Basin Ecosystem" where the latter is defined as: " . . . the interacting components of air, land, water and living organisms, including humans within the drainage basin of the St. Lawrence River."[1]

Such a concept of "integrity" demands analysis, because it is used in both its environmental (descriptive) sense and its moral (prescriptive) one. It is worth noting that "integrity" has such favorable connotations in a purely interhuman context, that it almost begs the question to propose to use it in a purely descriptive manner. Some have suggested as an alternative "integrality," and perhaps that is a good choice if the context is a purely scientific one.

On the other hand, in Aldo Leopold's famous statement,[2] the expression is somewhat equivocal, as it appears to have both senses, that is it is both descriptive and requiring approbation at one and the same time. Regier says:

> Like the terms *health* and *wholeness*, *integrity* has been applied to a broad spectrum of phenomena. At least implicitly, the underlying

21

paradigm is usually that of a living system, either in a natural biotic sense, or in a cultural noetic sense, or both.[3]

"Integrity" thus includes the wholeness of a living system. It is, first of all, a desirable state of affairs. Our use of the term in a human context suggests a person of character, not easily swayed, "all-of-a-piece" ethically, unassailable, as well as basically honest. In the biological sense the claim is made that that which is naturally one should not be interfered with or torn asunder.

If a natural system prima facie should not be interfered with, then some sense of value or appropriateness must be added into its "cultural" counterpart, as only the "natural" version (i.e., ecosystems) appears to be strong and valid enough to stand as it is, and hence to possess inherent worth and value. For instance, I believe the "vigor" and "health" of the South African political system do not amount, at this time, to an "integrity" which should not be disturbed or "dissected."

Regier speaks of "two polarities or subsystems within the Great Lakes Basin ecosystem: the natural and the cultural." He adds that "these can only be distinguished in a general way—we see no clear boundary between them."[4] He is correct, insofar as the difficulty of clearly separating "natural" from "cultural" integrity is concerned. I understand "culture" to mean the specific activities of some members of the biota, that is human beings, and thus as a (partially) natural activity. Now "integrity" while naturally present in undisturbed natural ecosystems, requires a constant, or at least a deliberate effort on the part of humans if "these two subsystems (which) are now interacting adversarially" are to complement one another instead.[5]

Therefore, Regier's use of the word "integrity" slips almost imperceptibly from being merely descriptive of a state of affairs, to being prescriptive, in the sense of manifesting an "ought," which should be brought about.

If I understand him correctly, it is in this way that: true "integrity" can be brought about: Regier further cites Thomas C. Jorling (1972 U.S. P.L. 92-500), who uses the concept of "harmony" to describe this desirable state of affairs.[6]

I will return to the concept of "integrity" below, after presenting some specific aspects of the problems concerning the Great Lakes Basin, primarily the presence and the effects of "toxics" in the region. In 1991, an intensive workshop was convened at Niagara-on-the-Lake, Ontario by the Great Lakes Institute (State University of New York at Buffalo), comprising lawyers, epidemiologists, toxicologists, and public health professionals, from both Canada and the United States, to discuss the need for new public policies based on findings about toxins in the Great Lakes. The main evidence for the latter is to be found in the states of health of species in the ecosystem, both nonhuman and human. Pesticides, heavy metals, PCBs, dioxins, all have documented effects on fish, birds, and mammals: fragile eggshells (leading to 80–100 percent loss of some bird species), reproductive impairments, and cancers and tumors in fish and mammals are some of the effects, as well as a wide range of deformities in insect larvae. Abnormal parental behavior is another factor contributing to species loss, and so is neurological dysfunction in many species, from birds to whales. Many of these abnormalities remain to affect subsequent generations.[7]

Against this background, "It should not be surprising that human tissues also reflect the trend and state of ecosystem contamination."[8] PCBs show up in mothers' milk, for instance, and congenital deformities have adverse effects on reproductive outcomes in females and significantly decreased sperm count in males. Decreased birth weight and head circumference, and increased rates of cancers of all types, as well as circulatory and immune system diseases, are some of the results documented.[9] Further, psychosocial conditions arising from exposure to high levels of hazardous substances are also to be expected. The impact of feelings of fear and anger at having no control over one's circumstances, on people trapped in homes and communities from which no escape might be financially possible, and within which— paradoxically—they find their only appropriate group support, has been documented from New York (Lewiston and Love Canal), to Three Mile Island and South Carolina.[10]

An aggravating factor in such cases has been that "a high level of distress was shown to be associated with significantly poorer DNA repair in lymphocytes," as compared to low distress, increasing the likelihood of cancer, infectious disease, and the like.[11] Technological and scientific "advances" have significantly extended our life span but, even in that context, "the public rightly perceives the risks around them to have become more severe."[12] In Canada, against this somewhat terrifying background, we are euphemistically (or optimistically) assured "the right to life" within the Charter of Rights and Freedoms (Section 7 guarantees the "right to life, liberty and the security of persons"), which does not now include, but someday may be interpreted by the courts to include, the right to quality of life, or a right to health.[13]

It is because of these and other similar problems that recent legislation has used the science of ecology and the concept of integrity, which goes beyond quantifiable science, to help recommend a certain change in our attitudes to the natural environment. The concept of "ecosystem integrity" has been used since 1972, in various legislative acts (such as the Clean Water Act, U.S. 1972; and the GLWQA of 1978, ratified 1988, U.S./Canada). It is also explicitly used in at least two national "constitutions," the 1988 "New Constitution of Brazil" (Chapter Six, "Meio Ambiente") and the failed proposal for a revised Canadian Constitution. Although the proposal failed on political grounds, the language of integrity was preserved and now forms the basis of both practical training and a "Mission Statement" for Environment Canada. Recently, the language of integrity was included in regulations and legislation, as well as "mandates" and "vision" or "mission" statements, such as those of UNCED (United Nations Commission on Environmental Development), 1992; the World Bank, 1992, and the 1993 American Fisheries Society Draft Policy statement regarding the Endangered Special Act and its reauthorization, as well as several 1991 documents, such as Ascend 21, 1991, and those of the Great Lakes Science Advisory Board (GLSAB), 1991.[14]

For all its common usage and its twenty-year history, "integrity" has not been exhaustively defined or conceptually analyzed in the field of public policy or in that of science, ethics, or the philosophy of science, although scientists have attempted to design Indices of Biotic Integrity (IBI) for both land and water (J. Karr et al., 1986). Through the work of recent meetings on "Ecosystem Science and Integrity"[15] and "Ecosystem Health and Integrity," James Kay (complex systems theorist) and I developed a provisional definition of "integrity," which was further enriched by the input of Henry Regier, Robert Ulanowicz, and Don DeAngelis. Our intent was to manifest its meaning and value, hence the reasons for its use in legislation. We have provisionally defined integrity as follows:

"Ecosystem integrity" is an "umbrella" concept that includes in various proportions which cannot be specified precisely, the following:

1. Ecosystem health and its present well-being (defined, for our purpose, below). This condition may apply to even nonpristine or somewhat degraded ecosystems, provided they function successfully as they presently are. Some examples might be (a) an organically cultivated farm, or a low-input operation; but also (b) a lake which, having lost its larger species because of anthropogenic stress, now functions with a larger number of smaller, different species. Hence, ecosystems that are merely healthy, may encompass both desirable and undesirable possibilities, and may be more or less *limited* in the capacities they possess (or

have become artifically or accidentally constrained by humans).
It is for this reason that health alone is not sufficient.

2. The ecosystem must retain the ability to deal with outside interference, and, if necessary, regenerate itself following upon
   it. This clause refers to the capacity to withstand stress. But
   nonanthropogenic stress is part of billions of years of systemic
   development. Anthropogenic stress, on the other hand, may be
   severely disruptive to the system in that it may contain realities that are radically new to the natural components of the
   system, or it may operate at intensities that are unprecedented
   in evolutionary history, hence the system may not have ways
   to correct or compensate for such stress.

3. Integrity obtains, when at point C (see Fig. IA, p. 49), the system's *optimum capacity* for the greatest possible on-going developmental options within its time/location, remains
   undiminished.

   The greatest possible potentiality for options is also fostered
   by the greatest possible biodiversity (dependent on contextual
   natural constraints), as the latter is a necessary but not sufficient component of C. Biodiversity contributes to integrity in a
   least two ways:

   (a) through genetic potential, based on the size and diversity
       of population and their respective gene pools (hence sup-
       porting and enhancing both structure and function of these
       populations);
   (b) through biodiversity's dimensions as purveyor and locus of
       both relational information and communication, of which
       existing populations and ecosystems manifest and embody
       only a small proportion. We can only theorize about the
       immense capacities for diverse qualitative interactions
       among individuals and species, which are not *presently*
       existing or knowable.

4. The system will possess integrity, if it retains the ability to
   continue its ongoing change and development, unconstrained by
   human interruptions past or present.

It is the latter two facets of integrity that differentiate it from the
notion of ecosystem health. Although this work is primarily concerned
with "integrity" rather than "health," it is appropriate at this time to
define the concept for our purpose by showing just how it differs from
integrity. What is the meaning of "health" in the context of an ecosystem? Is health to be classified simply as "the absence of disease"?[16]
Historically, once the "communicable diseases" were, to some extent,

conquered in the biomedical model, noncommunicable diseases such as cancer, heart disease, and other ailments of "middle and later life" became the main focus of study. Yet simple cause and effect relations are no longer sufficient to explain these diseases, nor to understand or even correct some of the complexities that lead to their occurrence. Lester Breslow says, "the World Health Organization (WHO) has defined health as 'a state of complete physical, mental and social wellbeing and not merely the absence of disease or infirmity.'"[17]

Health has also been defined as the capacity to resist adverse environmental impacts at the present time, and as "the imputed capacity to perform tasks and roles adequately."[18] In this sense, "health" places "individuals on a continuum with physical, mental, and social dimensions." This brief excursion into current "health paradigms," manifests a significant number of aspects of the concept which serve to separate it from that of "integrity," in the context of ecosystems.

The first difference is the most evident (keeping in mind, however, the limits of the single organism analogy): without one kidney, one may be healthy, albeit more prone to succumb to certain stresses and diseases; without one finger, one may be healthy, in the sense of being capable of resisting diseases as before the amputation. Yet in both cases, the organism's integrity has been diminished. This in turn diminishes either the capacity to withstand stress, or the potential for activities (e.g., one may probably not become a concert pianist with a missing finger). But there are many other differences as well, and perhaps a list of these differences would be useful, to compare and contrast the two concepts:

(a) health in its more recent paradigms, is understood as relative to population, social expectations and the like, rather than being defined substantially (as opposed to culturally);

(b) health is understood in relation to specific time frames and locations;

(c) health is limited to *actual* manifestations in existing populations or species, instead of manifesting the less constrained, long-term intergenerational thrust of integrity;

(d) health strongly emphasizes functional over structural features;

(e) health is, at least partially, a social construct (both as phenomenon and as criterion);

(f) health, even "optimum health" may be understood with reference to "support/manipulation" (e.g., a "healthy" diabetic, permanently functioning on insulin).

Hence, the "ecosystem health" paradigm is a useful one, but it is applicable only to instrumental landscapes, defined within this work as possessing I_b. The fact that "ecosystem health" is compatible with (a) cultural relativity; (b) short-term, and a limited time frame and scale; (c) present existing populations/species (vs. integrity's largely unpredictable genetic potential); (d) overemphasis on functional attributes; (e) social constructs; (f) support/manipulation—all separate it from integrity (as I_a), which is incompatible with all of the above.

Breslow concludes by raising the issue of a possible "agreement of a new (socioecological) paradigm for health."[19] A pristine ecosystem, or at least one which is as pristine as it is possible to be in today's world, is not so "by agreement." If it possesses integrity as per our definition symbolized by the point C, or optimum present and long-term capacity, then that is a real, objective condition, not one which is so only by cultural agreement. Whether or not precise, exact limits can be posited for the concept of integrity that satisfy all possible frames of reference, point C remains an objective one even though it may now exceed our capacity to characterize it.

In the final analysis, most of what we can "produce," or "use" is within the realm of ecosystem health, or I_b. It has been my aim to show the absolute value of I_a (pristine/wilderness areas), both as benchmark and as necessary support for I_b, because the latter cannot be sustainable if it is not used, manipulated, or supported with reference to areas where true (or full natural) integrity is the respected, actual goal.

This understanding uses the science of ecology in its most recent paradigm, that of complex systems' theory (of which chaos theory is a subset), and the laws of thermodynamics.[20]

Because the concept was first used by Aldo Leopold as part of the main expression of his teaching, and because it appears to have been brought into legislation and regulation in order to resonate with a meaning similar to that of Leopold's, the main focus of our analysis would be the meaning of ecosystem integrity and its relation to science. In this chapter, as in the well-worn parable of the four blind men and the elephant,[21] we will focus on many different aspects of integrity, in the hope that the final result, combining all of our observation and analysis, will yield an understanding of "integrity" as a defensible ultimate value. The aspects of integrity we will discuss will be (a) integrity and science; (b) legal aspects; (c) organismic aspects; (d) ecosystemic aspects (both regional and global); (d_1) ecosystem integrity: a valuable goal; (e) integrity, teleology, and nonequilibrium thermodynamic theory; (f) can integrity be restored?; (g) metaphysical aspects; and (h) ethical aspects.

When the value of integrity has been reached through this analysis and only then, can we hope to use it as the basis for the Principle of Integrity, which will be presented and defended in Chapter Three.

a. Integrity and Science (Of Facts and Values)

The principal problem to be faced at this point is whether questions leading to the support of a value *can* in fact be asked of scientists. Values are present throughout the scientific enterprise as (a) personal values and convictions, which may indicate, for instance, the sort of research scientists consider most interesting and worth pursuing; and as (b) institutional or corporate values which to a great extent also may shape and direct their research through selective funding; values can also be present in their choices of (c) preferred methodologies, and (d) their chosen epistemological approach.[22]

Yet a vast gulf remains between all of the above and the goal here pursued—*natural value*, to be *objectively* discovered by science. For our purposes, ecosystem science is being asked to supply at least a clear *limit* to what can be done without interfering with a basic ecological value. Why is the "restoration of integrity" or its preservation (if an ecosystem which exemplifies integrity could be found today) deemed to be good and desirable? Are there any scientific reasons why that is the case? It seems as though the belief that "integrity" is intrinsically good and valuable, thus preferable to other ecosystem states, is a necessary conceptual and factual prerequisite of both legislation and this new moral principle. In a seminal paper entitled "Fact and Value in Ecological Science,"[23] Mark Sagoff discusses the problem by providing a framework within which the "two tasks of ecology" can be appreciated for what they are, without necessarily expecting complementarity necessarily in their respective approaches and pursuits. Ecology, he points out, citing national Environmental Protection Agency policy, may be used "in planning a development of resource-oriented projects," in order to "attain the widest range of beneficial uses of the environment" (U.S. Code, title 42 [1976] sec. 4332). Yet the same statute includes sections which address the other task of ecology, namely, it "seeks to enrich the understanding of ecological systems" (sec. 4321), in order "to prevent or eliminate damage to the environment," and "to preserve important . . . natural aspects of our national heritage" (sec. 4331).

Our task here is also twofold. The primary task is seeking to understand "integrity" from various standpoints. First, the task is to understand integrity from the standpoint of ecosystem science, which is in line with the second task Sagoff cites. If "integrity" is the mandate of legislation, then answers should be sought about its value, and the understanding gained should be used to help support, protect, and respect ecosystems.

The second task depends upon the primary one. If the value of ecosystem integrity is understood, and the appreciation of its complex functioning is enhanced, then we will be in a better position to understand the limits required by the second task, that of using science better to understand ways of benefiting from nature without harming the source of such benefits. We will then be able to ensure sustainability and maintain maximum ecosystem health to support defensible human uses of such ecosystems.

Unless the first task is seriously undertaken, we will not have a paradigm case or, as Thomas Jorling puts it, a "benchmark" from which to understand what constitutes a defensible and sustainable human use.[24]

Two main difficulties emerge: the first is the problem of the passing from facts to values. The value sought herein is the prerequisite for all values and choices; it is the maximum capacity for life support, a value which is holistic and individual as well as anthropocentric and nonanthropocentric at one and the same time. Most discussions of ecosystem stress or degradation[25] occur in the context of some specific human goal beyond bare survival. For instance, the loss of certain fish species may be used to indicate a poor state in an ecosystem. Yet, while the specific loss indicates the condition of an ecosystem, it manifests at the same time a diminished capacity in relation to a human preference.

Therefore, from a consequentialist and anthropocentric position, it is the specific present or projected loss that renders a degraded system undesirable. From the standpoint of respect for nature and for all parts of the ecosystems' biota (including but not limited to humans), it is not the result of the condition (i.e., stress and ecosystem degradation leading to species loss), but the *condition itself* which is undesirable. This is because the condition is threatening to (a) the continuation of life itself, when stress becomes acute, and (b) the capacity of the ecosystem to regenerate itself.

In practical terms, one may answer the question of why one should restore integrity either from the standpoint of some particular purpose (e.g., we should restore this ecosystem so that it will produce more timber or more fish) or because we want to (a) respect and protect natural ecosystems as much as that goal is compatible with our own continued existence and the satisfaction of basic needs, and (b) because we want to maintain its potential to support the maximum number of choices and options compatible with that ecosystem. Regier says:

A living system exhibits integrity if, when subjected to disturbance, it sustains an organizing, self-correcting capability to recover toward an end-state that is normal and "good" for that system. Other end-states than pristine or naturally whole may be taken to be normal and "good."[26]

There is no conflict, in principle, in recognizing a number of separate possible ethical (and prudential) positions, supporting the *same* action and the *same* value (integrity). As long as they are clearly acknowledged and specified, this does not represent a problem.

What needs to be accepted is that many choices (although not the maximum number, based on maximum capacity) could be supported by a somewhat stressed ecosystem as well (Rapport and Regier, 1992), and this needs to be recognized and made explicit. In that case, ethical stances supporting that position would not be the same as the moral stance requiring, if possible, full integrity. It is only with respect to the optimum capacity, or optimum resilience, that optimum instrumental and optimum intrinsic value coincide.

Therefore, our position does not require taking a fact as a value. It simply proposes as a basic condition for the achievement of any valuable state whatever, the existence of biological life. As an example, "health" is a value, as is a somewhat subjective state such as "happiness": both are factual, yet neither is simply one among many possible goals that can be chosen. Both "health" and "happiness" are viewed as ultimate or intrinsic values in interhuman ethics. Because of its unique capacity to support all other values, including the two above, I propose a similar role and status for the value of "integrity."

The question arises, what does science make of this assertion? What can science be fairly asked to contribute to the answers we are seeking? It is difficult for some scientists to even consider intrinsic value in natural ecosystems. They can readily concede that, once a human purpose has been disclosed to them and projected, then they may be able to speak of whether a specific ecosystem might successfully support a chosen goal. In other words, they might be able to predict *approximately* the sort of behavior an ecosystem may exhibit within specific spatio-temporal constraints and environmental conditions, but they are not prepared to rank possible alternatives hierarchically, except by reference to human goals.[27] One reason why this is so is the joint ideal of scientific neutrality and objectivity; another is that ecosystems are neither clearly definable nor are they static entities, hence not easy to analyze, at least in principle. They are (partially open, and therefore not fully predictable) processes, and it is uncertain whether they are oriented toward a goal which is good and valuable, at least in their own "terms," that is, whether they can be seen as teleological.

From the scientific point of view only, some have suggested that since "teleology" as the intended move toward a desired goal cannot truly be proven even in the case of rational human agents, let alone nonhuman entities, populations, or wholes in general, it might be more appropriate to argue "as if" teleology might govern complex systems as well.[28] This brief discussion should be sufficient to give some idea of the scientific problems arising from the present enterprise: the next subsections will present further difficulties and add to what has been said.

b. Legal Aspects of Integrity

> The ambiguity of the concept of "integrity" which was not defined in the Act, proved fatal to implementations.[29]

Since the practical value of "integrity" lies in its policy applications, while its philosophical (theoretical) value lies in its strength as a basic concept supporting obligation, both conceptual and role analysis appear necessary. Thus it is entirely appropriate to turn next to the analysis of "integrity" from its legal standpoint, as it was first used in an environmental setting in U.S legal/political discourse. In 1972, the U.S. Clean Water Act adopted an "ecosystem approach" as a methodology or perspective, the objective of which was "to restore and maintain the chemical, physical and biological integrity of the Nation's waters" (33 U.S.C. (a)).[30]

Senator Edmund Muskie used similar terms in 1972 Congressional Acts; he added, "it is the national goal that the discharge of pollutants into the navigable waters be eliminated by 1985," hence "these policies simply mean that streams and rivers no longer need to be considered part of the waste treatment process." The call of the holistic goal of "restoring integrity" through the ecosystem approach was explicitly advocated as early as 1970 by Lynton K. Caldwell in his "The Ecosystem as a Criterion for Public Land Policy." He subsequently played a determinant role in the design of Great Lakes policy.[31] No matter how often the goal of "integrity" is enunciated, what appears to be constant is the emergence of two related problems: (a) a lack of definition for the concept in all regulatory acts, and as a consequence (b) a corresponding lack of prescriptive, binding force, easily traceable to the concept's imprecision. Based on the assumption that (a) and (b) are inescapably correlated, it seems imperative to undertake a thorough analysis of "integrity," not only for scholarly purposes, but also in order to help restore the urgently needed power of a law largely ignored in current public practice and policies.

Barry Boyer speaks of the goals of restoring integrity and achieving "zero discharge," thus equating disintegrity and pollution: "many congressmen . . . shared the EPA's leadership's opinion that zero discharge was 'hopelessly unrealistic.'"[32] In fact, "zero discharge" legislation "was branded from the start as purely symbolic legislation," whereas "integrity" was viewed as too ambiguous to implement. Boyer adds:

> (a) if "integrity" had any meaning, it referred to the pristine quality of water that existed before European settlements in North America. (b) Congress could not seriously have meant for the agency to implement requirements that would ensure pristine water, because that would be either physically impossible or prohibitively expensive in the context of modern economy.[33]

Lacking a clear definition, "integrity" is left with the status of a "moving target" rather than a positive goal. One could be a cynic and suggest that perhaps the concept was chosen primarily because lack of precision entails lack of political force, so that "integrity" may have served the dual purpose of sounding like a desirable vision, giving the impression of governmental concern and resolution as well as evoking a positive response, while at the same time ensuring that the status quo would not be disturbed.

More likely, I suspect, the initial choice of "integrity" by politicians was meant to resonate as an echo of those values that constitute a United States' "vision of the environment" (as opposed to simple consumers' preferences), as indicated for instance in Mark Sagoff's *The Economy of the Earth*.[34] Analogously, a Canadian "vision" could also be appealed to, in order to ground a different yet compatible set of values.[35] Both could be termed "ideal" legislation, however, rather than "symbolic" as Boyer suggests. The former represents an extremely valuable goal worth approaching as closely as possible, whereas the latter is a token representation of some other, unspecified value. Further "symbols" are culture-bound, thus limited in scope, whereas "integrity" is meant to be a multinational, or even global, goal.[36]

An example might be that of a doctor telling a patient that she is overweight, and counseling her to start losing weight through various means, keeping in sight her *ideal weight* as a goal. The "ideal" in this case represents a clear value, carrying with it a correlative notion of obligation—even if the precise "magic number" may never be reached—not simply the "symbol" of a vague "better" state.

Boyer's analysis demonstrates the importance of a thorough understanding of "integrity," well beyond the haphazard, brief definitions offered in the current literature on the topic, most of which appear to be concerned with one or more components, rather than ever attempting to harmonize all facets of the concept. The defining characteristics of integrity are important since they will, in turn, clarify the role it might play in international legislation. We must know what integrity is, before we can assess possibilities of its role.

Another problem with the present lack of definition, as Boyer accurately points out, is that as it stands in its roughly undefined state, "integrity" can be reinterpreted to mean whatever quality of water will result from implementing the operational programs of the act in a "reasonable manner."[37] The appeal to rationality or the "reasonable choice" of policy is too vague to be more than a token phrase, one that remains totally open-ended unless "rational choice" of means is coordinated to a specific goal. To assume that "reasonable" and "right" (in the sense of "good") are interchangeable, is to commit the so-called Platonic fallacy, assuming that an action which is expedient in order to bring about a certain goal, is therefore good or right. If one is a Mafia assassin, it is "reasonable" to ensure the possession of a gun in good working order with a functioning silencer. But it is neither right nor good to possess and prepare a gun for the purpose envisioned. A lot has been written about this problem in the context of modern business or policy choices that needs no duplication here.[38] Caldwell, for instance, makes a similar point. In his discussion of goals of public policy, the concept of "conservation" also appears unclear. Caldwell says: "Aphorisms such as 'conservation means wise use' are of little help in the absence of objective criteria for wisdom."[39] Second, the political barriers to the implementation of a global, holistic goal are exacerbated by the fact that precisely determined geographical boundaries of ecosystems may also be unavailable.

The legal system presents other problems and obstacles to the acceptance of the ideal of "integrity."

At this time, laws and legal systems are primarily individualistic in tone, hence their resistance to a holistic ecosystem approach. A brief look at current U.S. law in regard to constitutional "takings," where the conflict between individual and holistic considerations is most evident, and at past land use laws and attitudes, from which the present ones evolved, might be useful at this point, to show a major obstacle to the acceptance of a holistic goal.

Eugene Hargrove carefully traces the basis for the present difficulties with the value of land as such, in contrast to individual rights to it. The roots of the problem lie with the ancestors of the U.S. political system, the Saxons and German freemen.[40] The deeply embedded belief in the landowner's "absolute rights" to do as he pleases without considering any interests except his own, is based on practices and beliefs antedating the arrival of the first colonists to America. The basic argument advanced (implicitly or explicitly) in defense of individual rights, Hargrove shows, is based primarily on those early German and Saxon attitudes and customs.[41]

This earlier position is reflected in John Locke's work and thus transmitted through Thomas Jefferson, who "couched (it) in moral rather than historical terms,"[42] to the American consciousness with its emphasis on individual rights, in direct contrast with the "divine rights of kings," left behind in the original homeland of the colonists. The law of "constitutional takings" most likely evolved against this background. Mark Sagoff discusses such cases as the well-known *Just* v. *Marinette County*, drawing out the contrast between the usual legal requirement for clear, provable harms, in order to use "the concept of harm to others . . . (to limit) the rights of landowners."[43] As far as Locke is concerned, he lived in times when (a) the present environmental crisis could not have been foreseen, and (b) he believed that "one must leave enough for others." Thus one only has the right to use what one truly needs, and "that one does not possess a right to waste." Sagoff suggests substituting "justice" as a basic concept, for "individual rights." Justice is at the very least a communitarian term, although it is much harder to understand and use in a holistic sense.

The same basic problem lies in the distinction between individual and whole, according to Boyer, who contrasts "victim-oriented" with "perpetrator-oriented" laws.[44] The contrasting approaches disclose that the latter, whether in the context of pollution or racism, "avoids confronting the realities" of "institutional" unacceptable behavior. By "identifying and punishing individual bad behaviors," those who are not so identified in contrast, are characterized as "innocent," thus "free from the need to change."[45] Once again the problem is approached atomistically rather than holistically, thus manifesting a *second* clear obstacle to the implementation of the *holistic* goal of integrity. Both required "shifts" in values and perspective are basic: the restoration of integrity demands that—like a recovering alcoholic—we start by admitting the all-pervasive and crippling position we are in. We must admit that our society has "touched bottom," having drifted out of control, beyond a sustainable state we can justify, in the global context. It is not the case that once a few "bad apples" are removed, then we can continue business as usual, with minor changes. Just as the proposed solution, that is, restoring integrity is holistic, the problem too is holistic. The "victim perspective" Boyer recommends as the better alternative is also not an atomistic one.

From a legal standpoint, the goal of integrity emphasizes a perspective requiring an environmental protection act. It also suggests the adoption of a standpoint that goes even further, because it no longer needs to be able to "denote" "victims" as "denotatively identifiable individuals," to use Ernest Partridge's expression. He contrasts it with the designative duties to future generations which he advocates instead. In essence then, the concept of integrity, although it has been in place in legislation for close to twenty years now, is neither closer as a goal, nor fulfilling its proposed role. From the standpoint of its legal connotations, it suffers from serious problems of definition. Further, and equally damaging to its viability, it requires a massive reorientation of our common understanding of it, as well as self-understanding as a species. Without the complex value and paradigm shift required, little can be expected of the concept of "integrity." Like a seed dropped on arid, unwelcoming, and unprepared soil, it can neither take root nor grow and bear fruit. Yet this is not completely representative of the factual realities. After all, decisions like the one on the *Just* case are not unique, and "integrity" *is* presently the ostensible goal of legislation, it is working to some extent, and—finally—it *has* worked, for instance in the restoration of Lake Erie.

The next subsection will briefly consider the basis of "integrity" as a paradigm in the biological–organic sense, as a prelude to viewing it in the ecosystemic sense, in which it was first used in general or philosophical discourse.

c. Organismic Aspects of Integrity

J. Baird Callicott suggests that theories which ascribe value to individual organisms, such as "conativism," are "intractably atomistic."[46] It would then seem that to speak of single biological organisms is not relevant to the holistic concept of integrity. Nevertheless, the paradigm case of integrity is usually "that of a living *organism . . . in a natural biotic sense*."[47] Another definition says of a system, "its integrity has to do with its ability to maintain its organization and to continue its process of self-organization."[48] Integrity is valued on the basis of the paradigm case of organic unity.

The related concepts of "unity, completeness and value,"[49] are part of that paradigm, that is, the first two form the basis for the third. Why this should be so is the first question we should examine. Peter Miller, for instance, analyzes integrity in detail in a recent presentation[50] where he considers it under seven different headings, the last of which is particularly relevant to our purpose. There he defines a specific aspect of the concept as follows:

Functional–dynamic coordination, i.e., an interactive system with feedback mechanisms which preserve certain features or control a directional transformation–dynamic equilibrium (vs. functional failure and uncoordinated processes)

  (a) mechanical coordination . . .
  (b) communicative coordination . . .
  (c) *organic coordination* [emphasis added] i.e., possessing properties of organisms such as self-development, self-governance, self-repair, reproduction, etc. (vs. disorganization).
     1. *bounded*, e.g., a cell or organism (vs. disease and death).
     2. *open*, e.g., an ecosystem (vs. degradation).[51]

Several important points emerge from this analysis. The single organism paradigm refers to something which is "bounded," possesses "organic coordination," yet where "unity" may have a stronger role to play than "completeness," at least prima facie. Miller appears to be correct in defining an organism through the significant dynamic/process features it possesses. In other words, it is by what it *does*, by the way it *functions*, that an organism is primarily defined. Evolutionary theory also appears to redefine organisms through time by their adaptive capacities, as needed for a possible environmental "fit."[52]

This in turn demonstrates that the paradigm case for the goal of integrity is dynamic and a process, rather than a static "ideal." Thus a possible critique of "integrity" in the holistic sense, as a goal which seeks to restore and reenact a *specific historic* state of ecosystem pristineness, must be mistaken (since that state is something static and frozen in time).

The capacity to act and react as a unitary whole distinguishes an organism from, for example, an aggregate. A random collection of things, whether homogeneous or heterogeneous, has the capacity neither to initiate nor to sustain change, nor to fulfill any of the functions of growth, decay, or reproduction that are normally part of an organism's operation. Further, the health of an organism is manifested in its capacity to function in this manner. In this sense its function and its capacities, *present and potential*, define the organism. "Temporal and causal process is never complete," as Miller points out, from which it follows that to define an organism does not mean that the organism is "this *specific whole as it is at this particular moment and no other*." An "exhaustive" definition and description of myself purely as a physical individual (if such a thing were possible) at this time, would not be sufficient to characterize me, even aside from the additional aspects of spiritual, intellectual, and affective capacities, if it did not include my physical potential.

Interestingly, the potential to die is a clear component of the definition of any organism. The future certainty of death, however, does not negate the organism's other defining capacities: (a) to maintain (and recapture) health after outside interference or inner disturbance; and (b) to resist stress up to some point, not exactly specifiable because it may vary with each organism or kind of organism. These capacities are based on the organism's drive to maintain its structural integrity. Thus, even at the level of individual organisms, the applicable concept of integrity that emerges is both (1) structural and (2) functional.

Although structural and functional integrity are closely related, they represent two separate aspects of integrity even in the case of a single organism. Therefore, even if one accepts that the unity of integrity as a value is strong enough to support an obligation, the question remains whether structural or functional integrity is the most significant, as one might be present when the other is not. For instance, cutting off a part of one's anatomy that does not appear to be vital to one's health (e.g., the appendix), even if it could be done without causing any pain or future emotional or physical repercussions, is still an assault on one's integrity. Thus it is fair to say that, at least at the intuitive level, the "structural" integrity of individuals appears to embody a strong value and to represent the basis for moral considerability. Is there any other way that value can be defined, other than by an appeal to intuition to that which Mark Timmons might term our "core beliefs"?[53] For humankind, the value of the unity and the integrity of each whole is normally taken to be inviolable—the basis of the dignity of human persons—together with their rationality and their membership in the species *Homo sapiens*, although the last two criteria have been attacked on several fronts.[54]

Aside from metaphysically based doctrines, there appears to be no other basis for "rights" for individual humans, other than various forms of contractarianism, which ultimately rest on the same basic values, with the additional problem of placing an even stronger emphasis on rationality than some other positions. It is precisely because of the weakness emerging from the criteria of rationality and membership in the species for individual moral considerability that some thinkers take the unity of a live organism as a criterion on which to base viable doctrines. Unfortunately, these theories, like all rights-based doctrines, remain open to critiques based upon the difficulties of prioritizing rights-based claims, and the interests that support them. Yet, for all the difficulties that can and do arise, the living organismic unity appears to remain, minimally, a strong basis for claims of moral considerability. Thus, related functional and structural integrity at the level of individual organisms is a major component of value, and a necessary one.

d. Ecosystemic Aspects of Integrity

Because the "principle of integrity" is based primarily on ecosystem integrity and the closely related concept of global "ecological integrity," it is important that this sense of integrity is shown to be consistent with the previous one, and that it can be shown to represent a stronger basis for supporting ethical obligation.[55]

Now a philosopher may speak in general terms of "the earth" or the environment, but a scientist must be more specific. Even if she avoids the tight confines of the "reductionistic" approach (both as a methodology and as an ontology), factual descriptions and hypotheses meant to fit physical reality must be detailed in order to be useful. Consider the definitions of the useful terms "biome" and "ecosystem":

A biome is the largest land community unit which ecologists find convenient to recognize (Odum, 1971). It refers to a biogeographical region or formation; a major regional ecological community characterized by distinctive life-forms and principal plant and animal species.[56]

Ecosystems, however, are smaller units than biomes: An ecosystem comprises a natural community and its abiotic environment together as a functional system of complementary relationships in which there is transfer and circulation of energy and matter (Odum, 1971 [cp. E. P. Odum, 1993]).[57]

Jeffrey McNeely suggests that the biome is the best approach within the biosphere or the entire global ecosystem for defining a community capable of supporting living organisms.[58] It offers several advantages, such as: (1) recognition of the necessity of development based on natural systems of renewable resources, in turn based on a broad perspective; (2) identification of major common "ecological relationships, processes, potentialities, and vulnerabilities"; (3) identification of major common problems (thus fostering the quest for common solutions); (4) stimulation of interdisciplinary, comparative, and international studies and applications to common problems; and (5) identification of "priorities of conservation," based on scientific grounds, "regardless of the location of national frontiers."[59] The concept of "ecosystem" provides a unit whose smaller scale allows more ease of handling than a larger unit such as the biome. Yet when philosophers use the term "ecosystem," they might mean biosphere or the environment in a more general sense. The objects of their focus are the universal features of all ecosystems. This seems justified given the universality of the principles they want to reach. What do ecosystems have in common? Ecologist Eugene Odum, for instance, cites the dual role of ecosystems as not only "supply depot(s)" but the "home(s)" in which we must live. This "home" supplies us with services arising from "nonproductive landscapes": we need a "balanced CO_2O_2 atmosphere, . . . the climactic buffer provided by oceans amid masses of vegetation. . . ."[60]

It is worth noting that the "service" approach is clearly anthropocentric and utilitarian. Rather than conceiving of healthy, diverse ecosystems as commercially valuable monocultures, we see them as contributing "to the long-term creativity of nature—an area of great biotic diversity creates more diversity through time."[61] Various scientifically observable processes, creating a "more heterogeneous environment," result in and "explain why total diversity is self-augmenting in ecological time," as well as "in evolutionary time."[62]

On the other hand, its reverse has the reverse effect. Hence the far-reaching results of disintegrity: "Losses in diversity beget further losses." B. G. Norton adds:

> If a species goes extinct, other species that interact with and depend upon it are threatened. A well-known biologist has asserted that for every plant species that becomes extinct, fifteen animal species can be expected to follow.[63]

Thus, while species diversity is "a self-augmenting evolutionary phenomenon," and evolution of diversity makes possible further evolution of diversity"[64]—disintegrity fosters and accelerates species loss. Thus species loss is not "simply that," it is a "first step in a process of ecosystem simplification."[65]

Yet Norton suggests that the simplistic coupling of diversity with ecosystem stability does not do justice to the complexity of the situation. Indeed, a specific loss may seldom produce an immediate catastrophic effect. Yet the cumulative losses, accelerating as they presently do, suggest that extremely serious consequences will follow, even if: (a) the *specifics* of the time and conditions of this happening cannot be predicted with accuracy; and (b) our usual means of assessing risks, that is, economic calculations and preference assessments, are not appropriate, for various reasons, for such risks with low probabilities and serious consequences, sometimes called "zero infinity dilemmas."[66]

Holmes Rolston says:

> We want to value the lush life that ecosystems maintain in their diversity, unity, dynamic stability, spontaneity; the dialectic of environmental resistance and conductance; the generating life forces.[67]

This represents the basis for the "principle of integrity" we wish to defend. Since "unity, completeness, and value," are among the various dimensions of integrity, it goes beyond the concept of health. (See earlier discussion of the difference between "health" and "integrity" in this context, and our understanding of the concept.)

Callicott recently addressed the question of ecosystem "health." After speaking of the scientific and conceptual problems of ecology, and consequently its corresponding lack of conventional authority in environmental problems, he termed "ecosystem health" as the "conceptual saviour" instead.[68] Callicott speaks of Leopold's idea of "land health" before mentioning integrity. But the elements of Leopold's landmark statement, "a thing is right, when it tends to promote the stability, integrity and beauty of an ecosystem, wrong when it tends otherwise,"[69] are clearly three, not two. Thus collapsing "stability" and "integrity" within the concept of "health" may be inappropriate, at least within an ecocentric, rather than anthropocentric framework. The preservation of integrity is distinct and separate from the noninfliction of harm (including pain) on a single organism. Similarly, the infliction of harm aimed at reducing the healthy functioning of an ecosystem, may or may not be an aspect of a further interference with its "integrity." On the other hand, interference with the "integrity" of an ecosystem may have nothing to do with either pain or the diminution of its health. Substitution of one species for another would be a clear case of interference with the integrity of an ecosystem, while its health or even its stability would not necessarily be diminished.

The values of "health" and "integrity" appear to be independent, although often connected to one another. Further, even in the ecosystemic sense, the concept of "integrity" itself may be said to have two aspects: (1) structural integrity (I_1); and (2) functional integrity (I_2). Functional integrity might be easily associated with stability and with ecosystem health; Callicott, for instance, cites Leopold's concept of "land health" as "the capacity for self-renewal," which is "more functional than structural."[70]

In essence, our aim is to discover and defend a value strong enough to ground an obligation. For this purpose, "structural integrity" might be more significant than functional integrity since it facilitates the differentiation of "integrity" from notions of health, continued existence, or stability. Structural integrity may then form the basis for both the "dignity" of the environment, and the obligation of respect in regard to it. This appears to imply that "structural integrity" might relate to some kind of phenomenon that is both cultural and natural, even if no longer pristine. According to this model, one would need a further distinction between "pristine structural integrity" and "transformed structural integrity," and an example of the latter might be a restored ecosystem, supporting sustainable development. Yet "structures" may be understood as "slow processes or functions," and processes (functions) as "rapidly changing structures." Clear separation of the two concepts may not be as easy as it may first appear. In Chapter Five, dealing with policy and social issues, "pristine structural integrity" will be termed I_a, or "true pristine ecosystem" (see definition earlier in this chapter), whereas "transformed structural integrity" will be termed I_b. Robert Rosen discusses the concept of "function" in a chapter entitled "Entailment without States: Relational Biology," in his work *Life Itself*.[71] He speaks of "heterogeneous systems," wherein "one part looks different, or behaves differently from another part." He continues:

> If we leave the system alone, some autonomous behavior will ensue. On the other hand, we can ask a question like: if we were to remove, or change, one of these distinguishable parts, what would be the effect of that behavior? This is a pregnant question. It involves a new element, not merely observation, but willful active intervention. The result of that intervention is, in effect, the creation of a *new system*, which can be regarded as a kind of perturbation or *mutilation* of the original one.[72]

The natural, "autonomous" behavior of a system is contrasted with that of a system after "willful, active intervention." The intervention's result is *another* system, a "mutilation of the original one." It is not necessary to totally qualify, quantify, and define the former, to be able to say the latter is "mutilated," thus at best a healthy ecosystem (or I_b area), and at worst, a measurably degraded one. "Mutilation" is a pejorative term, although the ensuing ecosystem might be supported/manipulated for desirable human goals. Integrity (as I_a) refers instead to the ecosystem in its unmutilated condition.

To seek a possible answer to these difficulties, it is worth returning to the science of ecology and its main current paradigms. The
ecosystem approach is by no means the *only* available "window"
through which these can be studied. Indeed, the concept of an ecosystem itself is fraught with fundamental ambiguities. At any rate one
major approach views individual organisms, aggregates, and communities as the main basic units of study, thus reducing ecosystems to
"relatively constant backgrounds."[73] Another views ecosystems (however defined) as primary and considers the relevance of succession
and change first, thus reducing individuals and communities to the role
of members/parts of the ecosystems. Both approaches are valid and in
fact necessary for better comprehension of both composition and functioning of ecosystems.

The latter could be defined as "any system that . . . (is) open to
the flow of energy and matter and (contains) at least one living entity,[74] yet this offers no answers to persistent questions of time and scale,
without which ecosystems cannot be understood properly. Ecosystems
can also be defined as "the smallest units that can sustain life in isolation from all but atmospheric surroundings," although there is no
"simple method for specifying the size of an ecosystem unless recognizable boundaries exist."[75]

Hence, those who are accustomed to more easily identifiable objects of study, such as organisms or communities (although the latter
may not be totally precise themselves), tend to downplay the ecosystem approach, as based on entities too ephemeral and imprecise to
support a scientific theory. Aside from such debates, it is clear that
different scientific projects may well require different approaches. On
the other hand, the concept of "integrity" may well provide an "umbrella" under which both aspects, that is, that of function and that of
structure, retain their relevance. Integrity (as I_1) takes into consideration both organisms and communities within an ecosystem, as both
additions and subtractions of species. The addition of species alien to
the ecosystem under consideration is viewed as inappropriate—at least
prima facie—from that point of view, and the introduction of exotics
appears even less recommendable.

The functions and processes taking place within an ecosystem, therefore need to be understood through careful consideration of its structure; and the organisms and species that inhabit and form it, also
cannot be understood in isolation.[76] The same is true of human organisms: a human being's physiology can be studied as such, but stresses
and disturbances, that is its pathologies, require additional investigation of its environment. Viruses and bacteria, for instance, interact with

and within the human system, and so do food, water, and air that sustain its life, as well as the toxins, pollutants, and man-made chemicals that might be ingested, absorbed through outgassing of chemicals in its surroundings.[77]

In this sense, some of the problems concerning the precise definition and boundaries of ecosystems may need to be rethought as requiring too limiting and reductionist a view. Taking the example of the human organism once again, the same question can be raised: what are our "limits"? Is it simply our skin that limits the individual a scientist or doctor needs to understand? What of genetic background, medical history, lifestyle, present surroundings, and possible exposures, as well as emotional attachments or isolation? A doctor attempting to understand an organism without an understanding of these factors, would be just as handicapped as the blind men were, feeling only *one* part of the elephant.

But an ecosystem is not just a plurality of interacting processes and functions through which organisms and communities affect one another in various ways. It is also a unity, a whole, as I am, in spite of my temporal and geographical interconnections; and this is true to some extent, whether or not one can tell precisely when and where it starts and ends. Of course there is no claim made here that individuals and ecosystems are analogous in all respects. It simply appears that their status as developing and changing entities containing life, renders them similar to each other in some relevant respects. It is their complex, changing, developing *unity* that is addressed by the concept of integrity.

A basic disanalogy between a single organism and an ecosystem lies in their respective time scales. An individual organism is born, reaches maturity, then ages, and eventually dies. The organism will dissolve into its chemical components and give rise to other life-forms (grasses, plants, worms, and the like). On the other hand, the ecosystem integrity views ecosystems in their continuing, though sequential development. It might help to use C. S. Hollings's "figure eight" on the following page, which inspired that definition, together with its modified version manifesting the environmental position defended here.[78]

The first point to note is that James Kay's work makes use of the "figure eight" view of ecosystem functioning through time; Hollings's detailed presentation of that figure, based his own theory on "extensive comparative field studies," led him to postulate four principal "revisions" of existing ecosystem theories. The result represents a way of understanding, through the figure eight design, through which "devolution or evolution" are viewed as "revolution," and where the con-

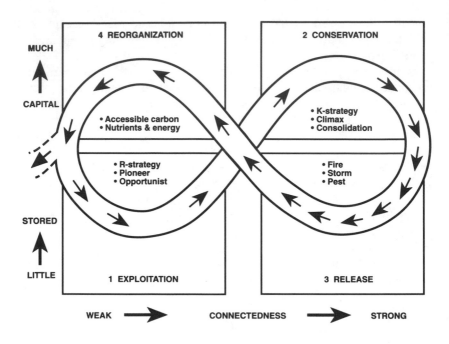

Figure 1. Hollings's "Figure Eight" (From C. S. Hollings, "Cross-scale Morphology, Geometry, and Dynamics of Ecosystems," *Ecological Monographs* 62 (No. 4, 1992): 447–502.)

cepts of release or "creative destruction" and "reorganization" must be added to the traditional functions of "exploitation" and "conservation."[79]

For our purposes, the "figure eight" has the following notable characteristics: it does not ultimately lead anywhere, except back to the beginning; it does not "culminate" in either harmony or stability, and its paths are not entirely predictable.

Against this background and framework of understanding, several points emerge. For the sake of clarity, these points can be listed under four major headings, although they cannot be completely separated from one another: (a) the concept of "well-being"; (b) the concepts of "optimum functioning" of an ecosystem, and the possibility of using ranking terms in that regard (e.g., "better" or "worse"); (c) the teleological aspects of Kay's perspective; and (d) the difference between "health" and "integrity" in ecosystems.

It is worth noting that ecosystem "health" is not identical to "health" in a human organism. It does not represent the "absence of disease"; rather, it is the capacity to remain self-organizing in spite of changes, such as the addition or subtraction of species (see "health," earlier in this chapter). Yet several analogies persist between organisms and ecosystems. Some individuals claim that "the health paradigm can be applied to ecosystems" and that it is "a useful strategy for dealing with society's concern about environmental degradation and the sustainability of natural resources."[80] Further, some may argue in support that human and other single organisms may *also* be viewed as "ecosystems," because of the existence of bacterial colonies and other species within such organisms. Kay advances the suggestion that the concept of "well-being" might be a better choice to describe the optimum state of an ecosystem. Can "well-being" capture both the capacity to reorganize and maintain itself (ecosystem health), and the maintenance of its structure (structural integrity, or I_1)?

The concept may be useful philosophically, in the sense that it echoes the ultimate human value of "happiness" in Aristotle. His concept of *eudaimonia* is best translated as "well-being" or "faring well." This concept differs from the types of "happiness" used in modern moral theory. For instance, in the work of John Stuart Mill, "happiness" represents a preponderance of pleasure over pain, over time, and is used as the goal of the theory of utilitarianism. For Aristotle, the concept transcends both pleasure, the absence of pain, or the presence of goods; instead, it introduces a metaphysical component. In order to understand what it means to speak of "well-being" (*eudaimonia*) in Aristotle, one needs to refer to what it is to be a human being, which represents the human *ergon*, or excellence. In that case, what a human being was meant *to do* defined what a human *was*, intrinsically. Hence, the intimate connection between structure (or essential being) and function provided by the definition sought. Thus, the notion of "well-being" may help bridge structure and function, so that the question of the meaning of integrity may be rephrased as the question of what is the *ergon* of an ecosystem.

In relation to the "excellence" of an ecosystem—its unique function or *ergon*—another question arises. Kay and others have maintained that ecosystems are complex, dynamic systems, that cannot be clearly defined, perhaps not even in principle. Can one also say that human beings are both complex and dynamic, rather than static entities (as Aristotle himself would have readily conceded)? Can both *nature* and *ergon*, imprecise as those concepts may be, in fact be ascribed to ecosystems? Intuitively, one can find both connection and similarity between the two, although one must not push the analogy too far, as ecosystems are not single organisms.

Integrity as "well-being" or "faring well" is a notion that clearly introduces a combination of both physical and metaphysical components, hence it accommodates both structural and functional aspects of integrity. Moreover, as we saw, the Aristotelian concept of "excellence" is implicitly introduced. (For Aristotle, man's *ergon* is man's function—his "excellence.") On the other hand, Kay maintains that a scientist may lay bare and explain any number of changes an ecosystem may undergo, including possible transformations after both usual changes and catastrophic events.[81] What is neither possible, nor appropriate, he adds, is to rank these in hierarchical order, nor to state which might be the "better" ecosystem. This might be done, if I understand him correctly, only in regard to a single ecosystem, viewed at different times, which could be in turn pristine, well-functioning or healthy, degraded, restored, or whatever. Even in this case, some ambivalence appears to be present in science, as no attempt is made to specify the "value" of an ecosystem except in respect to some human goal.

Yet for Aristotle not only single humans may change and improve or lose (moral) ground, but humans in general may be compared and ranked hierarchically, and the wise (happy) man can be distinguished from the less "actualized" or excellent, and the *Nichomachean Ethics* is devoted precisely to the task of discussing, making explicit, and defending these differences. This indicates a serious difficulty with the use of Aristotelian concepts and theory in the present context: Kay's explicit claim is that the introduction of value or comparisons is both separate from and incompatible with the scientific perspective. Yet several remarks in his published work and his presentations appear to be compatible with an Aristotelian approach. For instance, Kay indicates that a "natural" rate of species extinction is preferable to one that is too quick, because it arises from human interference.

Implicitly, if not explicitly, the possibility of an ecosystem's "excellence," or at least the existence of a "better" and a "worse" state, is here indicated and granted. But how is it possible to understand the "excellence" of an ecosystem? One possibility might be to relate the "excellence" to "exergy," or the ecosystem's optimum capacity for sustaining species while dissipating energy. Kay says:

> It could be argued that any environmental change that permanently changes the optimum operating point affects the integrity of the ecosystem. . . . It also could be argued that any time that the system can maintain itself at an optimum operating point, it has integrity.[82]

For Kay, the definition of integrity remains somewhat ambivalent: on one hand, there is some effort to distinguish different states of one ecosystem, and even to rank these as optimum, better, or worse. On the other hand, wary of espousing or endorsing values (even if only unwittingly) within such scientific discourse, a description of an ecosystem as embodying an "undesirable change," is said to "inject an anthropocentric component into the definition of integrity."[83]

Yet to simply relate integrity's definition to the individual observer's point of view (Kay says this can be seen as "equivalent to the exercise of defining the observer's frame of reference in physics") may ultimately be in conflict with any effort to judge ecosystem integrity in relation to an "optimum" point. The approach Kay terms "second law/exergy analysis," apparently deals mainly (or only?) with "immediate changes in an ecosystem caused by environmental change." Yet, as Kay himself admits, "Some environmental changes will not immediately affect an ecosystem. Rather, they affect the ability of the system to cope with future environmental changes." Hence, one needs to consider the relation between integrity and health within this context. If the capacity to self-organize and maintain species diversity are components indicative of integrity, then loss of this capacity, even if related to the future, is extremely significant.

The example Kay offers is that of "fenitrothion spraying of forests to control spruce budworm." Although this practice appears to have no immediate effect, it interferes with the ability of the forest to regenerate itself in the face of other environmental changes. This represents a loss of the ecosystem's capacities, a loss which is general enough to transcend individual observers' perspectives, making it a loss of integrity *intrinsic* to the ecosystem, totally aside from the specifics of any "regulatory and management" context.

Therefore, I cannot agree entirely with Kay's assertion that integrity is to be defined in purely instrumental terms, as means to some more or less desirable management goal. On the contrary, many states of any ecosystem, after certain surprises and environmental impacts, may well be intrinsically lesser, removed from well-being or excellence, or removed from its optimum point, without any reference to anthropocentric goals. The only anthropocentric component one must acknowledge is the enlightened one of deep ecology, which recognizes the intrinsic value in pristine or undegraded ecosystems, ones which still possess the maximum capacity to exercise their original (though evolving) *function* or *ergon*, within the spatio-temporal conditions of that specific ecosystem.

Kay's use of thermodynamics to measure ecological integrity (or rather, to provide a framework to define and understand it) goes beyond previous approaches; by showing that "all real processes are irreversible, it indicates a direction and an end state for all real processes."[84] This addition is extremely significant: it reintroduces teleology in processes described only in scientific terms, without appeals to metaphysics, to Aristotelian doctrine, or any other anthropocentric framework.

Here, teleology does not imply a necessary movement from a worse to a better state, even less the existence of an ideal state as an end goal. It simply shows that (1) ecosystems act as wholes; and (2) that they *tend* toward some specific state, without, of course, *intending* it. Both (1) and (2) are in evidence in the following statement:

> The thermodynamic principle which governs the behaviour of systems as they are moved away from equilibrium is that they will take advantage of all means available to them to resist the applied gradients. Furthermore, as the applied gradients increase, so will the system's resistance to being moved away from equilibrium.[85]

E. Mayr suggests substituting teleonomy for "teleology" in order to eliminate the metaphysical implications teleology carries. But this will not do, because the root of *nomos* implies a lawlike precision not available in principle in the context of Kay's use of complex systems theory.[86] Kay's work shows that Mayr's fears are unfounded and in fact that he is mistaken in this regard. The concept of teleology can and should be reintroduced within a newer scientific paradigm.

It is important to note is that Kay's approach suggests an optimum point or even an excellence, but does not find this to be a stable state, or a goal (see Figure 1A). Let us term the hypothetical "original position" or starting point from which the ecosystem proceeds through the figure eight, *C*—to indicate the point where the greatest capacity for alternative developments and patterns exists. Let us also follow the figure through a brief downturn, then a reascent to an optimum point, *A*, which manifests the ecosystem's excellence, eventually to be followed by a period of "constructive disruption" to *B*, before returning to *C* once again.

Earlier ecosystem science and my own work tended to focus on point *A* as the locus of integrity. This, while true, is not sufficient to capture the meaning of integrity, in the light of complex systems science. Within the new scenario, the excellence of *A* is not sufficient to denote the ultimate value of integrity, because it is neither stable nor, ultimately, steadily harmonious. *A* contains within it the seeds of its own destruction and "devolution." However, although this factual correction is extremely important, it does not eliminate the importance of our previous insights. The "optimum point" or "excellence" of the ecosystem *retains* its foundational meaning for "integrity." What has changed is that integrity, in order to be more than a fleeting stage

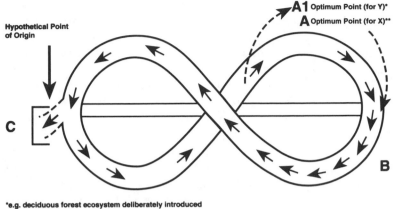

Figure 1A. (From C. S. Hollings, "Cross-scale Morphology, Geometry, and Dynamics of Ecosystems, " *Ecological Monographs* 62 (No. 4, 1992): 447–502.)

within ecosystem developmental unfolding, must also be related back to the conditions existing at the point of origin. "Point of origin" is intended to indicate any time in the ongoing development of an ecosystem which has suffered no major anthropogenic stress.

Surprises, disturbances, or "perturbations" are not only occurring through human interference. They are also, with some qualifications, representative of the way ecosystems flow *naturally*, and this must be clearly recognized within our quest for value. If *A* represents an optimum point, and *B*, say, a degraded point in a later stage of the ecosystem's trajectory, and further, if *A* is not unique in its status as optimum point, but there are other possibilities (let us call them, for the sake of argument, A_1, A_2, and so on), still *C*, as optimum capacity, manifests the fitness for the greatest range of possible options, thus the optimum capacity for resilience and regeneration of the system.

In other words, in this case, *C* represents integrity because of its relation to *A*; where *A*, rather than A_1 or A_2, represents the optimum point possible in the absence of human interventions, so that *C* is a necessary component of integrity if and only if it is such that it may support ecosystems having the greatest capacity for regeneration compatible with their spatio-temporal location. As Kay's paper indicates, a range of different healthy ecosystems, and therefore different optimum points, may be developed within the spatio-temporal limits imposed by *C*'s specific environmental conditions. An example might be in order.

Say that, without intervention, a specific ecosystem (X) will develop into a mature forest, primarily Douglas Fir, slated to reach its optimum operating point as maximum biomass production in about 500 years. Suppose that powerful human interests preferred to effect changes intended to bring about another *healthy* ecosystem (Y), through human intervention, in order to bring about a deciduous forest instead, in about 100 years. Both are possible paths to develop and reach optimum operating points, indicating their maturity and health. But the true test of integrity is not the optimum flourishing of *either* X or Y; rather, after all cycles and changes have taken place, the test is whether or not the *return* to C will once again reach a point that is equally resilient, hence a stage of undiminished capacities. Therefore, although Kay and others may not wish to say that either X or Y is "better" than the other, without a projected human goal as benchmark, the optimum capacity to regenerate compatible with the specific ecosystem's location and climate conditions, is the support basis for any and all preferences and choices, an indisputable value both intrinsic and instrumental, whatever our perspective.

The question that arises now is—given the uncertainty and unpredictability inherent in this view of complex systems—whether the possible intervention aimed at producing Y rather than X could be morally acceptable. The answer is that scientific uncertainty accompanies all human intervention; hence, even if there is no scientific basis for choosing between two healthy ecosystems (both X and Y are such by definition), it is more likely that healthy ecosystem X, or the "naturally" evolving one, which needs to cope only with natural disturbances and impacts, is the "more capable" and "more resilient" ecosystem. It is the ecosystem with the fullest range of capacities and the most likely to regenerate.

The excellence of an ecosystem is not its mature/optimum/climax point. It lies in its greatest capacity to regenerate itself, to be resilient in the face of natural surprises and perturbations, and to initiate again the processes leading to the path of reorganization. At the same time, the optimum point in time, or A in its relation to C, is what also supports the contention that indeed X is better than Y. When an ecosystem is interfered with to bring about an interest-specific state, we cannot be assured of either the proximate or extended range of consequences beyond the intended ones. Therefore, it follows that we are far more likely to reencounter resilience, the capacity to reorganize effectively and the ability to cope with the unforeseen,[87] when we *do not* add to environmental perturbations (many of which happen naturally), except in the most minimal form possible.

In an effort to design an "index of biotic integrity" (IBI), designed to help assess and monitor water, J. Karr says that biotic integrity "has been defined as the ability to support and maintain a balanced, integrated, adaptive community of organisms having a species composition, diversity, and functional organization comparable to that of natural habitat of the region.[88] The "potential" or capacity component is also present. Karr also states, "The ability of a water resource system to sustain a balanced biological community is obviously the best indicator of its potential. . . ."[89] Similarly, he also separates this understanding of the concept of the integrity of systems which are manipulated for specific purposes: "Biotic integrity however, is not essentially correlated with harvestable products or services of economic value. Indeed the presence in some systems of harvestable products in large amounts may indicate a loss of integrity."[90]

His findings are therefore not in conflict with the theory presented here; conversely, the understanding of the value of integrity, derived from scientific analysis attempted within these pages, appears to be supported by the practical quest for a theoretical basis, and the policy-oriented need for some clarification and a definition of integrity.

d₁. Ecosystem Integrity: A Valuable Goal

What emerges from this exploratory discussion is that we can attempt to understand an ecosystem in a state of integrity, by analyzing what it does, and what it can do. This appears to place our position squarely on the process/function side of the debate alluded to earlier. To some extent, whatever the "set of living organisms," the species and populations it may encompass, the ecosystem is constantly changing and evolving, so that the possibility of a static "ideal" for an ecosystem is not appropriate. The ecosystem is constantly evolving according to genetic information, some of which dates billions of years, and to recent information. However, it is not wholly predetermined, in spite of this genetic "load," because it retains its valuable capability for creativity (see definition of integrity, this chapter). Theoretically, creativity is a real value. Practically, this entails that complete control and predictability will elude us.

When ecosystems are viewed as they are by Robert O'Neill, Don DeAngelis, and their associates as "hierarchical systems," they may be "decomposed into subsystems or holons," the components of which may interact strongly with each other, but weakly with "components of other holons."[91] An ecosystem in a state of integrity comprises self-organizational processes both in its internal relations and its external ones with adjacent ecosystems. Thus the internal "self-organizing" or networking may well "transcend or penetrate what may superficially appear to be sharp physical boundaries."[92] This indicates that, rather than representing a valid objection to the ecosystem approach, the acknowledgment that it is the *very nature* of such open systems to be imprecise in this sense, shows the objection to be inappropriate.[93] Hence this objection cannot be used to disvalue either the ecosystem approach or the concept of integrity.

A further indication of the value of integrity emerges: the influence or impact an ecosystem in a state of integrity may have over *other* ecosystems (that is, its capacity to transcend its boundaries, which are neither hard nor fast supports the global importance of the concept of ecosystem integrity, particularly given its strong connections to both survival and sustained identity.[94] As O'Neill and his associates assert, through their work on "ecosystems as dual hierarchies," they "have shown that the natural world can be profitably viewed as a multilayered system in space and time," while at the same time providing a "framework for understanding" how the two schools or approaches in ecology can be reconciled without reducing one to the other.[95]

Without making any claims to novel scientific discoveries, I suggest that the concept of integrity might be said to give a name and a strong value to this reconciliation. Either approach in isolation may be seen to provide only partial, incomplete understanding without the other, evoking once again the allegory of the elephant and the blind men. From the philosophical standpoint instead, the quest for a morally acceptable environmental value, evokes yet another "allegory," that of the "cave" in Plato's *Republic*. Either ecological approach offers only a partial vision: when compared with the light shed by the holistic approach of integrity, the others represent only visions of "shadows," perceived by those who are constrained to one, limited point of view.

In the final analysis, the value of integrity, symbolized by point *C*, can also be supported on scientific grounds: the system under consideration is not "mutilated" (to use Robert Rosen's expression; see discussion in this chapter). This manifests *theoretically*, the intrinsic value of something which has not been diminished in some way! From the *practical* standpoint, the *instrumental* value of the undiminished system is evident in the necessary role it plays in supporting sustainability in all other systems ("used" and "manipulated"), such as those supporting forestry or agriculture.

e. Integrity, Teleology, and Nonequilibrium Thermodynamics Theory

Most of those who wish to dismiss or belittle holism sooner or later bring out the "Gaia" hypothesis as an example of how misleading, ludicrous, or unscientific the basis for this position is.[96] The first point to note is that "Gaia" is not presented as an ethical doctrine in either J. Lovelock's work or in that of Lynn Margulis. Yet, like all scientific "laws" (or "hypotheses" as some would prefer to term them), it suggests limits to appropriate or not-so-appropriate human actions. No doubt, it is primarily because of the laws of gravity that it might be morally inappropriate to drop a large rock from a second story window directly over some unlucky passerby. A norm that forbids causing harm must rely on natural laws about what is "harmful," or painful, without as a result of this taking any logically incorrect step, such as ignoring the fact/value dichotomy. What are the major assumptions, the controversial aspects of the hypothesis? Lynn Margulis has said:

> Symbiosis, rather than the accumulation of chance mutations . . . (is) the major source of evolutionary novelty; (and) the reciprocal action between organisms and the environment, rather than competition among individuals, . . . (is) the chief agent of natural selection.[97]

Margulis depicts "bacteria reacting in a meaningful way to stimuli," and claims widespread "consciousness" beyond the human realm.[98] Many do not agree with these claims. Yet the hypotheses upon which chaos theory is based indicate that a truer understanding of what comes about "naturally," that is, without human interference, is not simply a predetermined result. And if consequences cannot be predicted with any degree of assurance, or even brought about by consciously directed human action, then a certain degree of self-directedness, autopoiesis, in a word, "freedom" or "openness," may obtain in ecosystems. Perhaps the difference between humankind and the rest of the biota, as far as consciousness is concerned, is indeed one of degree only.

In that case, those who believe that the language of teleology is anthropromorphic and an outmoded Aristotelian legacy, may need to rethink their position. Probably the major problem with the acceptance of teleology, in both scientific and philosophical theory, is that the concept is by no means univocal, although attacks on it tend to assume that it is, thus giving rise regularly to "strawman" fallacies.[99] One of the clearest statements of the various confusing senses that may be imputed to teleology are listed by Rolf Sattler in his work, *Biophilosophy*.[100] He suggests that "teleology" incorporates at least four major aspects which can be distinguished:

1. The laws of nature are held responsible for the goal-direction of the sequential behaviour which is also called developmental teleology. . . . The role of consciousness is excluded . . . genetic programs are also considered to be important in this respect because they are selected. . . .

2. Intentionality, which presupposes consciousness, is held responsible for goal direction (. . . or "goal-intendedness").
3. A vital force immanent in the living organisms has been held responsible for goal-direction according to vitalistic thinkers.
    . . .
4. Finally, the direction toward goals is seen as the act of god, creator, or mind. . . . [101]

Although some speculation about the sense listed as (2) above by Margulis will be mentioned in our discussion, the use of the concept of teleology in the present work will refer exclusively to the first sense listed by Sattler, and exclude all others, unless specified otherwise.

This should help deflect some of the more outlandish critiques, such as a recent attack by George C. Williams, for example. In a paper entitled *"Gaia*, Nature Worship and Biocentric Fallacies," Williams confuses the "respect" advocated toward nature by biocentrists (unspecified) with "worship." He also suggests that damaging or catastrophic natural events are viewed by the same "biocentrists" as "diabolically perverse," a second strawman fallacy (assuming that others attribute moral agency to nature). The question of "worship" assumes either divine or similar status for the Earth as a whole, hence assumes also the fourth sense of teleology as implicit in the acceptance of any other sense of the concept. This is obviously not true in many cases. For instance, speaking of teleology and biology, A. Rosenberg says:

> Organisms have aims and purposes, which their behavior serves; their component parts serve to fulfill these purposes and have functions in meeting the needs of cells, tissues, organs, whole biological organisms. . . . Because the objects of biological interest have goals, purposes and functions, it is incumbent on biology to identify, describe and explain these teleological—end-directed—features.[102]

E. Mayr, speaking of the "Multiple Meanings of the Teleological,"[103] notes that Aristotle "invoked final causes not only for individual life processes (such as the development from the egg to the adult), but also for the universe as a whole." Yet, he says, for some time "teleological language was out of favor," as open to at least four objections: (1) it appeared to "imply the endorsement of unverifiable theological or metaphysical doctrines in science"; (2) the acceptance of teleology was taken to imply the rejection of "physicochemical explanations"; (3) teleology "appears to subvert causality, by making "future goals" causative of "present events"; and (4) to describe something as "purposive" or "goal directed" appeared to represent pure anthropomorphism.[104]

If newer scientific paradigms are accepted in ecology, including chaos theory, then all four objections lose much of their force. For example, (1) one need not go beyond science to theology or metaphysics, to speak of "directedness in the functioning of ecosystems"; (2) if some principle of choice or autopoiesis is inherent in material processes, then neither chemistry nor physics need to be rejected; (3) the question of the "directedness" of ecosystem change may be examined again: the answer may well be that the "goal" is not one and specifically describable. Shrader-Frechette says, "it is not clear what a community or ecosystem maximizes."[105] Perhaps it is simply the greatest possible "capacity for freedom" to be what it can be.[106] Finally, (4), no recourse to anthropomorphism is necessary if one accepts some degree of unpredictable self-determination for nonhuman organisms.

Rosenberg defines teleology as "an empirical, contingent, testable law of the form,

(T) Whenever a system of S's type in an environment of E's type has a goal of G's type, behavior B occurs, because it brings about (or tends to bring about) goal G.[107]

The example Rosenberg cites in regard to this law, the "so-called rule of intercalation," addresses "limb regenerative phenomena in cockroaches, amphibians, fruit-flies and crustaceans," and it is particularly appropriate for the paradigm of integrity. The "restoration of integrity," as a regulatory goal, cannot exist without the actual possibility that it *can* be done. Rosenberg adds that a specific condition needs to be present, in order to restore "continuity," and to regenerate the lost limbs: ". . . the environment, E . . . includes the absence of forces developmental biologists have identified as interfering with regeneration."[108]

The relevance of both teleogy's "testable law," and the one of the specific conditions that define it, as above, to the condition of "optimum capacity" in our definition of "integrity" (Introduction, this chapter), is obvious. Therefore we can accept Rosenberg's position that although teleological claims are "mysterious and have the appearance of backward causation," nevertheless, "the goal, the function determines the behavior that enables the system to attain it." Such claims are "unimpeachable in respect to testability."[109] Although ecosystems and single organisms are not totally analogous, they are alike in some important respects, hence the actual existence of goal-oriented processes and functions is sufficient to respond to those who object to appeals to teleology on the grounds that they are unscientific and obscurantist at the ecosystems level. Further, the existence of "substitute function" is, to some extent, analogous to the organismic "rule of intercalation" cited by Rosenberg. Examples of species performing the functions of another species' "niche" abound. A "niche" can be defined in several different ways: as (a) "the animal's place in the biotic environment, its relation to food and enemies (Eltonian niche)" (Class I); or (b) "a specific set of capabilities for extracting resources, for surviving hazards, and for competing, coupled with a corresponding set of needs (Class II); or, finally, (c) "niche as quality of environment" (Class III).[110]

On the other hand, nonequilibrium thermodynamic theories, when applied to ecosystems, imply nonrandom, unpredictable, and inherently directed change, a teleology; but the "directedness" applies only to the first sense of "teleology," as listed by Sattler and cited above. Hence, unlike Aristotelian science, they do not necessarily imply progress.[111] Directedness itself is "an inherent property of the ecosystem when the latter is defined through complex systems theory, but it is not inherent when the ecosystem is defined as a collection of interacting organisms," and I am indebted to Robert O'Neill and Don DeAngelis for this clarification. The change is not entirely predictable, because tiny variations, often not measurable with available instruments, or maybe even not measurable in principle, may eventually produce very different results from what could have been predicted from a thorough scientific analysis of the original conditions of the ecosystem at a certain point in time, or even of it in the context of exposure to some disturbance. The importance of chaos theory to ecology is pointed out by J. Gleick:

> In the emergence of chaos as a new science in the 1970's, ecologists were destined to play a special role. They used mathematical models, but they always knew that the models were thin approximations of the seething world they knew.[112]

Therefore, when Shrader-Frechette raises the question of "testable implications" of the theories of those "working within the organismic-ecosystem paradigm," she is pointing to a difficulty that is not specific to ecology, but implicit in all the natural sciences,[113] although testability is established for single organism teleology as shown above by Rosenberg's example. James Kay and Eric Schneider, for instance, say, speaking of ecosystems, "the difficulty is that by their very nature bifurcations and flips can be unpredictable."[114] What happens is that the fact that "bifurcations and flips" will happen is predictable; what is unpredictable instead are the consequences that will ultimately ensue, and the exact point when the flip and bifurcation will occur.

From the practical standpoint, one must acknowledge that the use of the ecosystem approach and the goal of restoring integrity has been successful in the Great Lakes Basin Ecosystem, in the recovery of Lake Erie, for instance, as well as in many other cases.[115] There are many cases where the ecosystem approach must be used, because it is superior in explanatory power. For instance, a case involves the adaptation of tropical trees to nutrient shortage, "where such trees have symbiotic relationships with fungi," which has "important implications for ecosystem stability."[116] Another case hinges on "the difficulty of documenting ecological covergence, especially at the community level."[117] Finally another example can be taken from the freshwater wetlands of the Florida Everglades and the Okefenokee Swamp, and the relation between *Utricularia* (or bladderwort), the prey they capture, and their ecosystem. (I am indebted to Robert Ulanowicz for this example.)

Perhaps what is needed is not an "all-or-nothing" approach, in the sense that *either* we need to adopt a scientific paradigm indicating that everything must be predictable and testable, according to linear scientific models, *or* we are left with a holistic approach that is often untested, untestable, and not truly science, in fact "no better than magic."[118] We have noted one way of combining approaches through "hierarchy theory," and Shrader-Frechette too appears to have chosen a better alternative. Rather than choosing simply *one* paradigm, model, or method of explanation, it is appropriate to maintain a dialogue between the reductionist and the holistic modes, and perhaps devote some attention to the discussion of each perspective's appropriateness to address different aspects of the environmental problems we face.

f. Can Integrity Be Restored?

Finally, from the standpoint of the meaning and value of integrity, the question of "restoration" needs to be discussed. Although science has no problem with restored limbs or any other form of restoration, environmental philosophy does. Robert Elliot, for instance, argues convincingly that there is "normative appeal" in a system which, "will make valuation depend, in part, on the presence of properties which cannot survive the disruption-restoration process."[119] This position does not discount the value of "restoring integrity," understood as restoring as much as humanly and naturally possible to an ecosystem suffering from catastrophic or crippling anthropogenic stress. It simply recognizes that any restoration is not going to result in the "real thing," although there is a great deal of difference between—say—substituting plastic penguins or trees for the real thing, and the conscientious effort to remove pollution and toxins from the degraded ecosystem, and attempt to reconstruct its structure by reintroducing species, in order to restore its health and function.

Both are, in Elliot's sense, "faking nature," but the respective value of those choices are quite different, and we might want to invoke the value of "health," rather than integrity, for the carefully restored ecosystem. In another context, Scott D. Slocombe analyzes possible states of an ecosystem as (a) change, (b) restructuring, and (c) transformation; whereby only the last (transformation) changes both "system identity" and "system organization" (e.g., its integrity is both structural and functional senses is only changed in transformation). Thus we can remove (transformation) from our consideration of "ecosystem integrity," because it represents another ecosystem altogether: "a re-organization of the entire system, new connections and forms."[120] The more difficult problem (as noted) is whether a restructuring or reordering of the whole system, often "a function of catastrophe, in which direction is changed or reversed," constitutes a return to integrity.

Possibly the first question one needs to ask is, to what extent has the "catastrophe" changed the identity of the ecosystem? Its integrity, as we saw, was based on both structure and form. Has the structure been affected? If so, has the change affected the function? If the ecosystem originally supported the life of, say, 50 species, then even without attempting to fine-tune the life span of all 50 after the changes, a restructured ecosystem which eventually supported 50 species after a catastrophe, would appear to still possess functional integrity (I_2).

The "structure" question is even more complicated. If the 50 species in the "reconstruction" were not exactly the same as the original 50, although the numbers had not changed, would "structure" have been maintained? Would it matter if it had not? In other words, the question is now, whether I_1 (structural integrity) or I_2 (functional integrity), is the most important aspect, if both do not appear to be present. Perhaps an answer to this question will emerge as we proceed. Because I_2 is to a large extent dependent on I_1, however, the answer is not an easy one. Yet if we don't wish to abandon the project and return to the legal confusion outlined in section b of this chapter, that question will need a clear and detailed answer. What is, precisely, the ideal of ecosystem integrity we must restore? A possible approach may be to view the "ideal" or "vision" we are seeking to restore in terms of an unfolding process—a "history" as long as we do not accept all historical processes or directions as equally valuable. In essence then, even the "historical" approach of an unfolding process requires a limiting vision in order to avoid adopting a totally relativistic position.

Minimally, we can affirm that using "ecosystem health" as our primary goal is too limiting. To understand ecosystem functioning is to acknowledge that an ecosystem's structural integrity must ground its identity through change, thus it is (and should be) primary, if we can speak of an ecosystem at all. It is true that change itself is a constant factor and must therefore remain a necessary part of an ecosystem's definition. Integrity, therefore, cannot be static nor represent a specific "moment" in the history of an ecosystem; it must recognize and accommodate change, at least up to the point of a possible restructuring or reordering. The latter though, if identity is to preserved, must be understood as a reconstruction *approximating* a previous state in its most significant aspects, coming close to the "ideal," without, however, needing to be a precise copy of an identifiable historical moment in the life and process of an ecosystem. This precision is not only impossible but also inappropriate for an entity *defined* (in line also with the paradigm case of integrity) as constantly changing and evolving.

Yet the fact that even "restored ecosystems" may not be capable of "optimum capacity" within their own context, as indicated, hence that they may not be equally valuable as a protected ecosystem possessing integrity, does not entail that from the practical standpoint restoration is not valuable. It simply underlines the fact that the value of integrity in its paradigm instantiation (that is, in the sense defined earlier, manifested in a wild, undisturbed ecosystem), is primary.

If even the best-intentioned restoration efforts are insufficient to achieve a perfect result, then it is all the more vital to guard jealously whatever might still be as close as possible to "wild" or "pristine," while redoubling our efforts to do the most we can for the rest. True integrity remains the benchmark case of an ecosystem possessing optimum capacities, and any and all other approximations can only be judged in relation to it. Hence "integrity" denotes both an ideal and a practical goal: the ideal remains the point of reference—the standard our actions aspire to—while we admit, at the practical level, that it might be unattainable as such. Once "integrity" is lost, even though both similar structure and function might be restored, it cannot be recaptured. Yet, even knowing that we cannot take a stressed, degraded ecosystem and restore it to pristineness, since all efforts on its behalf are *also* manipulative interference, the goal remains. Similarly, knowing that even the most careful restoration of a Regency building will not reembody that same building today, does not negate either the goal or the feasibility and worth of the project itself. One must guard, however, against "giving in" to what Eric Katz terms "The Big Lie."

He says, "Nature Restoration is a compromise; it should not be a basic policy goal." At best it represents "health" or what I have termed I_b.[121]

g. Metaphysical Aspects of Integrity

The project of integrity, as a goal of the ecosystem approach, requires changes in both perspective and mindset, on our part: the reduction of human being to parts of the ecosystem's biota. In the context of metaphysics, this perspective can be understood as (a) the recognition of external, "other," nonhuman entities as "beings," possessed of specific "natures"; and (b) the acceptance of "natural connections" within an "ordered system," that is, our interdependence and kinship within creation.

A further dimension needs to be brought out, that is, the reference to "true development." This expression acquires a specific, determinate meaning, when it. is understood in the context of Thomistic metaphysics and its conception of "truth," for instance. As noted in the previous section, Aristotelian teleology is not excluded from either biology or ecology, although it might appear in a different guise in those fields. The difference, if I understand it correctly, hinges primarily on (a) the fact that "the end of the process is determined by its properties at the beginning" (these processes are termed *quasi-finalistic* by C. H. Waddington);[122] and (b) as the process is still governed by "simple consequences of natural law," and systems' operations depend on a "program," that remains material and detectable, unlike the Aristotelian form or "final cause."

In essence, according to Mayr, these differences are the reason why he chooses the expression "teleonomic" as preferable to "teleological." Mayr suggests that, "a program is (1) something material and (2) it exists prior to the initiation of the teleonomic process. Hence it is consistent with a causal explanation."[123] He also cites Max Delbrück as correctly employing "terms like *genetic program* for *eidos*" for Aristotle, in order to separate clearly Aristotle's *eidos* from the same expression when used by Plato. Mayr adds that, just as Aristotle could see neither *eidos* nor even "soul," so "the modern scientist does not actually see the genetic program of the DNA either."[124] The final quote he offers from Delbrück, however, may well give pause to even the most open-minded Aristotelian: "And yet 'unmoved mover' perfectly describes DNA; it acts, creates form and development, and is not changed in the process."[125]

One wonders whether too much is lost of the heuristic power of teleology, when all "vitalism" is ruthlessly extirpated from it, and thus from the understanding of live systems as Mayr prefers it: "Teleonomic explanations are strictly causal and mechanistic. They give no comfort to adherents of vitalistic concepts."[126] Perhaps one might accept some similarity between the DNA and the Aristotelian "unmoved mover," if one considers its efficacy within *one* generation only: "it expresses itself and never gets reprogrammed (barring somatic mutations)."[127] Yet, unlike the "unmoved mover," natural selection "moves" the DNA instead. The role of the latter is not only causal, it is also cybernetic, and its responsiveness to outside processes and conditions appears to make it more than physical or mechanistic causation, when live organisms are involved. In that case, the limitations Mayr imposes on the term "teleonomic" make it less than acceptable in the present context.

Now a metaphysical account of reality, cannot ignore the "life" component of systems it attempts to explain. It also needs to account for the basis of "truth" (as in "true development" or even "true beings"), as well as the reason for the existence of the "programs" or the DNA. The scientist may have no need to raise these questions, but the metaphysician must. The scientist, policy maker and even the philosopher may discuss integrity and think about the structure/function distinction, but the metaphysician may also want to ask a further question: what accounts for the relation between the two?

Possibly, neither the reasons we are seeking here, nor the answers we might arrive at can be "seen" or tested any more than the "programs" Mayr discusses can be. Yet a metaphysical perspective will serve to add another dimension to the consideration of integrity, and at least help to raise questions other perspectives do not raise. For instance, let us return to the question of "truth." In the Thomistic–Aristotelian context, truth is not, primarily, propositional; truth is grounded in the actual things, (for Aquinas, for example, in creation), so that one can speak of "true being" or the "truth of beings." Although these terms cannot be used in scientific explanations or definitions, nevertheless their meaning may help in pinpointing integrity from yet another perspective. A "true river" is certainly one with all its potential, all its capacities intact. A "true river" possesses integrity: it is composed of all the elements it should have *structurally*, and its also *functions* the way a specific river of that size, in that location, at that time of the year, should. Its "truth" refers precisely to its "nature and operation" both, and it is based upon the origin of these in creation. In other words, fish are "made" to live in water, carrots are not.

Nor is the idea of a "paradigm fish" returning us to a static Platonic world of ideas. Its potential and capacities for change, growth, reproduction, maturity, and death are implicit and manifest an "integrity" that is based on identity through change, even, possibly, through evolution. To say that science proves that today's fish or lake was not "created" at a specific point in time, "as is," is not to deny the existence of sets of evolving capacities whose potential is to change according to "feedback loops"[128] as Mayr has it, and does not negate their completeness, unity, or identity, hence their integrity.

Moreover, states Mayr, a "true river" or fish is one which is viewed in its totality, as it is, hence not one that is analyzed separately from its "vitalism." Thus perhaps teleology, with all its aspects cannot be abandoned yet, as Rosenberg indicated as well, so that the heuristic function it performs can be used to cover, maybe in novel ways, every aspect of the"truth" of the being or the entity. Hence, from this perspective, to speak of "integrity" as such, is to speak not only of "ends," but of the "truth" of beings, thus to consider the question of *origin* as well.[129]

William Desmond, for instance, raises the question of "origin" as well as that of "ends" when he speaks of the integrity of the whole as a value: "I suggest that to speak of integrity of creation raises just this extreme issue of the ground or groundlessness of all value."[130] The metaphysical perspective, unlike others, requires one to consider the meaning of the integrity of the whole. It also raises the question of the value of it. Desmond notes that Nietzche saw that "modern science and culture effectively lead to a neutralization of all being. They lead to a deadening of the earth."[131] The result is a deep nihilism: nothing really matters. Nietzche's solution is a reevaluation of the human will. Yet if all in the cosmos is ultimately interrelated and interdependent as we have learned since Nietzche's day, then it makes little sense to single out *one* being (a human one) and capriciously assign value without considering that we have granted no value to the whole of which she is a part.

We are forced, by our awareness of the factual background of the issue, to choose, and thus to deal with "this extreme issue of the ground or groundlessness of all value." If humankind is part of the whole, then either the whole is valuable, or nothing is. In that case, to project value on any part of the cosmos if it is itself void of value, is "mere metaphysical whistling in the dark."[132] If this argument is accepted, it seems that a metaphysical approach to integrity may add a transitional step to value.

This supports either the ecocentric position or a "weak anthropocentrism" that incorporates aesthetic and other environmental values.

In *either* case, the necessity of incorporating environmental values raises the question of how to support these values, and indirectly, a position that does. Why is the natural beauty and integrity of natural systems a value strong enough to ground obligation? Hence Desmond correctly raises the question of the basis of value of the whole, a question that is clearly metaphysical, rather than based on either preferences, however chosen, or nominalism. He says, "In sum: if being itself has no value, man can give it no value, for his own being itself ultimately has no value."[133]

From this perspective, pursuing the more modest project of seeking a *coherent* rationale for environmental ethics *only*, is fundamentally misleading, because it is still seeking a Cartesian, mathematical model. It remains simply an effort to "totalize nature," to render it yet another "integer," available to us, its "masters" and to the pride of our "*ratio*." It is still the "subjection of the ambiguity of the world to the univocity of mathematical determination."[134] Thus neither the analytic approach with its logically contained, cautious attempts to propose answers to the"basic value" question, nor yet the deconstructionist approach will serve, although the latter does "help us be wary if totalizing claims."[135]

How can integrity escape this further problem, that is, the problem of being viewed as "totalizing?" It can be viewed as a valuable, somewhat open whole—a community of being. This in turn raises the question of whatever it is that "integrates" that community of being, beyond the individual human being, who is part of that community. Now, it is clear that to look for something "other" and both "in" and beyond the community of being is to assume a metaphysical stance, not to prove the need for one. Nor do I claim that logic and consistency *alone* force this additional step upon us.

I simply claim that, while it is possible—as we shall see—to defend the value of integrity aside from metaphysical underpinnings, the latter help to make what I take to be a stronger case, and a more defensible one, for both value and obligation, as I will argue in Chapter Three. For now, the recognition of the possibility of a metaphysical component to the value of integrity is sufficient. What might help us keep an open mind, rather than ignoring that possibility, is the acknowledgment of the weakness of a purely anthropocentric basis for value, a position which I share with many who do not speak of metaphysics at all. Although some may recognize that only humans (to our knowledge) argue about environmental values or perceive and appreciate beauty or wholeness in the natural world, they may wish to establish these values as objective, whether or not they are perceived.

Even if the argument is not explicitly made, nevertheless, even the claim that humans who do not perceive these as "values" ought to, or that they might be educated or brought to do so, ultimately assumes the existence of the values prior to human effort/understanding/appreciation and assent finally. Otherwise, one could well ask the question, *why* weaken our anthropocentrism or even displace it? Why is a non-degraded, nonpolluted world better aside from prudential reasons? Why do we "need," as Peter Miller suggests "a counterweight to . . . the homocentric value theories that dominate the Western world?"[136]

Desmond refers to Plato's "belief that no proper accounting of things is really possible outside some invocation of the absolute Good."[137] My claim, however, is not that environmental obligation has no ground at all, unless a metaphysical basis is accepted. My claim is a more modest one, or perhaps one that is wider reaching: a metaphysical basis, I believe, strengthens all claims in moral theory, including environmental ethics. As we will see in Chapter Three, these claims are not a necessary part of the "principle of integrity" I defend; they are, however, entirely compatible with it.

h. Integrity in the Ethical Sense: Its Value

This whole chapter has been exploratory in regard to the concept of integrity, its meaning, and its role as catalyst in legislation. Its main purpose has been to discover integrity's value before using it as a basis of moral obligation not only to the environment, as a separate issue, but as a first consideration of moral life. Integrity is required to bear a heavy conceptual load, because it is not sufficient to show it to be valuable, a value among many to be juggled in the pursuit of diverse interests, but as the foundational or ultimate value that must be respected and defended before any other values or choices are considered. Given the magnitude of this task, the reader will perhaps be disposed to forgive the length, broad range, and detail of the foregoing discussion. Has the task been accomplished? The following summary will show that it has.

The first section of this chapter (a), addressed the problems of considering scientific notions in the quest for value in general, given that integrity is intended as a partly scientific notion, because without a carefully drawn understanding (though not necessarily a precise definition), it could not be successfully used either in policy issues or in environmental ethics. But if science is an integral and important component of integrity, then another problem arises, aside from that of the fact–value dichotomy: the question of a philosopher's competence to undertake such a task. The whole discussion admittedly takes place within the constraints of a philosopher's limited understanding of the natural sciences. In that context, concepts and hypotheses that appear to stand out as philosophically relevant and significant may not be considered so within the scientific community, or may be considered "mainstream."

I have no solution to this problem. On the other hand, the present discussion is intended to be both theoretical and practice-oriented. Given the fact that the scientific community is hardly ever monolithic in its position on any issue, and that various theories *are* in fact presented to the educated (though nonspecialist) public, it is appropriate that a member of this public be allowed to consider various positions, understanding them as well and as deeply as the noninitiated citizen can, and then judge according to her own lights.

No doubt it would be helpful for any citizen (including the philosophers) to have a more specialized grasp of scientific facts and of the meaning of scientific explanations. Yet if these "facts," "laws," and "explanations" have an impact on public policy, then whatever information *can* be communicated to (and understood by) the public *must* be ultimately sufficient. Each member of the public would of course retain the obligation to seek explanation and understanding of debated points and issues to the best of her ability.

Yet, in the final analysis, although that was done here, even after seeking out deliberately different and often diametrically opposed viewpoints on difficult issues, the decision as to what to accept ultimately rests with the author, as it will with each citizen. Therefore, no further apology is required for the lack of scientific sophistication exhibited in the previous pages. The positions discussed were those of a member of a concerned, somewhat educated public faced with complex and threatening issues of public policy.

In essence then, section (a) is more methodological than foundational in the quest for value in integrity. Section (b), instead, is far more useful for our analysis. If the notion was first used outside ethical discourse by politicians, one can assume that the concept was deemed—minimally—to resonate in the mind of citizens/voters as a desirable, acceptable goal, as something the great majority would find appealing, and as a positive value for most people. Perhaps this is one assumption that can be made with a reasonable degree of assurance.

An interesting corollary of this aspect of integrity is that it suggests a *universal* value, comparable to peace or health perhaps, knowing no national or geographical borders. Thus, globally it might support the value of nondivisive, noncompetitive interaction among nations, and might even suggest a better political option than the present world structure, based on clearly defined national states. The specific value of integrity in this context is that, unlike "health," which could ultimately be fostered through individual policies still within national states, and "peace" that could also be maintained severally, in groups of few countries in a specific area, "integrity" is an environmental goal that requires global application.

The ability of the concept of integrity to suggest ideas that are revolutionary in their application is one of the most disconcerting aspects of the notion. It represents a value that can be used to question seriously the viability of existing, entrenched political and social beliefs and institutions. North American entrenched beliefs about individual rights and liberties, and traditionally evolved land use attitudes provide similar examples. From the standpoint of integrity, the only remedy for these long-established obstacles to environmentally concerned policies is nothing short of revolutionary: a turn-around or complete paradigm shift.

In essence then, "integrity" may be viewed in this context as a *catalyst for peaceful global interaction*, based not only on many individual national "visions," but also on one of the few truly revolutionary universal goals. Any goal that could serve to undermine militant individual nationalism must be viewed as extremely valuable in itself as an ideal guide for action as well as the promoter of clearly better circumstances.

When turning to section (c), one needs to be careful not to slip into anthropocentrism, because the value of one single organism, ours, has been the basis for most normative moral theories to date, although the biological aspect of humans has not been viewed as the dominant one as a basis for value. Nevertheless, some of the "purely physical" aspects (if such a thing exists) of human organisms did play a strong part in the ascription of value. At any rate, no theory could recommend respect for an individual's rationality but remain neutral in the face of possible physical harm. One can say generally, that in the context of single organisms, value is primarily seen in the obligation to act in a way consistent with "freedom from" harm, and without stunting, diminishing, or limiting in any way the capacity of any individual organism to maintain itself and unfold according to a specific "program."

At the level of a single organism, one can also often speak of "pain" as well as harm and other more general terms, as many single live organisms have a nervous system (unlike ecosystems as a whole), which indicates that pain is clearly a disvalue to them. In this regard then, an organism's integrity cannot be regarded as paradigmatic in regard to ecosystem integrity. However, as the "paradigm" case of integrity, as Regier suggests,[138] the biological organism represents "unity and completeness," therefore, once again, value. The "unity and completeness" of the paradigm, suggest that one can borrow from its human sense once again and *also* speak of an organism's "freedom to" actualize itself, something it can only do while it maintains its capacity to react as a unitary whole, in contrast with an aggregate, for instance.

It is worth emphasizing that the "actualizing" leads to a conception of completeness or maturity that is somewhat open-ended, rather than representing a precise, specific, and predictable state. The discussion of chaos theory and the present state of the "ecosystem approach" in ecology make this qualification necessary at the level of wholes. Without doubt, similar considerations apply at the level of individual organisms. No two humans or animals are precisely alike, although they share many qualities and capacities, broadly speaking.

Another valuable aspect of a single organism is its capacity to maintain identity through change and even strong variations. It too manifests the close interrelations of structural and functional integrity that supports identity.

Summing up then, values emerging from section (c), are primarily those of *freedom in its two senses* (i.e., positive and negative), and the *capacity to develop and change while retaining identity.*

In section (d), containing the basis and core of the "principle of integrity," the value of integrity was shown to reach beyond "health." One could say that "health" is a necessary but not a sufficient condition of integrity in that context. The "ecosystem approach," by making integrity the goal, offers a basis for making claims about human obligations to the environment. Both the use of integrity and the reference to humans as part of the biota of ecosystems, consciously or unconsciously echoes the words of Aldo Leopold and his insight. In his mind too, humans were viewed as "mere citizens" of ecosystems. Nevertheless, it is not clear whether or not the wording of the Great Lakes Water Quality Agreement of 1978, or the earlier and current numerous expressions of "integrity," *deliberately* use Leopold's words, thus accepting his work as foundational.

Whatever the historical, factual answer to that question, I take that to be the case, as the only holism that is (and was at the time) both new and defensible is precisely that of the "land ethic." This, however, brings us to the core problem, the major stumbling block in the quest for integrity in the holistic sense required by legislation and its acceptance by ethical philosophers. Humans are mere "citizens," akin to all other life in the ecosystem they inhabit. But their activities exceed animal/plant activity, directed by the "interest" (desire? instinct?) in survival of both individuals and species. Humankind has "culture" as well, and through that and in that alone, it is *not* in "nature."[139]

Environmental ethics and the goal of integrity can and should recommend harmonious, respectful interaction with the rest of the biota, and even respect and moral consideration for the ecosystem as a whole. In fact, in the interest of spelling out these categorical (not hypothetical) obligations, the goal of integrity can specify the negatives pertaining to this interaction. It can say, "thou shalt not pollute"; it can insist on, "zero discharge" and "sunset chemicals"; it can even demand a changed mindset, a new lifestyle, but only in regard to environmental interaction. What the call to "integrity" cannot do is appeal to holistic goals in the social/political sense, as the values that support it and constitute it are not primarily social or political and are even less interpersonal.

Its aim is "to restore" humankind to its rightful place as part of the natural biota. It is not "to *restore*" (per absurdum) trees, rivers, fish, bees, and beavers within political, societal, or cultural frameworks of organization. Nor are the two ideals of "restoration" interchangeable. Hence the value of integrity must represent an ideal for humans in all societies, but it is not and cannot be a *social* ideal, and the history of the many critiques directed at Leopold by those who misunderstand his point, as well as possible responses to these attacks, new and old, can be found in Chapter Four.

It is because holism and even the ideal of integrity are often treated in a dismissive manner, rather than accorded the serious consideration they deserve, that the "principle of integrity" I defend is meant as a "proposal for ethics," *simpliciter*, but it is also admittedly limited in its scope. Its primacy is emphasized, even while its limits are acknowledged. My principle gives no guidance whatever about interhuman, interpersonal interaction (Rolston says the same of Leopold's principles); although some attempt will be made to trace a tentative program of what might constitute a *compatible* interhuman ethic, that is not the object of this work. Ecocentric holism, or the quest for harmony between humankind and their environment, is simply the recognition of nonanthropocentric value or values implicit in integrity. To say how a human must interact with her environment, basing obligation on carefully supported values constitutive of ecosystem integrity, is not to choose a way of adjudicating between conflicts of human rights, priorities, and social goals.

For example (and more on this in Chapter Five), harmonious rather than hostile or confrontational interaction with an ecosystem, between its human and its nonhuman components, is a definite value. If it is translated into political/societal interaction, it may not be. It might be the sign of quietism under the rigid rule of an oppressive society, or it might be symptomatic of a society that has abandoned the vigorous confrontational defense of minority opinions or rights, or has stopped agitating for better laws, or more justice. Making "harmony" primary could thus hide compromise, despair, and even the abandonment of ideals. Thus the *harmony* fostered by the goal of ecosystem integrity is an important value, as is *biodiversity* whether or not it is a necessary condition of stability, and—in general—the *life-support function* it provides.

Section (e) defends the viability of teleological explanations in biology, thus reinforcing the Aristotelian flavor of the philosophical analysis of integrity: both Aristotelian science and metaphysics appear to be compatible with it. But the scientific viability of "restoration," the official goal of the ecosystem approach, raises questions about its ethical defensibility. Clearly, different gradations of "value" will need to be ascribed to various forms of what Robert Elliot terms "faking nature"; the paradigm case of integrity lies in wild, largely undisturbed ecosystems (as much as they can be in today's world of global pollution).

In a descending scale from that near "absolute," we find what can be reproduced and restored: harmony to begin with and health, both of which we saw were subsumed under the heading of integrity. This realization places our efforts in context and reinforces the need for a strong ecocentric position, given the rarity of the value we seek.

Finally section (f) questions the position of humankind within the world. Integrity, as a goal, represents the common denominator of value, globally. It may well be the *lowest* common denominator, but it is also the *most necessary* one, the one supporting the basis of life.

The Value of Integrity

The analysis of several different aspects of integrity in this chapter discloses a number of values that can be attributed to it. They are primarily nonanthropocentric, although most have further anthropocentric applications, not constitutive of the value of integrity as such. These values can be listed under ten headings.

Integrity's value may be based on the following intrinsic aspects:
1.   It is a *universal value, global* in a sense different from both peace and health, the only other values that may compare in relevance with it.

2. It is a *revolutionary concept*, a catalyst for the necessity of rethinking both *national* basic beliefs about just human interaction and human rights, and accepted standards of previous *international* interaction.

3. It emphasizes the meaning of its paradigm case, organic unity, and the *value of freedom in its two senses*, negative and positive, in that regard. Negative freedom requires no interference with the organism's biological identity; positive freedom requires that the organism's conditions be such that it may continue in its capacity to develop and change while retaining identity.

4. It includes the *value of health* in a nonanthropocentric sense.

5. It indicates and supports the *value of the whole*, while correspondingly emphasizing the reduced role and status of individuals including humankind. This emphasis is *only* applied to biological interaction, *not* to social or cultural activities.

6. It supports the *value of harmony*, including that between individuals and whole, and structure and function, once again, *only* in the biological sense indicated in (5) above.

7. It encompasses the *value of biodiversity*, and (a) the *life-support* and (b) the information/communication functions it supports.

8. It subsumes the *value of sustainability*, hence *stability*. In fact it is absolutely necessary in some proportion, for the sustainability of all other parts of the landscape.

9. It emphasizes the *value of life/existence* as such (that is, for *all* individuals and wholes).

10. It shows the *congruence of morality, science/empirical reality, and metaphysics*, in integrity as an environmental value.

Not everyone will accept each of these separate, interrelated facets of the value of integrity. Nor do I claim that these and only these are all its possible valuable aspects. Nevertheless, even some of these aspects manifest the existence of a cluster of values that can be discovered as implicit in the concept of integrity. And even accepting some of these might be sufficient, in order to support the principle of obligation arising from integrity.

In the next chapter I will turn to the use of "integrity," established here as a basic yet ultimate value, through this chapter and the previous one as well. The "principle of integrity" will make use of the notion in order to establish a categorical imperative, in two related formulations. The Kantian flavor of the formal aspect of the principle is deliberately adopted to indicate the deontological, nonnegotiable status of the principle. On the other hand, other thinkers have attempted to base obligation on biocentrism and ecocentrism. It is therefore important to show why and how the "principle of integrity" is different from those theories and thus original, although appealing to similar values. This task will be accomplished in the next chapter, and the "principle" will be presented and defended.

Notes

1. Henry Regier, et al., "Integrity and Surprise in the Great Lakes Basin Ecosystem," in *An Ecosystem Approach to the Integrity of the Great Lakes in Turbulent Times,* Great Lakes Fisheries Commission Special Publications 90-4 (Ann Arbor, Mich.: Great Lakes Commission, 1990): 17–36.
2. Aldo Leopold, *A Sand County Almanac*, 224.
3. Regier, "Integrity."
4. Ibid., 3; see also George M. Woodwell, "The Challenge of Endangered Species," in Ghillian Prance and Thomas Elias, eds., *Extinction Is Forever* (New York: New York Botanical Gardens, 1977).
5. Regier, "Integrity."
6. Ibid., 6; cp. Thomas C. Jorling, "Incorporating Ecological Principles into Public Policy," in *Environmental Policy and Law* 2 (1976).
7. Thomas Muir and Anne Sudar, "Toxic Chemicals in the Great Lakes Basin Ecosystem" (Burlington, Ont.: Environmental Canada, 1987), 44ff.; cp. *Science Advisory Board Report to the International Joint Commission* (Windsor, Ont.: IJC, Sept. 1991); esp. 15–41.
8. Muir and Sudar, 31.
9. Ibid., 44ff.
10. M. R. Edelstein and A. Wandersman, "Community Dynamics in Coping with Toxic Contaminants," in *Human Behavior and Environment Advances in Theory and Research*, Vol. 19 (Mahwah, New Jersey: School of Social Sciences, Ramapo College, 1987); cp. M. Sagoff, *The Economy of the Earth*, 24ff.
11. Muir and Sudar, 82.
12. William Frendenburg, "Perceived Risk, Real Risk: Social Science and the Art of Probabilistic Risk Assessment," *Science* 242:44; Kristin Shrader-Frechette, *Risk and Rationality* (Berkeley: University of California Press, 1991), especially Chapters 11 and 12.
13. Paul Muldoon, "The Fight for an Environmental Bill of Rights," *Alternatives* 15, No. 2 (1988):35.
14. Great Lakes Science Advisory Board–Great Lakes Regional Office, Report to the International Joint Commission (Windsor, Ontario: 1991).
ICSU (International Council of Scientific Unions), and TWAS (Third World Academy of Sciences, Conference Statement: International Conference on an Agenda of Science for Environment and Development into the 21st Century (Ascend 21).
IJC (International Joint Commission), Research Managers Report; Proposed

Framework for Developing Indicators of Ecosystem Health for the Great Lakes Region, (Windsor: IJC 1991).

IJC/GLFC (Great Lakes Fisheries Commission), Integrity the Context of Surprise: Proceedings: Proceedings of a Workshop (Windsor, Ontario: IJC 1990, and Ann Arbor, Mich.: GLFC, 1990).

National Institute of Public Health and Environmental Protection, The National Environmental Outlook 1990–2010 (Bilthoven: RIVM, 1991).

OMEE (Ontario Ministry of the Environment and Energy), Toward an Ecosystem Approach to Land Use Planning: A Biophysical Environmental Perspective (OMEE, July 1992).

RAAS (Rawson Academy of Aquatic Science), Towards an Ecosystem Charter for the Great Lakes–St. Lawrence (Ottawa: RAAS, 1989).

WCC (World Council of Churches), Integrity of Creation: An Ecumenical Discussion. Discussion Document for an Ecumenical Consultation (Granvallen, Norway: February 25-March 3, 1988).

WCC, "American Fisheries Society's draft Policy Statement i.e., Endangered Species ACT" in *Fisheries* 18 (No. 7, July 1993): 34.

15. A meeting on "Ecosystem Science and Integrity" took place at the University of Waterloo (Ontario), in conjunction with the meeting of the International Association of Great Lakes Researchers (IAGLR), June 2, 1992 (Focus Group No. 1), with the support of SSHRC and an interdisciplinary thematic grant for environmental ethics (L. Westra, Principle of Integrity). A further meeting took place June 28, 1993, at the University of Guelph (Ontario) under the sponsorship of Dean O. Nielsen, College of Veterinary Medicine, on Health/Integrity (Focus Group No. 3).

16. Lester Breslow, "Health Status Measurement in the Evaluation of Health Promotion," *Medical Care* 27, no. 3, Supplement (March 1989):S206.

17. Ibid.; cp. World Health Organization Constitution, in *Basic Documents* (Geneva: WHO, 1948.

18. Talcott Parsons, "Definitions of Health and Illness in the Light of American Values and Social Structure," in E. Gurtly Jaco, ed., *Social Structure and Personality* (New York: Free Press of Glencoe, 1964), 208, on Breslow.

19. Breslow, S213.

20. J. Kay, "A Nonequilibrium Thermodynamic Framework for Discussing Ecosystem Integrity," *Environmental Management* 15 (1991): 483–495. See also J. Kay, "The Nature of Ecological Integrity: Some Closing Remarks," in *Ecological Integrity and the Management of Ecosystems*, S. Woodley, J. Francis, and J. Kay, eds. (Delray Beach, Fla.: St. Lucie Press, 1993).

21. D. DeAngelis, Robert O'Neill et al., *The Hierarchical Concept of Ecosystems* (Princeton, N.J.: Princeton University Press, 1986), 15.

22. Kristin Shrader-Frechette, *Risk and Rationality*, 39–46.

23. Mark Sagoff, "Fact and Value in Ecological Science," *Environmental Ethics* 7 no. 2: (2), 99–116.

24. Thomas C. Jorling, "Incorporating Ecological Principles into Public Policy," *Environmental Policy and Law*, 2 (1976).

25. D. J. Rapport, "Symptoms of Pathology in the Gulf of Bothnia (Baltic

Sea)," *Biological Journal of the Linnean Society*, 37 (1992): 33–49. See also Rapport and H. A. Regier, "Disturbance and Stress Effects on Ecological Systems," in B. C. Pattern, ed., *Complex Ecology: The Part-Whole Relation in Ecosystems* (New York: Prentice-Hall, in press); and also J. Karr et al., "Assessing Biological Integrity in Running Waters, a Method and Its Rationale," *Illinois Natural History Survey*, Special Publication 5.

26. H. A. Regier, "The Notion of Natural and Cultural Integrity," in S. Woodley, J. Francis, J. Kay, eds., *Ecological Integrity and the Management of Ecosystems* (Delray Beach, Fla.: St. Lucie Press, 1993), 3–18.

27. J. Kay, "A Nonequilibrium Thermodynamic"; see also Kay, "The Nature of Ecological Integrity: Some Closing Remarks," op. cit.

28. A. Rapoport, *General System Theory* (Cambridge, U.K.: Abacus Press, 1986).

29. Barry Boyer, "Building Legal and Institutional Frameworks for Sustainability," Annual Meeting of the International Association of Great Lakes Researchers (June 1991), 13–14.

30. Congressional Record–Senate (U.S.), October 17, 1972; Volume 118, Part 28, 92nd Congress, 2nd Session; Speaker Senator Edmund Muskie, citing Clean Water Act (1972), section 101 (1): "To restore and maintain the chemical, physical and biological integrity of the nation's waters."

31. Lynton K. Caldwell, "The Ecosystem as a Criterion for Public Land Policy," in *Natural Resources Journal* 10, no. 2 (April 1970): 203–22, especially 208.

32. Boyer, 14; cp. John Quarles, *Cleaning Up America: An Insider's View of the Environmental Protection Agency* (Boston: Houghton Mifflin, 1976).

33. Boyer, 14.

34. Mark Sagoff, *The Economy of the Earth* (Cambridge, U.K.: Cambridge University Press, 1989), primarily Chapter 5.

35. See L. Westra, "Endangered Earth: U.S. 'National Vision' and Canadian 'Survival'." Manuscript prepared with the support of the Canadian Embassy, Washington, D.C., Summer 1991.

36. For this point I am indebted to Chris Westra, my son.

37. Boyer, op. cit.

38. John Ladd, Alaisdair MacIntyre, Kristin Shrader-Frechette have all addressed this point in some detail.

39. Caldwell, 208.

40. Eugene Hargrove, *Foundations of Environmental Ethics* (Englewood Cliffs, N.J.: Prentice-Hall, 1989), 55; cp. 56–61.

41. Hargrove, ibid., 56.

42. Ibid., 62.

43. Mark Sagoff, "Takings, Just Compensation and the Environment," in *Upstream/Downstream*, 158–79; compare 160–61 with E. Paul, *Property Rights and Eminent Domain* (New Brunswick, N.J.: Transaction Books, 1987), 138.

44. Boyer, 10–11; cp. Alan Freeman, "Antidiscrimination Law: The View from 1990," *Tulane Law Review* 64 (1990): 1407.

45. Boyer, ibid., 11.

46. J. Baird Callicott, "Intrinsic Value of Non-human Species," in *Why Preserve Natural Variety?* (Princeton: Princeton University Press, 1987), 163.

47. H. Regier, et al., "Integrity and Surprise in the Great Lakes Basin Ecosystem: Implications for Policy," in *Proceeding of An Ecosystem Approach to the Integrity of the Great Lakes in Turbulent Times*, eds. Clayton J. Edwards and Henry Regier, July 1990; Great Lakes Fisheries Commissions Special Publications 90–4; 17–36.

48. James J. Kay and Eric D. Schneider, "Thermodynamics and Measures of Ecological Integrity," 1992, in *Ecological Indicators,* Vol. 1, D. H. McKenzie, D. E. Hyatt, V. J. McDonald, eds., *Proceedings of the International Symposium on Ecological Indicators* (Fort Lauderdale, Fla.: Elsevier, 1992), 159–82.

49. Both William Desmond and Peter Miller referred to integrity in that way as part of a panel discussion they participated in, Central American Philosophical Association, Chicago, Apr. 29, 1991.

50. As above.

51. Peter Miller, "Is Integrity Enough?," presented as above, p. 6. It is important to realize that "openness" is a relative term.

52. Kristin Shrader-Frechette, "Biological Holism and the Evolution of Ethics," *Between the Species* no. 4 (Fall 1990):186.

53. Mark Timmons, *Conduct and Character* (Belmont, Calif.: Wadsworth Publishing Company, 1990), 16–18; cp. K. Shrader-Frechette, "Ecological Theories and Ethical Imperatives," in W. Shea and B. Sitter, eds., *Scientists and Their Responsibility* (Canton, Mass.: Watson Publishers, 1989), 84–85. She refers to these as "first order (intuitive) ethical claims," and speaks of intrinsic value in nature.

54. See for instance Paul Taylor, *Respect for Nature: A Theory of Environmental Ethics* (Princeton, N.J.: Princeton University Press). Peter Singer, "Animal Liberation," in VandeVeer, 24–32; Tom Regan, *The Case for Animal Rights* (Berkeley: University of California Press, 1983); Donald VandeVeer "Interspecific Justice" in *People, Penguins and Plastic Trees*, 51–65.

55. It is important to note that the concept of "ecosystem integrity" is elastic. In Regier, "The Notion of Natural and Cultural Integrity," 1–2, it is stated that some people have noted that the human organism "serves as a habitat for a variety of other species, together with some non-living material as in the gut, so that a single human may rate as an ecosystem."

56. Jeffrey A. McNeely, "Learning Lessons from Nature: The Biome Approach to Sustainable Development," in P. Jacobs and D. Munro, eds., *Conservation with Equity*, Proceedings of the Conference on Conservation and Development; Implementing World Conservation Strategy, Ottawa, May 31–June 5, 1986 (Gland, Switzerland and Cambridge, U.K.: The International Union for Conservation of Nature and Natural Resources, 1987), 25.

57. McNeely, 253–54; cp. E. P. Odum, "The Ecosystem," *Ecology,* 2nd ed., (Sunderland, Mass.: Sinaver Associates, 1993), 38–67.

58. McNeely, 253–54.

59. Ibid.

60. Ibid.

61. B. G. Norton, *Why Preserve Natural Variety?* (Princeton, N.J.: Princeton University Press, 1986), 49–50.

62. Ibid., 51–57.

63. Ibid., 57.

64. Ibid., 59.

65. Ibid., 58; R. H. Wittaker, *Communities and Ecosystems* (New York: Macmillan, 1970), 103.

66. Norton, 63.

67. Holmes Rolston III, *Environmental Ethics* (Philadelphia: Temple University Press, 1988), 163.

68. J. Baird Callicott, "Aldo Leopold's Metaphor," in R. Costanza, B. G. Norton, and B. D. Haskell, eds., *Ecosystem Health* (Washington, D.C.: Island Press, 1992), 42–56.

69. Leopold, 224.

70. Callicott, "Aldo Leopold's Metaphor."

71. Robert Rosen, *Life Itself, a Comprehensive Inquiry into the Nature, Origin, and Fabrication of Life* (New York: Columbia University Press, 1991).

72. Rosen, 116.

73. O'Neill, DeAngelis, et al., 3.

74. Ibid., 4.

75. Ibid., 5.

76. Ibid., 16–17.

77. William Vayda, *Psychonutrition* (Port Melbourne, Australia: Lothian Publishing, 1992).

78. C. S. Hollings, "The Resilience of Terrestrial Ecosystems; Local Surprises and Global Change," in W. C. Clark and R. E. Munn, eds., *Sustainable Development of the Biosphere* (Cambridge, U.K.: Cambridge University Press, 1992), 292–317.

79. Ibid.

80. N. O. Nielsen, *Ecosystem Health and Sustainable Agriculture* (University of Guelph, Ontario: The Science Council of Canada, 1991).

81. J. Kay and E. Schneider, "Life as a Manifestation of the Second Law of Thermodynamics," in *Advances in Mathematics and Computers in Medicine* (Waterloo, Ontario: University of Waterloo, 1993), 30 pages.

82. J. Kay, 483–495.

83 Ibid., and also Kay and Schneider, "Life as a Manifestation of the Second Law of Thermodynamics" (in press) in *Advances in Mathematics and Computers in Medicine*, 30 pp.

84. Kay and Schneider, ibid.

85. Ibid.

86. E. Mayr, *Toward a New Philosophy of Biology* (Cambridge, Mass.: Harvard University Press, 1988).

87. D. H. Meadows, D. L. Meadows, and J. Randers, *Beyond the Limits* (Post Mills, Vermont: Chelsea Green Publishing, 1992).

88. J. Karr, et al., "Assessing Biological Integrity in Running Waters, a Method and Its Rationale," *Illinois Natural History Survey*, Special Publication 5 (1986).

89. Ibid., 1986.

90. Ibid., 1986.

91. O'Neill, et al., 79.

92. H. Regier, "Ecosystem Integrity in the Great Lakes Basin: An Historical Sketch of Ideas and Actions," *Journal of Aquatic Ecosystem Health* 1(No. 25, 1992):25–37.

93. Kristin Shrader-Frechette and E. McCoy, "Community Ecology, Scale and the Instability of the Stability Concept," in *PSA* 1992, M. Forbes and D. Hull, eds. (East Lansing, Mich.: Philosophy of Science Association).

94. H. Regier, "The Notion of Natural and Cultural Integrity," op cit.

95. O'Neill, et al., 186.

96. The notion of Gaia we are referring to here can be found in J. Lovelock, *The Ages of Gaia: A Biography of Our Living Earth* (New York: Norton, 1988). "Gaia" is used to refer to "the idea that Earth is alive" (p. 3) and to "the concept that the Earth is actively maintained and regulated by life on the surface" (pp. 3–4). Also, "The name of the living planet, Gaia, is not a synonym for the biosphere. . . . Gaia, as total planetary being, has properties that are not necessarily discernable by just knowing individual species of populations of organisms living together" (p. 19).

97. Lynn Margulis, as cited by Charles Mann in "Lynn Margulis: Science's Unruly Earth Mother," *Science* 252(April 19, 1991):380.

98. It must be acknowledged that Margulis's claims do not represent "mainstream" scientific consensus at this time. Further, that systems may indeed be open/indeterminate and cognitive/cybernetic, without being conscious. I am indebted to H. Rolston III for the last point.

99. George C. Williams, "*Gaia*, Nature Worship and Biocentric Fallacies," *The Quarterly Review of Biology* 67(no. 4, December 1992): 479–96.

100. Rolf Sattler, *Biophilosophy* (New York: Springer-Verlag, 1990).

101. Sattler, op. cit., 153; The "four senses" of teleology are here cited in part, without the extensive footnotes and details that appear in the text.

102. A. Rosenberg, *The Structure of Biological Science* (Cambridge: Cambridge University Press, 1985), 43.

103. Mayr, 38–66.

104. Ibid., 40.

105. Kristin Shrader-Frechette, "Organismic Biology and Ecosystem Ecology: Description or Explanation?" in Nicholas Rescher, ed., *Current Issues in Teleology* (Lanham, Md.: University Press of America, 1990), 78–91 and passim.

106. I am indebted to Henry Regier for this point. Private communication, May 1991; in contrast the concept of "openness" may be substituted.

107. Rosenberg, 49; for another example of this law see Marcia Baringa, "Viruses Launch Their Own Star Wars," *Science* 258(Dec. 11, 1992): 1730–31.

108. Rosenberg, 49.

109. Ibid., 50.

110. Paul Colinvaux, *Ecology* (New York: Wiley, 1990), 29–32.

111. Scott D. Slocombe, "Assessing Transformations of Sustainability in the Great Lakes Basin," in *Geo Journal* 21 (No. 3, 1990): 252–72.

112. J. Gleick, *Chaos, Making a New Science* (New York: Penguin Books, 1987), 59.

113. Shrader-Frechette, "Organismic Biology," 82.

114. Kay and Schneider, 18.

115. Literature abounds on *specifics* of Lake Erie's restoration to "health," although no one, to my knowledge, has written a holistic account of its recovery. See, for instance, Noel M. Burns, *Erie: The Lake That Survived* (Totowa, N.J.: Rowman and Allanheld, 1985).

116. Colinvaux, 439–40.

117. John A. Wiens, *The Ecology of Bird Communities* (Cambridge, U.K.: Cambridge University Press, 1989), Vol. 1, 417–20.

118. Schrader-Frechette, "Organismic Biology," 83.

119. Robert Elliot, "Faking Nature," in *People, Penguins and Plastic Trees*, 143.

120. Slocombe, op cit.

121. Eric Katz, "The Big Lie: Human Restoration of Nature," in *Research in Philosophy and Technology* 12(1992): 231–41.

122. Mayr, 44; cp. C. H. Waddington, *Toward a Theoretical Biology I* (Edinburgh: Edinburgh University Press, 1968).

123. Mayr, 48.

124. Ibid., 57.

125. Ibid.; cp. Delbrück "Aristotle-totle-totl" in J. Monod and E. Borek, eds., *Of Microbes and Life* (New York: Columbia University Press, 1971).

126. Mayr, 60.

127. I am indebted to Holmes Rolston III, and to Kristin Shrader-Frechette for much of this discussion of Mayr's claims.

128. Mayr, 60.

129. William Desmond, "The Integrity of Creation," presented at the Central APA, April 29, 1991, p. 2.

130. Ibid., 2.

131. Ibid., 2.

132. Ibid., 3.

133. Ibid.; cp. p. 4: "Ethics is inseparable from metaphics. Without proper metaphysical ground, ethics is groundless."

134. Desmond, 5.

135. Ibid, 6.

136. Peter Miller, "Is Health an Anthropocentric Value?," *Nature and System* 3 (1981): 193–207, especially 199.

137. Desmond, 9.

138. Regier, "Integrity and Surprise," 18.

139. Rolston, *Environmental Ethics*.

3

"Respect," "Dignity," and "Integrity": An Environmental Proposal for Ethics

Introduction

The previous chapter concludes with a list of intrinsic aspects which attest to "integrity" as a value, possibly even an ultimate value. The analysis of the concept of "integrity" was undertaken because the notion could not boast, at least prima facie, the same credibility and the same traditional support possessed by other proposed "ultimate values." The concluding remarks in Chapter Two addressed both similarities and dissimilarities between "integrity" and other "ultimates" such as "happiness" or "rationality."

If ecosystem integrity is to be accepted as a fundamental value, the obligation to act in accordance with it, or—as the legislative understanding of the "goal" has it—to "restore" it, will engender an ethic of respectful interaction with the life-support system and thus with the environment of which we are a part.

The understanding of our place in "nature" also counsels respect. Accepting integrity as a value entails that it is forbidden to treat the environment as only instrumentally valuable. Further, the rejection of the absolute of anthropocentrism, implicit in the recognition of "integrity" as a fundamental value, also requires that respect be extended first beyond our species. However, I am not the only one or even the first person to argue for an environmental ethic of respect. For instance, Albert Schweitzer did so, with the "reverence for life" ethic, and Paul Taylor, with his own "ethic of respect for nature." The two ethics are by no means equal, yet they both share the component of the quest for a ground for respect which might be similar to Schweitzer's concept of "reverence," which in turn holds the place of primary aspect of my own ethic as well. Therefore it is necessary to show that my position is (a) different from the other two (prior) major positions mentioned, and (b) more complete than they are or, at least, capable of resolving some of the puzzles the others leave unsolved.

Thus a question may arise in regard to "respect" as a requirement (in my case) for an environmental/animal ethic supported by the value of "integrity," in the sense in which I develop the notion. Is my sense of "respect" only duplicating the "reverence for life" which represents instead Schweitzer's highest "court of appeal"?[1] But should that be the case, appealing as that position might be to me, it is too flawed to be useful, according to J. B. Callicott and K. E. Goodpaster, among others.[2] Therefore two questions need to be addressed. First the question of the difference between Schweitzer's position and mine; second, the validity and viability of my position. My main contention has, as does Schweitzer's, its grounding in a "biocentric outlook on nature," as Paul Taylor, the second thinker I want to examine, terms it.[3] Taylor in fact is the main proponent today of this ethical approach, and his work is not only very useful for evaluating the viability of "respect" as such, but also for trying to reach beyond it to whatever we can accept as engendering and eliciting it, both in its regular ethical version (that is, as respect for humans), and as respect for nonhuman natural entities.

I believe that my approach has a wider reach than either Schweitzer's or Taylor's for various reasons to be discussed below, and in order to attempt to move beyond their positions, one needs to start by understanding well their basic principles. My interest lies in attempting an analysis of "respect" as well as a discussion of "inherent worth" (Taylor's term), and particularly of "dignity" as a possible basis for both, as the latter is a notion often used even in purely human ethical argumentation but seldom defined or analyzed in itself.

Both Schweitzer and Taylor do not concern themselves directly with ecosystems, rather, with individual life-forms and maybe with aggregates or communities. Nevertheless, as I maintain, there is no conflict, at least prima facie, between respect for individuals and respect for systems, even though a separate argument needs to be made for the value and the moral considerability of the latter, as was done in the previous chapter. Other "deep" positions based on ecosystems' "interests," such as the deliberate Spinozism of Freya Matthews or Lawrence Johnson's position, are clearly quite different from my position, so that no presentation of their detailed argument is necessary.[4]

I will start with Taylor's position before turning to Schweitzer's, then returning to my own in the concluding section. Throughout I will keep in mind the foundational concept of "dignity" and attempt to shed whatever little light one might be able to shed on such a difficult and elusive notion.

Taylor's Biocentric Ethic of Respect for Nature and the Concept of Dignity

"Dignity" is a concept which is thrown into the ethical arena when one needs to justify either "rights" or "respect" (in our cases) in some way that is not dependent on contractarian premises. Now it is only aside from such arguments that the notion is at all interesting and deserving of serious consideration. In other words, if the term indicates something we can contract, to view each other as having, then it is of no more moment than any other title or property we may bestow upon one another. Examples might be Member of the Order of the Knights of Columbus, or the Loyalist Daughters of the Empire, and so on. We define what membership in these groups entails, therefore there is nothing deep, puzzling, or even objective about those terms, other than the way we (subjectively) decide to understand them.

Respect for human beings, on the other hand, is not meant to rest on pacts or group decisions. It is meant to be a universal aspect of all ethical doctrines. Taylor discusses the difference between nonmoral rules and universal moral rules: the latter "must be intended to be applied disinterestedly, as matters of principle. They serve as categorical imperatives. . . ."[5] In human ethics, these rules require "respect for persons," he says.[6] My question goes beyond this statement: what is the ground or basis for this "respect for persons"? As Taylor's argument goes from the general requirements for human ethics, to the equivalent (and equally acceptable) requirements for a biocentric environmental ethic, it is imperative that we start with the former in order to see whether it might be transferred to the latter. Taylor says:

> . . . it is possible to establish the truth of this claim that a person has inherent worth by showing that only this way of regarding persons is coherent with the conception of every person as a rational valuing being—an autonomous center of conscious life.[7]

The context of this argument tends to show that it is inconsistent to view oneself in such a light but refuse to extend our self-respect (based on the properties listed above) to other human beings. But Kantian rationality and conscious autonomy seem to me to be poor candidates for grounding "inherent worth" such that it can eventually be extended beyond the human realm. Taylor does in fact affirm that "there are no good reasons for affirming human superiority,"[8] yet, just like most others who argue for environmental or animal ethics, he tacitly appears to believe in at least one form of human superiority: that of moral capacity.

When a lion stalks and eventually kills his prey, he is not performing an immoral action, although this might entail breaking all the rules
Taylor sets up as following upon the biocentric "ethic of respect for
nature" (these are, the rule of nonmaleficence, the rule of noninterference, the rule of fidelity, and the rule of restitutive justice).[9] Therefore, nature just "is," while we instead "ought" to do this or abstain
from that action. Taylor's own enterprise clearly assumes that to be
moral is a good thing and—given his Kantian approach—probably also
a necessary aspect of being a rational, autonomous human being. Thus,
the argument may run, humans have no "inherent worth" which makes
them superior to any other species on earth or even to ecosystems as
such, yet they possess a capacity which represents their primary characteristic, but which does not exist in any other individual creature:
the capacity to be moral agents. This position appears to be inconsistent; unless our "way" is better why should we not be governed by a
natural "is" as other entities are? Why attempt to behave in our "superior" way and consider our actions from the standpoint of morality?

But, as many contend, it is both inappropriate and illogical to go
from an "is" to an "ought" in interhuman ethics, and perhaps this
position is the correct one, at least as far as it goes. The problem
then is far deeper than Taylor, among others, implies. First, to feel
impelled to view our situation vis-à-vis nonhuman entities and systems as one where we are bound to act "better than they do," in a
sort of "noblesse oblige," as I have heard it phrased at the XVIII World
Congress of Philosophy in a session devoted to animal ethics, is to
depreciate implicitly individual entities, ecosystems, and even the rules
and laws that govern them. This attitude, while overtly nature-regard-
ing, is covertly disrespectful instead, as its claim must be that it is
"more enlightened" to treat wild nature in ways other than the "law
of the jungle." It is anthropocentrism pure and simple; it claims that
"we" are the measure of all things moral and correct in the universe.

Second, in trying to extend our "measure" or standard, we run into
serious logical and methodological problems. As we saw, Taylor speaks
of "every person as a rational, valuing being—an autonomous center
of conscious life."[10] We can claim that all live entities, and even whole
ecosystems are also "autonomous centers of life," but rationality, consciousness (in the strong sense of being self-conscious, rather than the
weaker sense of being sentient and aware), and even more the capacity to be a "valuing being," are much harder to extend across the
species barrier.

What, if anything, can be so extended is a question many, including Taylor, have attempted to answer in various ways, more or less

satisfactorily, and I will return to this topic in my conclusion.[11] The first question is—I believe—even harder. In essence, Taylor's argument is that, because we respect what has "inherent worth," and that is not exclusively or essentially human, then human morality necessarily extends to the environment and all within it in "wild nature." His argument for morality toward "domesticated" nature, or what he terms "bioculture" is too vague and inconclusive to be helpful. To be fair to Taylor, he excludes "bioculture" or all that is not "wild" from his main argument, simply counseling to devote some moral concern to these creatures as well, in a very brief section titled "A Note on the Ethics of the Bioculture."[12]

Now the fact that a very large proportion of nonhuman creatures, that is, domestic animals, is thus hard to fit within his "respect for nature" ethics, should alert us to the fact that a problem exists. Any ethic that starts as interhuman is bound to be limited, thus limiting in its usefulness when "natural" barriers are exceeded, and its logical problems (if any) are magnified by the recalcitrant subject matter it is applied to. Taylor argues that it is important to maintain the "logical gap" between the "is" statements of the biological sciences and the "ought" statements of ethics,[13] whereas there is—for him—a symmetry "between human ethics and environmental ethics."[14]

If the "logical gap" is accepted as basic, thus foundational in this enterprise, then we lose the main link to the rest of nature and the kinship we need to embrace in order to accept that its laws are our laws and—ultimately—its interests and goals are ours too. To say that there is one world of nature, to which a simple "is" is appropriate, but there is also another world of humans where an "ought" must reign, is to introduce a vast and unjustified gap that does not facilitate the adoption of an ethic of respect, but rather appears to foster the very anthropocentrism we need to combat.

An example of this paradox may be found in Taylor's rule of "Fidelity," an extension of a human virtue. We must not lie or break trust, intraspecifically, and this is in line with what obtains in wild nature as well: wolves do not break faith with other wolves in their pack. Moreover, humans can "cheat" birds or other wild animals by imitating their distress calls (the example Taylor offers of humans "breaking trust" with wild nature), precisely because in wild nature these calls are always truthful, never used by animals as pranks or to mislead (within their own specific boundaries).

However, animals themselves walk stealthily when they need to stalk prey; for some, their very appearance is meant to serve as a camouflage, a decoy. Taylor would be the first to admit there is nothing "immoral" about the situation. Similarly, I want to argue, the Canadian native or Inuit who equally stalks and kills his (animal) prey and then uses it fully for the sustenance of his family or his tribe is also not breaking any moral law. "Fidelity" and "trust" may only come into play when the motive for the hunt is immoral: "sport," curiosity, trivial uses for the prey, and so on. But in this case, the breach of fidelity or trust, is peripheral; it is the kill itself that is unequivocally wrong. To speak of immoral means to bring about an immoral goal seems somewhat superfluous. There is no "moral" way to rob, in human ethics, though one can readily agree that torture or other "worse" ways may in fact aggravate a crime.

In essence then, a biocentric ethic of "respect for nature" is—I believe—the only and best way to proceed toward an all-encompassing environmental/animal ethic, but Taylor's own carefully argued version is not totally satisfactory. This is mainly because (a) it attempts to extend (mainly Kantian) interhuman ethics, and that leads to problems such as (b) the ethic's self-contradictory aspects (mentioned above), and (c) its incapacity to deal with the problem of millions of nonhuman creatures which are not in "wild nature." Much as I too see the great need to incorporate everything that exists in the realm of the "morally considerable" as Mary Midgley for instance argues,[15] it does not help to maintain the coincidence of intraspecies (i.e., interhuman) ethics and interspecies ethics. This tends to contradict "what is in wild nature" as Holmes Rolston puts it, and as I pointed out earlier, manifests a problem with respect for natural rules and laws which govern what is.

And what about "dignity"? To phrase this in a different way, what grounds and elicits our respect? Taylor replies:

> Having regard for the natural world in this sense, arises from a consideration for the wholeness and integrity of the system of nature as an independent realm of reality existing in its own right. Regard is the due recognition we give to that realm of reality as something worthy of our respect. It is seen to be sufficient in itself, not dependent on human agency for making possible the good of life.[16]

"Regard" is thus elicited by the natural world's "wholeness," "integrity," "independence from human agency," and "self-sufficiency." Thus the "attitude of respect" can be fostered and justified without recourse to the notion of rights,[17] which Taylor claims cannot "logically" be ascribed to either animals or plants, as they can to us, given that "personhood" is required to guarantee them.[18]

Thus, in the final analysis, for Taylor the appropriate attitude of respect is elicited from us simply through "inherent worth," to which rights, involving the "claim to be respected" add nothing from a conceptual standpoint.[19] Thus we return to "inherent worth." For humans, it is based on "simple personhood"; but what about the rest of the environment? "The attitude of respect for nature is not only a moral one, but an ultimate one," says Taylor. It is therefore very important to provide such an ethic with a truly solid basis. For Taylor, this basis is the fact that human life itself is "an integral part of the natural order of the biosphere," and that (a) the physical requirements for survival impose on all living things, human and nonhuman alike, the constant necessity to adjust to environmental changes and to the activities of other organisms within the environment; (b) they (like we) are entities having "a good of their own," one which is not under our control any more than it is under theirs, human *hubris* and self-deception notwithstanding;[20] (c) we share with other creatures one specific sense of freedom (not free will or social/political freedom), that of being "able to preserve one's existence and further one's good;" (d) we share a common origin with all other living things; and finally (e) "humans are absolutely dependent upon the soundness and good health of the earth's biosphere, but its soundness and good health are not in the least dependent upon humans."[21]

Taylor claims that "From the perspective of the biocentric outlook on nature, we see human life as an integral part of the natural order of the Earth's biosphere."[22] Conversely, these facts (clearly detailed in (a) through (e) above) confirm a reality that may well engender the desired attitude. However, if our respect for persons is based on their "personhood," we may still have grounds to disprove the superiority of humankind, but I see no specific ground to extend any other moral principle. We may not be superior, but according to the human criterion Taylor adduces, we are indeed different enough to allow a human chauvinist to deny any possible symmetry between a purely human and an environmental ethic.

Further, his concept of "inherent worth" for nonhuman entities centers on the disproof of human superiority and the affirmation of kinship between the two realms. This may be sufficient to dictate an attitude of general respect. It does not, however, appear to manifest the basis for a specific regard or a determinate content for the "inherent worth" Taylor wishes to defend. Kinship is not sufficient. For example, I may well readily admit to being (a) governed by the same laws, (b) free to pursue my physical good just like him, (c) sharing a common source, (d) following like him a good of my own, and (e) having exactly the same physical requirements for survival as some mean, unintelligent felon I might share quarters with for a time. Yet all of that does not entail that I may be persuaded he has "inherent worth," other than—perhaps—that which I might grant him as belonging to the same species. Rather than respect him, I might well despise him, in spite of (a), (b), (c), (d), and (e), and deem him inferior. Take away "personhood" and what would serve to elicit regard becomes strained or nebulous, and the grounds for dignity disappear. The attitude of respect for nature may still be desirable on those grounds, but I see a problem with seeking a strong obligation in regard to nature.

Schweitzer's Biocentric Ethic
of "Reverence for Life"

Here I outline and discuss not only Schweitzer's ethic, but also Callicott's and Goodpaster's critiques of its viability. Schweitzer's starting point is the requirement that a truly ethical system should be "working in the world and upon the world,"[23] whereas

with the Chinese and the Indian, in Stoicism, with Spinoza, Scheiermacher, Fichte and Hegel, and in all mysticism of union with the Absolute, it reaches only the ethics of resignation, consisting of inward liberation from the world.[24]

Schweitzer is seeking here an "activist morality," which neither presupposes nor acknowledges any hierarchy of existing beings:

Since no motives to ethical activity are to be discovered in the course of nature, the ethic of self-perfecting must allow both active and passive ethics to originate side-by-side in the bare fact of spiritual inward self-dedication to Being. Both must be derived from actions as such, without any presupposition of any sort of moral quality in Being.[25]

The cosmic kinship advocated on factual grounds by Taylor has a deeper, metaphysical basis in Schweitzer: "Every world-and-lifeview which is to satisfy thought is mysticism."[26] Although, particularly in the Christian tradition, the ethical content in mysticism is "extraordinarily small": "Mysticism is not a friend of ethics but a foe. It devours ethics. And yet the ethics which is to satisfy thought is born of mysticism."[27] Mysticism, for Schweitzer, allows us to reach a truth out of which we can formulate a deeper ethic than the shallow ones prevailing in the Western world. These are "collapsing, because they are not true."[28] They are not "true" in the sense that they are human constructs, but not true, faithful (thus objective) reflections of the reality of Being. And if they are not true and objective, they are and have been "abstract," and "abstraction is the death of ethics, for ethics are a living relationship to living life."[29]

Schweitzer does not unpack the meaning of his doctrine as systematically as Taylor does, but the relation to "living life" he envisions is one which he characterizes as that of a man who obeys "the compulsion to help all life which he is able to assist and shrinks from injuring anything that lives."[30] In this endeavor, a human being does not ask for either merit or worth (e.g., he does not ask which case is more deserving or valuable), nor for degrees of sentience or capacity to suffer in living things, but deems them all as worthy of his help and "reverence." The basis for this largely indiscriminate position in his recognition that all entities share his own primary characteristic, that is, the "life-affirmation is my will-to-live, given by nature."[31] That is why abstraction appears to sever the very link to reality we must not only study and analyze but—more importantly—feel, as a "spiritual relation to the world," which allows our thinking to remain "elemental."[32]

For Schweitzer, knowledge, scientific analysis of nature, is not a step forward, toward a better way of dealing with the world. On the contrary, scientific understanding promotes abstract thinking and leads one to be "puffed up with vanity at being able to describe exactly a fragment of the course of life."[33] He adds:

> The unlearned man who at the sight of a tree in flower is overpowered by the mystery of the will-to-live which is stirring all around him, knows, more than the scientist who studies under the microscope . . . a thousand forms of the will-to-live, but . . . is unmoved by the mystery.[34]

Schweitzer blames Descartes' "I think therefore I exist," which he terms a "paltry, arbitrarily chosen beginning," for the irretrievable movement to abstraction, thus away from Being and the mysterious will-to-be which surrounds us and lives in us.

The way through mystical appreciation of the mystery involved leads us instead to consider life as such as sacred, and to an "ordering and deepening" of the "principle of the moral" and "a widening of the current views of good and evil."[35]

The factual, real basis for the moral attitude of reverence for life is not sufficient, as it is in Taylor. The additional requirement is a frank affirmation of the spiritual component of cosmic kinship, which manifests itself in a deep reverence for life, making us unafraid of being labeled "sentimental" or absurd when we save a drowning insect or remove a worm from the trodden path: "Ethics are responsibility without limit towards all that lives."[36]

Taylor's criteria for "inherent worth," especially that of "freedom" to attain one's biological goals comes closest to Schweitzer's "will-to-live," but lacks its depth and its mystical, metaphysical aspects. Schweitzer's philosophy offers as its basis an undeniable bond between all natural entities including ourselves. It is however open to several objections, one of which, to my mind the most serious one, I deal in my concluding section, and others, such as those voiced by Callicott and Goodpaster, of which more below.

For now, another question may be raised—why must we feel reverence for life? For the will-to-live? If we say, "because it is the deepest, most essential facet of being human," we appear to have little ground for such a position, aside from religious ones, and we are still reduced to a anthropocentric ethic. We have the lowest common denominator, the most widespread characteristic shared by all that exists. Callicott terms it "the essence of the self" and sees it as a further step in "The neo-Kantian voluntarist ethical tradition which begins with Schopenhauer." He sees Schweitzer's ethic as a "recent exponent of conativism," and claims "it exhibits the clearest traces of Schopenhauer's influence together with an explicit illustration of the modern method of generalizing from egoism to altruism."[37]

Callicott admits "conativism" or "will-to-live" has the advantage of being distributed throughout the live universe, from sentient entities to ecosystems, a claim which cannot be advanced for either rationality or the capacity to suffer. As such, it is a strong point in favor of its inclusion as a principle for a sound ethic. It is also cause for wonder and even awe, but only if we admit the mystery, perhaps a divine source. We cannot ourselves create life. It is, so far as we know, a unique phenomenon on Earth. Could that be the source of a special "dignity," one we share with all life?

I want to return to this question in my concluding section, and turn instead to possible critiques of Schweitzer's ethic. The main critique is Goodpaster's, through his generic notion of "moral considerability." He views the principle of respect for life as "self-refuting"; he adds, "the clearest and most decisive refutation of the principle of respect for life is that one cannot live according to it . . . we must eat, experiment to gain knowledge, protect ourselves from predation (macroscopic and microscopic). . . ."[38]

Schweitzer attempts to deal with this objection: we would not respect our own will-to-live if we allowed ourselves to starve rather than harm another living being. Schweitzer suggests the rule "never to pass the limits of the unavoidable," an attempt that Callicott finds less than enlightening. What is unavoidable? Whose judgment represents the final court of appeal? Both an economic or another strictly humanistic "must" may be brought to bear against the respect we have to live; hence Goodpaster is probably right in claiming that, while a respect for life ethic represents a noble ideal, it does not offer a principle through which we can operate on a day-to-day basis. Surely an ethic ought to offer more than a distant, unapproachable ideal.

Further, it is such an intensely individualistic ethic that it requires me to consider every leaf I might pick from a tree, every foolhardy insect that might burn against my light, every earthworm that might be lying across my path. It will also be extremely difficult to apply to aggregates, such as species, or communities, such as ecosystems. Goodpaster ultimately suggests as primarily morally considerable "the biosystem as a whole: not as a mere collection of biotic particles, but as an integrated, self-sustaining unity which puts solar energy to work in the interest of growth and maintenance."[39]

Once again this is a noble ideal. But, in the very next paragraph, Goodpaster's own words show the weakness of his and all positions we can contrast with human concerns, when these are given primacy instead: "Much less do I want to suggest for a moment that biosystemic respect should dilute human concerns for happiness and justice."[40] His critique of Schweitzer can be turned around and redirected against his own principle: it is equally hard to decide what constitutes "unavoidable" destruction of a "critical habitat for an endangered species,"[41] as it is to decide how to balance human happiness versus "biosystemic respect." If Goodpaster's critique is valid, then his own argument is flawed in the same way as Callicott affirms Schweitzer's is.

Still, Callicott prefers "reverence for life" ethics to an "animal liberation/animal rights hedonic ethic." He sees the ultimate message of the former to be that, "one's cardinal duty is not to interfere, to live and let live," and views it correctly as based on a "conation-based moral metaphysic."[42] His answer to what he perceives as the failings of these metaphysics is to propose an ethic of Bio-Empathy, a Humean/Darwinian approach which suggests that egoism and altruism are "equally primitive" and "both . . . explained by natural selection."[43]

Schweitzer's ethic is—at the very least—not clear or specific enough to give us guidance when conflicts arise. The depth of his metaphysical intuition cannot be denied, but the translation of that intuition into a workable, viable ethic is incomplete, leaving us with an intuitively desirable ideal, but also with many practical problems, perhaps as many as we had before Schweitzer's metaphysical principle.

"Dignity" is briefly mentioned by Goodpaster, but the concept is used mainly as a token of the "content" of whatever it is that we find elicits our respect. It is not defined, and neither discussed nor analyzed; it is a concept which is largely left untouched by the argument and undefined within it.

Problems In Taylor and Schweitzer: Is Integrity a Better Guideline?

The element of "respect," foundational in my own principle, is present in both Taylor's and Schweitzer's doctrine. But respect extending to *all* live organisms *equally* (*not* my position) is normatively vacuous and, ultimately, self-contradictory if consistently applied. If I respect all organisms and their right to exist, then my own corresponding "right" to life cannot be respected, as I can neither feed myself nor defend myself from attacks of any sort, even bacterial ones. Their respective approach encounters these difficulties, because it is simply biocentric but not holistic.

If one adopts an ecosystemic perspective, then implicitly one places every single organism within it in a functioning niche, and it has only the "rights" predicated by its natural interaction with other elements both biotic and abiotic at the most basic level, at which the principle of integrity functions. A general respect for life-support systems will therefore provide an answer to the "paralysis" problem (to use Rolston's expression), posed by the other two doctrines. Organisms *can* both feed, defend themselves, *and* be food, or be attacked by others in their self-defense.

Provided I act within the limits appropriate to my ecological niche, I am thus free to pursue my natural interest in self-preservation and the continuation of my species. These limits are exceeded when I attack the integrity of the ecosystem and its capacity for life-support, not only of myself and my species, but also of all others. Some ecosystems demand absolute respect because of their fragility, their rarity, or other factual reason; wilderness ecosystems need to be protected and preserved as benchmark cases of environmental fitness and paradigms. Others may be simply respected as healthy, rather than wild, as those used for organic farming or other sustainable function compatible with respectful human "culture," and permissible or appropriate interaction with the latter will not be exactly the same as comparable interaction with the former. The precise limits of our interaction with either, meant to be guided by the principle of integrity in principle, will need to be practically modified in order to be consistent with what is right for the ecosystem with which we intend to deal. These limits will therefore remain factual and require investigation. The principle will remain universal, the specific norm flexible, as is the case in the examples given in the Aristotelian ethics. Moderation in food intake dictates different amounts of food for a large wrestler and a lightweight philosopher, although the universal rule dictates moderation as an equal standard.

A question may be raised here: why continue to use the label "biocentric" when that term has been appropriated in the literature by proponents of respect for individual organisms? Why not simply switch to the expression "ecocentric," which appears more appropriate to represent our emphasis on ecosystems? Perhaps in some contexts this might be a clearer, less confusing option. On the other hand, the expression "biocentric holism" does not lend itself to polarizing wholes and individuals; rather, it proposes the recognition of a basic prima facie commonality between the two, based on their respective interests in life-support and regenerating capacities of natural systems.

A Proposal for a New Ethic of Respect and a New Categorical Imperative

In a recent issue of *Environmental Ethics*, Christopher Stone remarks that after the first decade of attempts to form an environmental ethic we must ask the question, "Where does environmental ethics situate itself within the larger world of moral philosophy?" He claims that we "have reached a plateau" and need to refocus our philosophical energies, after having "reached a certain level of maturity" in the subject.[44] While I agree that a change in focus is indicated, I would rather situate interhuman ethics in the context of environmental ethics instead. He is right that the past and present lines of argument which try to fit a recalcitrant subject matter within their (usually human) domain, have gone as far as they can go, and that is not far enough. Stone's solution is to turn from moral monism to moral pluralism, which he carefully distinguishes from relativism instead: one need not subscribe to one and only one moral approach when the circumstance and the "clients" to be served by the ethic are so disparate. Together with the pluralistic approach, he suggests the possibility "to formulate a lexical ordering rule"[45] to facilitate the resolution of conflicts.

By contrast with Stone, my position is one of two-level monism, starting with concrete reality. Our first step, I believe, is to acknowledge that about which we have no choice—our inescapable membership in the ecosystem of which we are a part. That is something we cannot ignore or bypass in any of our actions, therefore it ought to have primacy in moral consideration as well, particularly because (and Stone acknowledges this) moral theory is directed at action. Thus, whatever else we need in a moral theory, we cannot consistently design or discover one that is totally divorced from the most basic realities of our existence. Schweitzer had it right here: whatever else our ethics is, its first requirement is not to be abstract but to deal with *life* (see previous section).

Just as science needs, in order to prove its hypotheses to be valid, to return from abstract models back to reality, so too ethics cannot counsel, and even less command, something which does not fit the reality of our physical existence. Even the most Platonic and irreducible dualistic doctrines of morality require that the theory should not fit angels only, or disembodied spirits, but real, live human beings. This ought to be our first step, even prior to reaching decisions on monism versus pluralism, utilitarianism versus Kantianism, and so on. It can easily be objected that such a principle is just a truism, is too general, and does not really offer any guidance in our dealings with either man or nature. I think it is very helpful in limiting the parameter of our ethical argument by presenting us with a solid and incontrovertible starting point. At any rate, let us start with it, and see where we may go from there:

(1) The first moral principle is that nothing can be moral that is in conflict with the physical realities of our existence, or cannot be seen to fit within the natural laws of our environment.

The principle may sound like a truism, but contemporary Western civilization and Third World aspirations view the "laws of nature" or the "physical realities of our existence" as an obstacle to be overcome, an impediment to our freedom (and right) to self-affirmation. Even technology impact studies, required of all projects that might be hazardous to the public, are primarily based on cost/benefit ratios, hence on economic justifications, and second, on human health considerations, which apparently represent the true goal of the mislabeled "Environmental Protection Agency."[46] No explicit consideration of laws of nature and long-term consequences is normally present in their regulations.

Further, the principle appears to be paradoxical: How can we act or design policies that "contradict" or "fail to fit within natural laws," when all our acts are as much a part of nature as we are? I argue that while animals' actions and reactions cannot fail "to fit," human agency indeed can fail; witness our interference with laws that will eventually affect the survival of our species. We cannot act outside natural laws, in the sense that whatever we affect will deteriorate according to these laws. But our freedom to choose and implement ends independently of natural goals (always specific or holistic, rather than purely individual) allows us to choose not only to make ourselves "unfit" but also to curtail our species' own fitness for survival. It also permits us to adversely affect the whole environment, that is, to interfere with the persistence of life in all its aspects.

Holmes Rolston holds a similar principle, but he restricts it to a principle for environmental ethics,[47] whereas I see it as all-encompassing. At any rate, it is worth noting that even to say that our "ought" cannot and must not contradict nature's "is," is not to claim that all and any natural "is" translates into a human "ought."

Our next step should be to unpack that "is." Briefly, I argue that it means to understand nature primarily as an arena wherein the basic principles are (a) respect coupled with indifference, and (b) opposition or competition.[48] "Respect" is found in the limited, selective "unavoidable" (in Schweitzer's terms) killing that animals practice purely for survival, that is, not for sport, trivialities, or curiosity (science). I argue that ecosystems naturally should function this way, as all entities within the biota will use everything else which serves to facilitate their own survival. In this manner, they will manifest their own specific (i.e., favorable to their own species) will-to-live. Thus "opposition" and "respect/indifference" (the latter applicable analogically by animals to those species which are not vital to their own survival), serve to help reconcile an environmental and animal ethic, saving some aspects of both Schweitzer and Taylor's doctrines, yet differing from both, as I show below. I will now proceed instead with my proposed "categorical imperative,"

(1a) Act so that your action will fit [first and minimally] within universal natural laws.

This position it is perfectly compatible with a theistic viewpoint or—even more generally—with a religious point of view.[49] Neither the Christian God, nor a religious First Principle (a nonorthodox one, such as the One of Plotinus, for instance) may require us to act in conflict with the laws that govern all their creation; whatever freedom we possess, as part of our humanity, as moral agents, cannot negate physical reality.

In essence then, what I propose is a principle that is general enough to ground any and all other principles we might want to espouse but which stipulates a basic condition, thus ensuring that environmental concern is present from the beginning, rather than being a hard-to-fit afterthought. The reference to the primacy of "natural laws" not only prohibits environmental abuse, but solves the difficulties of joining animal and environmental ethics, while avoiding the inability to cope with the problem of domestic animals, forcing us to vegetarianism or—worse yet—to a position of guilt and outrage, at the use of anything we might need to survive. That is—to my mind—the major problem with Schweitzer's ethics. His reverence stops at individual lives, rather than extending to all nature. He says, for instance, "The world is a ghastly drama of will-to-live divided against itself,"[50] and "The ignorance in which the world is wrapped has no existence for me; I have been saved from the world" and even, speaking about "yielding to the necessary" against the will-to-live, that it "leaves me with guilt."[51] Such judgments against the natural functioning of the world (and all these passages are directed to the user stance, in our own survival), manifest a total lack of respect for life's laws as they truly exist in nature, and therefore contradict the basic principle of his ethic. In this sense, the principles and the ethic I propose eliminate this dichotomy and reconcile systemic with individual concern by extending respect and reverence to the ways of the environment as well as to the specifics and the wholes within it.[52] The second way in which my first principle and categorical imperative may be used is to permit a hierarchical ranking of approaches and to sanction as permissible, rather than contradictory to fairness and justice, an interhuman ethic which is not exhausted by our environmental ethic stance. In other words, just like the wolf will act in certain ways within his pack, giving primacy to his own survival, followed by that of his spouse and offspring perhaps, then exhibit certain appropriate behavior in regard to others within his pack but in a very different manner with prey, on one hand, and with other entities to which he is indifferent, on the other, some form of this sort of behavior is appropriate to us as well, in our interaction with other species.

We need not extend to animals and other environmental entities, species, and ecosystems, human "fairness," "justice," and so on. In fact to do so simply manifests a disrespect for the ways of natural entities and a general depreciation of the entities themselves, to whom we see ourselves as imposing benevolently our "higher" standards. It is right and just for a wolf to treat other wolves in a way which is quite different from the way in which he treats us. Indifference, non-interference, and—in the case of special need—predation are the hallmarks of a wolf's possible treatment of humans. The same should obtain interspecies, that is, between us and others that do not belong to our species. Of course, if we have interfered previously, then it is fair to use interhuman (or intraspecific) ethics as our guide, and apply retributive justice, as Taylor, for instance, suggests.

But—in general—the ranking of intraspecific, interspecific, and environmental attitudes and priorities, starting, of course, with the latter (as indicated by the first principle), and working inward so to speak— rather than extending purely interhuman ethics "outward"—is the main claim I have tried to defend. I have suggested that such an approach is (a) true to life and the scientifically knowable realities of our existence, (b) solid in its defense of environmental and ecosystemic values, while still allowing us (c) to hold on to our cherished interhuman ethical doctrines. Even more importantly, the first principle and its corollary "categorical imperative," by allowing a unitary though multilevel approach, will permit the resolution of some of the puzzles inherent in other "respect for life" doctrines. As we saw, Goodpaster believed that Schweitzer's ethic could not be lived, because of its failure in the face of "macroscopic and microscopic predation." The addition of "respect for natural laws," permits us (1) to invoke "self-defense," in the case of bacteria and viruses as well as actual (but rare) physical attacks by wild animals; (2) it also permits us to invoke "self-defense" without guilt for limited, painless, and respectful research into life-threatening diseases only; (3) it allows us to draw certain natural creatures into the human community, wherein the ethical ways of the community must prevail. Therefore, while noninterference is moral toward animals fighting, or diseased in the wild, it is totally inappropriate toward pets, domestic animals (free-ranging only), or research animals. The first group, pets (as Rolston himself states),[53] becomes part of the family and is to be treated as such, the second and third group are to be used, to be sure, but respectfully, in living conditions which are not worse or too different from what they would normally encounter.

"Use," in itself, is not necessarily wrong. I discuss in detail its required limits, and the meaning of respect within it elsewhere.[54] For now it is sufficient to restate that all entities in nature are users. A book review by a self-styled environmental philosopher states that it is "natural" for man to be technological, just as it is for beavers to build dams, or bees hives.[55] The obvious answer is that beavers and bees do not destroy the ozone layer in the biosphere, or give occasion to á Chernobyl; their interaction with natural habitats is neither a threat to whole ecosystems, nor to life on our planet as a whole. That is the force of the first principle and the categorical imperative: "use" fits under natural laws; abuse, use in conflict with respect and consideration for the rest of whatever shares the ecosystems, does not. As we will see in the next section in our discussion of "dignity" and "integrity," a mutually beneficial or at least respectful interaction between "natural" and "cultural subsystems" restores harmony and "integrity" and represents an ideal to strive for, the only way to interact morally with the world.

The Role and Dignity of Natural Laws and a Reformulation of the Categorical Imperative: Some Objection to the Principle

Our examination of these difficult notions should start by tracing their philosophical roots, at least in the case of "dignity," a term which appears to have a meaning which is social or political, which should be avoided in the present enterprise. If we look at Latin sources, most passages using "dignitas" use it just in that sense, although a few exist where a different use can be found, in Cicero and Apuleius, for instance. In *The Golden Ass*, Lucius Apuleius speaks of "French mares" possessing "dignitas." It is based, however, on their "long anteced-ents" or their parentage—still a socially based meaning, extended for the occasion.[56]

Yet if we reach even further back to Greek terminology and mean-ing, we find a much more useful connection. First of all, "dignity" has the dictionary senses of both "value" and "worth." This of course does not help, because it leads to a circular argument: we need to respect persons or ecosystems because they possess "inherent worth." This is based on their innate "dignity" ("worth" or "value")—a circu-lar argument which tells us absolutely nothing of this obscure proper-ty which must elicit our respect. To interpose "rationality," "humanity," or "sentience," does not help, unless the argument is consequentialist and utilitarian instead. We simply need to ask why is "rationality" worthy of respect, and what gives it "dignity." Once again, we en-counter a dead end.

It is only when we turn to the Greek term (*semnotes*), that we find a further meaning: "fittingness." Xenophon for instance claims that "it is not fitting for Zeus to move around from place to place" using his limbs, like ordinary mortals, and that is why he moves through his mind.[57] If we can accept conceptually this link between "dignity" and "what is fitting" or "fittingness," then we have a rather solid basis for our first principle, one that is philosophical, scientific, and reli-gious, at one and the same time. In requiring reverence or respect for all that is "fitting" in an environmental context, it permits inclusion not only of live individual entities, species, and ecosystems, but also of the laws that govern their interaction. We no longer need to view all natural intercourse as a bloody "drama" we are "saved from," as Schweitzer does, nor need we feel—as he does—guilt when we give in to "necessity" and force ourselves to kill some living thing, say a carrot or a fish. The acceptance of "kinship" need not translate into acceptance of "brotherhood" interspecies; in fact, respect is compatible even with hostility, as I will argue, citing Thomas Nagel.[58] The painful, paradoxical dichotomy Schweitzer experiences is thus resolved.

The apparent divergence between "fitting" in the social sense, as exemplified by the concept in ancient Greek works and Roman sources, and the environmental "fit" we wish to defend is reconciled through the "natural law" connection. In more recent times, what is "fitting" to a ruler, for instance, is understood in terms of social conventions; in the sense cited from ancient sources, "fittingness" is as natural as the succession of seasons or the freezing of water at low temperatures. Hence the comparison is more accurate than would appear at first glance.

Today, and in our sense of what "fits," continued ongoing scientific investigation of these natural laws is vital. At the same time, the status and dignity of these laws and processes, as well as that of the natural world itself, which functions according to them, must be upheld. The "categorical imperative" derived from the first principle or (1a) needs a slight rephrasing now:

(1b) Act so that you manifest respect and understanding acceptance of all natural processes and laws (although self-defense is acceptable).

When it is restated in this form, it clearly requires that everything about ecosystems that is possible to learn, should be learned. A hierarchical pluralism reigns there; for instance, nothing that happens spontaneously (that is, without our interference) is not in some way or time, enhancing of life-support systems within certain time constraints. When conflicts arise between individuals or species as a whole, they are usually resolved within the larger picture, that is, in favor of ecosystemic integrity even at the expense of some individuals or even species.

However the behavior appropriate to individuals need not copy this approach. Observation discloses that within any group, that is, intraspecies—animals will observe their own pecking order and strive to enhance first of all their own existence, then that of their close kin perhaps (in some cases), mates and offspring, then they will show concern for the species or group. K. Wiredu claims that the possibility of rational universals for human beings is grounded (and perhaps continuous with, thus manifesting a difference in degree rather than in kind with it) in the instinctual ways which are universal to other species and which are the base of their commonality of understanding.[59]

Our "lesson from nature" here is that, as long as we do not allow this to interfere with the ecosystemic "laws" (or the hypotheses that express our present understanding) which sustain survival, it is appropriate, "fitting," that (a) each species should have its own "specific" ethics (or mores in the case of animals), and that (b) that intraspecific and interspecific ethics should differ (that is, that what we do to other humans and to those in others species can be different. Now, while (a) is easily acceptable to all moral philosophers, (b) smacks of anthropocentrism, chauvinism, unfairness, and the like. Intraspecies, anthropocentrism (in the sense of not accepting the first principle, and viewing humankind as the only species that is morally considerable) and chauvinism, whether it emerges as sexism, racism, or speciesism, are indeed wrong. When it is combined with the first principle (of "fittingness") the result is simply that no action of any individual within a species should conflict with the life-enhancement of the whole ecosystem except for survival (immediate) or survival-related activities (future), and the latter must not be wasteful or proceed through disrespectful means, but need not be minimal to be morally appropriate. For instance, just as bees can store honey and squirrels nuts, so too we can cultivate and perhaps eat both the carrot and the fish referred to earlier, without guilt.

Thus, within our species, our rationality engenders a larger freedom of choice (both qualities and capacities natural to our species) and we may have a choice of ethical principle, of purely human laws and mores, and a choice of lifestyles which, although still limited by ecosystemic priorities, is nevertheless larger than that of the bee or the wolf. Yet we need not practice "moral extensionism," to use Rolston's well-thought term, to "stretch" our laws and ethics, which are appropriate intraspecies, to interspecies activities, and thus encounter the difficulties well summarized by Stone, and tacitly or explicitly acknowledged by many others.[60]

The direction of our moral discourse is altered, in fact, it is reversed. We have an all-encompassing monism as the ground of our moral reasoning. Within it we can fit various "fitting" ethics, somewhat like a set of nesting wooden Russian dolls, one inside the other. A parallel common case might be the commonplace of belonging to a profession, say nursing, thus having to subscribe to the appropriate code of ethics (of the state, county, or province within which one practices). The nurse, lawyer, or accountant, while required to practice under the constraints of the code of her profession, need not assume that therefore the obligations of family, citizenship, or membership in the human race are thereby no longer valid. In the case of conflicts, she remains first and foremost a human being, then a family member, citizen, and professional. Distinct group requirements must not interfere with her basic morality; when they do, they introduce an illegitimate dichotomy.[61]

The wider mandates of interhuman morality do not normally introduce such quandaries. "Do Not Kill" is just as true for a human in human context as it is for the wolf in his own group, although for interhuman ethics, this is simply an observation and not meant as justification. Nor do animals normally "lie" to one another within their own milieu (although exceptions exist). Other purely human moral laws might be not to steal or not to commit adultery. Neither activity has any application outside a purely human context.

Now, there are obvious objections that can be made to my position: (1) it is a fallacy to move from an "is" to an "ought"; (2) the position for which I argue is a defensible one within a Stoic or Plotinian context, or within a "religious" one of some sort, but has no philosophical value as such, outside these traditions; (3) that I indeed argue convincingly for what is "better" or even "right," but I provide no strong obligation to follow my imperatives, other than prudential considerations.

I will briefly address these objections in turn. First, it is not necessary for my argument to move from an "is" to an "ought." It is sufficient that the "is" should be seen as a *limit* to whatever "ought" we might be able to defend. This is a broadening of a purely environmental ethics, but it is also an implicit premise in all ethical doctrines. For instance, we could not prescribe the use of a utilitarian calculus, unless we possessed the ability to calculate, and unless pleasure and pain were *facts* of our existence. Although the obligation does not stem from that capacity, it could not be there unless the capacity was there as well, thus that capacity provides the factual limit to our prescriptions. Second, the respect I advocate as foundational, for a principle which is in a sense both transcendent and immanent, does not require a commitment to an act of faith (this is the objection, I take it, which would make my position "unphilosophical") and to an exclusive religious belief, and even less to a personal deity. However it might be viewed as a first step in a direction which might ultimately permit either of these positions; but, precisely as a first step, it also stands alone, and as such it is defensible as a separate position.

Finally, on the question of "obligation," it may be the case that—following Kant—too much emphasis has been placed on the absolute division between obligation and prudence. For instance, neither virtue ethics, such as the Aristotelian concern with isolating the "truly human" activity while tracing the link between contemplation and happiness (as "living well"), nor Plato's quest for the "good" and the Socratic appeal on behalf of the "philosophic" life, with its concern for goodness and harmony and the health of one's soul, exclude a somewhat prudential component. Nor is it possible or necessary to exclude enlightened, universalized prudence from ethical doctrines which consider happiness or rationality as an ultimate value.

In this case, it is even less obvious why a prudential component should render an approach to morality less credible if it is extended to the human race as a whole, particularly when the latter is not even singled out by the "imperatives" I suggest.

What has emerged from this discussion? Stone has shown the recent status of environmental ethics to be interesting, but not as "productive" as it could be. He pointed to the main reason for this: the desire to cling to modes of argumentation and principles which, initiating as they do in interhuman ethics, manifest problems as they are "extended" to "exotic clients," as Stone puts it, such as fetuses, future generations, and ecosystems.[62] Loving one's neighbor is easier and logically (and practically) more comfortable if the neighbor is at least in some basic way like us. Stone says: ". . . trading places is a blind alley. It is one thing to put oneself in the shoes of a stranger, perhaps even in the hooves of a horse—but quite another to put oneself in the banks of a river."[63]

On the other hand, I would like to argue that "cosmic sympathy" or viewing one as kindred, in the sense of the religious, interhuman maxim just cited, requires no linking, but attests instead to the kinship we have with others through creation. In that sense, my neighbor and the river are not different from one another at all, and as far as plain liking goes, I may even like the river far better than my neighbor. Thus, unless we start with a solid reason for the neighbor's special status, by referring to his "dignity" or singling out some capacity such as reason as ground for our respect, a problem exists. "Dignity," at best, harks back to "fittingness," or is simply a synonym for "worth" or "value." Rationality, on the other hand, is debatable and may be absent on many different grounds (e.g., age in infants, injury, and so on), and can also be viewed as circular in this argument.

If what distinguishes a human being from the rest of creation, in fact what "makes" her a woman rather than something else, is reason, then the answer to "what makes her morally considerable" cannot be "what makes her essentially a human being." It works in interhuman ethics for some (I believe it does so only in a very limited way), but it is nothing other than a restatement of anthropocentrism, in a wider environmental context. Thus we need to return to "dignity" as "fittingness," unless we are willing to accept a metaphysics or ontology to ground our contentions. While I cannot claim to have proven beyond a doubt that the interpretation of "dignity" I suggest is the correct one, it seems to me that it is the only possible satisfactory candidate, moreover, it is one which permits, albeit without demanding it, a theistic view of the universe. As indicated, the value of "dignity" in relation to integrity is its historical connection with value for both processes, regularities, and the universe as a whole. In the chapter devoted to integrity's value, the notion was not discussed, because that discussion belongs here, in the context of the second formulation of the "categorical imperative" (1b) derived from the principle. In other words, the obligation is not only to study the natural entities and communities within a whole, an ecosystem, but also to accept, study, and respect the rules of their interaction (something that many biocentrists, for instance in animal ethics, do not accept).

The Principle of Integrity and "Deep Ecology"

As was noted in the discussion of the first two sections, the difference between the doctrine following upon the principle of integrity (PI) and other current environmental theories of intrinsic value is clear. Schweitzer's holistic, all-inclusive ethic was detailed in the first section, and Taylor's rights-based theory of individual intrinsic value, in the second. Yet even if the originality of the principle of integrity in regard to these two theories has been demonstrated, two questions remain: Is the "principle of integrity" a deep ecology position? And, if so, what is its relation to Arne Naess's "ecosophy"?

The first question is easily answered: indeed PI fits under the heading of deep ecology. It resembles it in two ways: first in its original appeal to the "gravity" of the environmental threats that face us (cf., "The Gravity of the Situation," in *Ecology, Community and Lifestyle*).[64] The second point emerges from Naess's own words. In his "Introduction," David Rothenberg (Naess's editor and translator) cites a dialogue with A. J. Ayer. Naess says:

> As an acting person I take a stand, I implicitly assume very many things, and with my Spinozist leanings towards integrity—being an integrated person is the most important thing—I am now trying to close down on all those vagaries.[65]

The "integrity" referred to is personal, not ecological; but the reference to Spinoza clearly opens the door for a traditional, metaphysical outlook similar, though not identical, to that which manifests itself in my own "stance," and which further permits a certain closeness between the two, at least in spirit.

Further, the passage also hints at "vagaries": too strong a word perhaps, but indicative of a certain openness in Naess's work. To speak of what we are "called to," in a somewhat Heideggerian manner, is to suggest the possibility of a path to be chosen freely and perhaps "authentically," starting with "intuitions," giving rise to principles (autonomously formulated), and finally leading to a "direction," an "arrow" pointing to the "better" activity, in harmony with both intuitions and principles.[66]

Rothenberg suggests that "the whole designation "ecocentrism" is closer to an equivalent for what Naess means by "deep ecology" "centering on the ecosphere." On the other hand, he also cites T. O'Riordan, charting "environmentalism" and recognizing the existence of a spectrum of positions, ranging from "deep ecologists" to "soft technologists," under the heading of "ecocentrism," but placing varieties of (hard) "technocentrism" at the other end of the spectrum.[67]

"Deep ecology" is clearly closer to the position required by PI, except that I would have no qualms about describing the latter as a principle, giving rise to a doctrine and to categorical imperatives expressing it. Rothenberg instead does not like the description of "doctrine" for deep ecology, because it is too "fixed" to do it justice. Reading Naess's work, one is indeed struck by its fluidity or the deliberate lack of precision and definition. In his effort to appeal to individual, personal integration within nature, and to a "revision of value standards in favour of all-round experiential values,"[68] a prescriptive, universal theoretical stance cannot be his main priority.

Still, "deep ecology" is well able to generate a set of principles, in the form of basic stances from which to judge the appropriateness of various alternatives in personal action or community policy. But the deliberate phenomenological approach, almost a Heideggerian parallel, precludes the quest for a formal moral doctrine. Naess says:

> I'm not much interested in ethics or morals. I'm interested in how we experience the world. . . . If deep ecology is deep, it must relate to our fundamental beliefs, not just to ethics. Ethics follow from how we experience the world. If you articulate your experience then it can be a philosophy or a religion. (20.)

Rothenberg further asks, "Just how should we experience the world?" And if the question of "what should be done" is raised (from an environmental standpoint), then not only an interest, but a commitment to morality appears to be necessary, such as the one advocated by PI. Nor is the reference to either *a* "philosophy" or *a* religion sufficient to suggest or even less base an "ought."

For the "initiates," those whose "experiencing" is similar and who in fact participate in an understanding and a valuing that is *not* shared by "technocentrists," Naess is both inspiring and moving (in both the emotional and the literal senses). But the acid test, I fear, in the face of the urgent questions Naess recognizes, is whether "technocentrists," not the "converted," can be motivated by an appeal to return to the mountains and the earth, and attempt to "experience" in a novel way before modifying their lifestyle and the public policy options they presently embrace.

Would this appeal work, pragmatically? I am not convinced of its effectiveness.

Hence, it is because of this concern that PI uses as a tool a concept that is presently embedded in international legislation and in legal and regulatory discourse. It is for the same reason that "integrity" is examined as an ultimate value and then used in deontological formulations. The concern with "depth" is tempered and directed by the pressing need for effective legislation. "Deep ecology," as it emerges from Naess's work, is neither "ineffectual" nor unimportant, as some would have it;[69] it is indeed a foundational position. But in the face of the necessity for immediate (and changed) action, it appears to be problematic in two ways: (1) the required, deeply personal, "authentic" and *new* experience of nature can neither be legislated nor be forced overnight; hence, it represents only a one-sided approach, too individual to yield the required immediate policy changes; and (2) the appeal to subjective experience giving rise to a philosophy or a religion carries within it a certain relativism that is equally undesirable in the context of policy options governed by the choices of a "technocentrist" majority.

Unless we appeal to a firm principle or to rules not open to negotiation there is ultimately little one can say to the "non-initiate," the "technocentrist" whose experience leads her to prefer "plastic trees," or whose religion appears to recommend unthinking "domination" of the earth. Hence, although the initial "call" in Chapter One was a call to responsibility in the sense Hans Jonas advocates, and Heidegger's ontology was also briefly mentioned, the responsibility is filtered through a deep urgency to be translated into concepts and terms—even values—that can be accepted and supported universally, and a principle and directives that *cannot* be relativized or rejected on personal or cultural-relative grounds.

Further, rather than attempt, as Naess does, to suggest activities at all levels of human interaction, including the social and interpersonal levels,[70] PI is more *categorically* demanding, but far less inclusive. It proposes as a strict rule, *no* individual "freedom" to harm the life-support systems of the earth, but other wise allows choices of social/ethical/individual priorities, provided they do not conflict with the absoluteness of the "harm principle" dictated by PI.

To attempt to categorize or systematize totally Naess's "deep ecology" would be as difficult as it would be to do so for Aldo Leopold's "land ethic." Both represent the sort of inspiration and the "visions" the "converted" need in order to produce their philosophy, their thinking, and their contribution to policy dialogues. But any attempt to convince scientists, policy makers, or bureaucrats must, regretfully, translate the very "depth" that grounds and nourishes their inspiration into principles and rules that have a wider appeal, even if some of the "depth" is temporarily obscured or not manifested. In essence, as long as I and others like myself *can* internalize the "deep" aspect of Naess's thought, and then think and write from that authentic experience, it is not absolutely necessary to stamp the "experience" on the banner we fly. If my own experience of hiking in the Dolomites prompts me to write about the "principles of integrity," and my public policy decisions in the Great Lakes Basin Ecosystem, by participation and dialogue with the policy makers themselves, there seems to be no further need to demand that policy makers *also* follow my path and start with the Dolomites as well.

Granted, the latter might guarantee a deeper "conversion, if the experience sought were to yield the desired result. But this certainty is not available, and the time constraints of the present crisis will not permit a tentative restructuring of everyone's experience. Far better, at least from the practical standpoint, to support changes in laws and regulations *first*, and hope that the changed mindset will follow, or perhaps proceed apiece with the more ecologically enlightened choices. In essence then, PI is inspired, in part, by the "deep ecology of Naess, but it takes a different path and addresses perhaps a different audience in quite a different way. The goals and ideals of "deep ecology are present within it, nevertheless. "Deep ecology" is not a systematic doctrine, and some believe it is not meant as a doctrine at all. In contrast, PI is presented as a doctrine, and so more needs to be said about the obligations it demands. What is the justification of the principle of integrity? And even if we can offer a satisfactory defense of its justifiation, to what extent are we responsible in our interaction with the Earth? These questions will be discussed in the next two sections.

The Principle of Integrity and
the Problem of Justification

I have offered a strong defense for "integrity" as a multifaceted value, a worthwhile moral goal, and even for the necessity of adopting an environmental ethic before all other ethical considerations. A question, however, remains. Neither the defense of a value, nor the preferability of a certain position over others may be sufficient to indicate clearly enough the obligation I believe to be implicit in my "proposal." Chapter Four represents a defense of biocentric holism as a viable principle, and of that approach, in general, as a foundational "good," or even an "ideal." But even there the source of the obligation is not emphasized. Thus, even if "integrity" is accepted as a basic, ultimate value, and biocentric holism as a defensible basis from which to pursue it, the obligation is still not spelled out.

This is a difficult question indeed. However, I take heart from the fact that both John Rawls and Bernard Gert see this as a major flaw in *Utilitarianism*, by John Stuart Mill. Both Rawls and Gert show that the defense of "happiness" as an ultimate value is not sufficient to justify the obligation imposed by the Greatest Happiness Principle. If a man of Mill's stature had a problem with justification, perhaps one should not be discouraged by discovering the same difficulty, but try instead to redress the problem.

In moving from value to obligation, Rawls suggests two possible forms of justification one might use: the first he terms "Cartesian," moving from necessarily true "first principles," to conclusions. The second he refers to is "naturalism," so-called "by an abuse of language"; its approach is

> to introduce definitions of moral concepts in terms of presumptive non-moral ones, and then to show by accepted procedures of common sense and the sciences that the statements thus paired with the asserted moral judgments are true.[71]

He opts for neither of these procedures because "there is no set of conditions or first principles that can be plausibly claimed to be necessary or definitive of morality." Thus "the principles of justice are argued for on the basis of reasonable stipulations concerning the choice of such conceptions."[72]

Rawls's procedure clearly cannot be adopted in our context. It is the main contention of the present work that "integrity" as an environmental value and goal is beyond "stipulations" in the sense that it remains basic to national and international justice whether or not "rational contractors" today find it to be so. The second moral theorist mentioned as pointing out the "obligation" gap in Mill's "utilitarianism" is Gert. According to Gert, Mill commits the fallacy of "assumed equivalence" when he claims that "the question concerning the *summum bonum*, or the greatest good, is the same as the question concerning the foundations of morality."[73] Gert adds: "We might discover that the *summum bonum* does not provide us either with the evidence or a source of authority for the moral rules."[74]

What does Gert suggest as possible grounds for an obligation or justification of the moral rules? To begin with, Gert makes his position clear: neither contracts nor stipulations will serve. On the contrary:

> Moral rules have a status similar to the laws of logic or of mathematics. No one invents the laws of logic, though the articulation of them, or perhaps the discovery of them, may have taken place at some definite time or times. . . . I do maintain that any account of moral rules which makes them subject to human decision is inadequate.[75]

Gert's position is clearly a lot closer to the one defended on these pages; we are not "agreeing" to what might be right morally, but rather articulating what is already morally right, objectively. If discovering the "good" is neither an intuitive, subjective procedure, nor a matter of agreeing to define some action or state of affairs, then how do we go about "discovering" the moral rules that the philosopher articulates?

According to Gert, there are some moral rules that "would be offered by almost everyone," being "completely universal" and "known by all rational persons." They are, further, "unchanging" or "unchangeable." The first rules Gert lists are (1) don't kill, (2) don't lie, (3) don't steal, and (4) don't commit adultery. Additional ones he suggests are (5) keep your promises, (6) don't cheat, and (7) don't cause pain (*sic*).[76] At first glance Gert's approach, moving directly to "rules" rather than outlining a value or values, then justifying the obligation, appears more fruitful for our purpose. For Gert the values are clearly objective, not a matter for stipulation among contractors.

They are to be "unchangeable" and completely "universal," and both of these are characteristics compatible with both integrity as a value and the principle that follows from it. The problem that persists is that "they must be known to all rational persons." The last three he lists, for instance, do not appear to have quite the same force as the others. Further, in another section of his work, Gert wonders whether "don't kill" may apply to a fetus in the first trimester or later, and adds that "*some* people" may want to include one set but not the other among those who might have a right to life. In fact, "a moral system must be public; that is, it must be known to all those to whom it applies, and it must be such that it could be accepted by all of them."[77]

Hence, although stipulative and contractarian considerations have been eliminated from a proper understanding of morality, still the absolute requirement for a "public morality" remains problematic from our standpoint. Environmental concern, like animal ethics a few years back, is a novel stance in some respects (though not in all). It is not new in its basic tenets, "don't kill," "don't harm," "don't inflict pain"; its radical novelty, however, lies in the respective "clientèle" of these requirements—the moral "patients" with which they are concerned.

It is commonly taken to be wrong to inflict violence on living things (primarily sentient ones) without good reason. Gert's analysis, however, does not indicate which living things are covered by this rule, nor whether his understanding of morality could adjust, bringing an expanding "sensitivity" to bear upon the range of entities that can be harmed. His position on moral rules does not appear to consider the possibility of a changing consciousness through which moral paradigms that are new may not be equally available to *everyone* in the sense required by his "public morality." This brings into question the very possibility of a critical morality over and above positive morality as it exists in various societies.

Probably this is a general problem in Gert's analysis, not one that is specific to environmental ethics. One can speculate, for instance, that the "public morality" in Nazi Germany *also* included the "moral rules" Gert lists, such as "don't kill." However, the problem in that context was that moral *considerability* did not extend to certain groups, such a Jews, who were not considered to be "fully human" in the sense that other, Aryan, Germans were. Hence, the avoidance of the "stipulation" problem that renders Gert's approach preferable from our standpoint, and, in general, more objective, still does not "cure" the problem of changing or evolving standards of "considerability." Similarly, "rights" considerations have also been expanding, as R. F. Nash, for instance, shows. Starting from the "rights" of white male individuals, the range of rights-holders has been extending through blacks, women, workers, native and aboriginal populations, animals, species, to ecosystems.[78]

With this expanding consciousness, the public "moral rules" that Gert identified, against "killing," "harming," and "hurting," have also been acquiring new meaning through the wider reach of their commands. Most people view this "expansion" as an improvement of morality. This raises three questions: first, when each of these "improving" steps was not yet accepted as a "public moral rule," what was the status of the rule? Second, if a further expansion to ecosystems or life-support systems, such as the one defended in this work, were envisioned, would it have to wait for the hypothetical status of public "moral rule" before it could be so defined? And third, what would be its status if only a significant minority decided that it was indeed a "moral rule" worth adopting?

This problem would make moral "advancement," if such a thing exists, or any visionary efforts on behalf of morality, impossible. Jesus himself would not have been talking about a "moral rule" when he spoke of "loving one's neighbor," because it was not part of the "moral rules" as publicly understood at that time. Thus, given the radical novelty of the principle of integrity (PI) I propose, according to Gert I would have no right to term the principle a "moral rule" at all.

The question of PI's justification remains, as no answer appears to arise either from the work of Rawls or that of Gert, two different, but influential thinkers theorizing on morality. Once again then, why should one adopt PI except for prudential reasons? Chapter One showed the reasons why one is led to consider seriously the primacy of environmental concerns. The concept of "integrity," in use in North American legislation and probably originally taken from Aldo Leopold's thought, suggests as a focus a complex, rich value, well worthy of respect and capable of being the focus of obligation. One wonders whether the fact that "integrity" is already codified as a bi-national and international goal of laws and regulations is sufficient to term the requirement to "restore integrity" a "moral rule" in Gert's sense. It still might not be sufficiently a part of common moral language to permit that claim.

Nevertheless, the goal "to restore integrity" posits a duty to comply and represents minimally a *legal* obligation. Normally one needs to argue *from* moral values (or rules) *to* a change in legislation in order to render the latter coextensive with some "new" or reaffirmed tenet of morality. An example might be most Western nations' confrontation with South African apartheid, where sanctions were introduced with the purpose of persuading the government to adopt new laws on moral grounds.

The principle of integrity, when viewed from this perspective, exhibits one more aspect of that radical novelty already discussed: it proposes that, for once, law is indeed "ahead" of morality, and that "moral rules" need to be reunderstood and expanded in the light of the goal and ideal proposed. Ideals, in turn, are intimately connected with the reasons why one should be moral: "virtues, moral and personal, define a human being of integrity and dignity."[79] On the other hand, this might be considered a circular argument; "one should be moral as the person who possesses virtues and morality is 'better' than one who does not" is based upon the tacit acceptance of the premise that morality is good and preferable to its absence in a person. Yet, acting "toward an ideal," particularly when that ideal represents a universal good, seems like a reasonable ground for obligation. Nor does the obligation thus proposed remain limited to the prudential realm. Unlike the "obligation to increase the amount of pleasure for most"—which prompts Gert to respond that "universal obedience to the rule 'Improve your sexual technique' . . . would undoubtedly increase the pleasure in the world by vast amounts" but can hardly count as a "moral rule"—the obligation to "restore integrity" demonstrates impartial, rational, and universalized respect.

Since the ideal sought is not intraspecific, then the major characteristics of *this* (human) species, rationality, is *not* the basis of the respect engendered by PI. Its flavor, Kantian, and even somewhat Stoic, is retained through the persistence of two other major values: life and freedom, the latter, however, only insofar as it is compatible with natural laws. We can, therefore, say that the "good" or value represented by "integrity" is at least as appropriate for supporting nonstipulated obligation as any other value currently or previously proposed. This is especially true as, in spite of the richness of the value of integrity, the obligation it imposes is extremely limited. PI only obliges us to refrain from interfering in the healthy functioning of life-support systems and to curb whatever choices or activities might disrupt the freedom of such systems to develop to their full potential, both structural and functional. This is particularly true because their healthy functioning, their function as life supports, is so closely dependent upon their structure that some even maintain that structure is nothing but a very slow "function."

The appeal to an ideal is apt. In present times much is made of the possible conflict and opposition between our (unchecked) desires and inclinations and the ponderous, reflective, and rational approach of morality. The former is what we *want* to do, what appeals to us; the latter is what we *ought to do*, and is, almost by definition, *not* something that appeals. The first step is to set aside this paradigm. We need to be reminded that in Aristotle's "good," the *kalon*, the noble-and-the-good was beautiful, attractive in and of itself, totally aside from the possibility of other favorable consequences of its adoption. Hence, "integrity," intimately connected with both abiding health (stability) and beauty, can easily exert an appeal similar to that of the Aristotelian *kalon*, although it does not represent a human, individual ideal. According to Aristotle, the good man needed neither punishment nor threats to "keep him in line," nor strict imperatives to force him along the moral path. The beauty and attraction of the goal, the ideal, in and of itself, was sufficient. We pursue the appropriate good because it is *kalon*, beautiful, attractive, and appealing; it commands one by its very existence.

Responsibility Reexamined

The trouble with global, holistic goals is that they overwhelm us by their sheer magnitude. Environmental threats are vast and all-pervasive; they represent an evil well worth the term *summum malum*. Perhaps the reason why so many people are recalcitrant about taking up the challenge of redressing environmental wrongs is precisely because of their size and reach. We are, after all, finite human beings. Most of us have little time and energy to spare, beyond our necessary commitments to the support and well-being of ourselves and our families. It seems that a global crisis is not "our size"; we feel singularly ill-equipped to deal with it. Further, it is hard to convince ourselves that whatever tiny ripple our individual actions may cause could have any real concrete effect. It is far easier to limit ourselves to group or social problems, where some tangible result might be anticipated.

Nevertheless, an ant is a tiny creature, yet the cooperative efforts of ants produce anthills, which actually alter the shape of the earth in a specific location. Further, the goal of integrity and the holistic approach to moral action it requires, indicate precisely why environmental problems are not "out there" beyond our reach, and therefore possibly also beyond the ambit of our responsibility. It shows clearly instead that they are "here" as well, and that all our closest personal responsibilities *start* with the imperative I propose.

It would be ludicrous to say that we are fulfilling our responsibilities to our children by setting up education funds for them or saving hard to leave them an estate, while at the same time we neglect to provide them with the necessities of life. We cannot neglect to feed them, house them, or protect them from childhood diseases through inoculations. All these responsibilities are primary and neglect in any of these areas would surely negate any other "good" we might achieve in the pursuit of educational goals or financial security for them. The thrust of my argument becomes obvious: environmental negligence is as culpable as neglect in the case of other life-support practices. Failing to ensure, by our utmost efforts, that our child has air that is safe to breathe and water that is safe to drink and food that is free of toxic substances is as negligent and culpable as not providing nourishment, shelter, and medical protection.

Nor is this appeal in conflict with our holistic goal. Support-for-life systems have primacy, and there is nothing to prevent each species within them from concerning themselves with their own, within this framework of responsibility, at the survival level. Thus, even in the case of our so-called "primary obligations," the call to integrity may remain primary or at least on a par with the other provisions for the necessity of life, mentioned above.

It is important to note, however, that in general our environmental obligation does not command specific actions. The obligation is a negative one; we are expected to *abstain* from certain activities regarding the environment. The only positive obligation might be the one to vote, or raise consciousness and stand up in ways that will indicate to specific governing bodies our determination to end environmental disintegrity, although individual activities that are restoring (rather than disintegrating) are to be performed (e.g., recycling, diet changes to reduce land stress, limiting the use of energy, and so on).

Our responsibility, then, is at least co-primary with other life/death activities directed toward those for whom we might be directly responsible: members of our own family, friends, co-workers, fellow citizens, and so on, in an ever-widening circle, because the damage we may possibly cause by negligent action will extend well beyond those to whom we have immediate responsibilities. Our status as cosmic citizens indicates the reach of this responsibility, as well as its immediacy. PI is directed at ecosystems, natural "wholes," not at persons.

But even those who are reluctant to accept the principle's requirements for the reasons offered may need to accept them anyway, in order to avoid culpable negligence toward those whom they have, traditionally, a strong obligation not to harm. The latter's obligation will be different, in the sense that motivation will be entirely anthropocentric, rather than holistic, as the principle requires. The obligation would be perceived as less extensive. An action that caused disintegrity in a location where the lives of family and others they cared about were not affected, would be treated with indifference, or even with acceptance. Only actions or policies tangibly affecting life "in our own backyard" would be considered immoral, given the anthropocentric thrust of their belief and the limit of their "special obligations." In essence then, only those who might be convinced of the *global* impact of their activity would still accept the requirements of PI on anthropocentric, and thus limited, grounds. This point has been emphasized throughout this work as the main reason for the necessity of a "holistic" ethic, admittedly a much more difficult choice, rather than a more traditional, intraspecific one, and therefore it needs no further defense here.

What does need clarification is the *extent* of our responsibility in the face of scientific uncertainties, limited resources, and lack of knowledge on our part. Setting aside cases of deliberate "ecosabotage" (in the sense discussed earlier, e.g., Saddam Hussein deliberately spilling oil into the sea) or deliberate minimizing of environmental threats for the sake of gain (a practice that is not essentially different from that of Saddam Hussein), when is the average citizen environmentally culpable?

The general question of whether we might be guilty through negligence when an action is performed (or omitted) is a difficult, debatable one. A discussion by Steven Sverdlik touches upon the salient aspects of the debate.[80] Negligence, for Sverdlik,

> seems to consist in three important features: 1) Behavior that poses an excessive risk to the well-being of others; 2) an agent who is unaware of this risk, but 3) who "should"—as we say—have been aware of it. As we use the term it seems generally to carry implications of wrongdoing and blameworthiness with it.[81]

Now there may be cases of negligence which are not morally wrong, but an analysis of those which are is discloses that causing actual harm, while adding to the blameworthiness of an action, is not absolutely necessary for culpable negligence. Another necessary condition for possible culpability is that the agent in question should accept and be committed to the following principle (N):

> Every person ought to take reasonable precautions to avoid *excessive* risks to the well-being of others posed by her person her property or the persons and property under her supervision.[82]

Now, in our context, it is worth noting that the problem with this "principle" is that "excessive risks" are undefined and thus ultimately open to individual judgment calls. What is the difference, in the final analysis, between exposing others to "risks" and exposing them to "excessive risks"? Is not any risk to which we expose others against their will and knowledge "excessive"? Another problem can be found in the qualifier "reasonable" precautions. Because "responsibility" is not the main quest of this work, I will not at this time attempt to revise Sverdlik's "principle" in order to render it environmentally cogent. Sverdlik's intention was not to speak of environmental ethics, hence, for now, I will simply point out the fact that some qualifications are necessary if the principle is to be adapted to this area. As it stands, it is insufficient for environmental ethics.

At any rate, as we noted, there are problems with the predictive capacities of ecology and the life sciences in general that might affect our knowledge of what might pose "excessive risks" and what might constitute "reasonable precautions." Yet positive knowledge of posing a risk is not absolutely necessary for blameworthy negligence. Sverdlik offers two examples, one of negligence by "commission," and the other by "omission." The first recounts the episode of someone (R) backing out of a driveway without checking his rearview mirror and hitting someone on a bike (although this is not really necessary to establish blameworthy negligence, as noted); the second, of someone (L), normally careful of the state of repair of her property, but neglecting to envision the possibility of falling masonry until after this happens, and a passerby is harmed.[83]

Assuming that both R and L subscribe to principle N, and that there is no question of evil intention, previous knowledge, or anything deliberate about their behavior, still, can both be termed "negligent"? In L's case, it seems hard to talk of blame, yet there might be a responsibility entailing blameworthiness even in "not knowing," or not seeking to acquire information about all aspects of one's behavior in regard to risk, or of property, or in regard to possible harms or dangers that might arise through the latter.

In essence, negligence is blameworthy because our beliefs about it, including the principle (N), the acquisition of knowledge and information to correct and inform our beliefs, is mandatory: "we cannot be blamed for not knowing the way the world is, but we can be blamed for not using the evidence we have."[84]

And we can also be blamed, one might add, for not seeking additional information about "the way the world is" as part of our responsibility not to impose "(excessive) risks." Thus, at some point in time, the agent must decide that further investigation into the risk-causing aspects (possible, not only probable), of her actions and omissions is necessary.

Environmental and business ethics textbooks abound in cases where a deliberate decision is made at some point, "to avert one's eyes from evidence that we had pointing in the direction of excessive riskiness."[85] A case in point would be the well-known textbook example "The DBCP Case." In it, a pesticide manufacturer in California, having evidence that his product was causing tumors in rats, not only withheld that information as a "proprietary" or "trade secret," part of company research, but also elected *not* to commission further studies relevant to human exposure to the substance. Eventually, as a high percentage of male workers were found to be irreversibly infertile, further testing disclosed that the substance *also* caused extensive shrinking in the size of rats' testes.[86]

This information was not available when the earlier decision was made to continue production as usual. But the indication of previous tests ought to have suggested that further tests be done and that workers ought to have been fully informed of possible risks. In this case, a clear example of the Aristotelian analysis of blameworthy negligence, "the agent must decide not to bother herself with seeing where troublesome evidence leads, knowing that this decision is risky."[87] Speaking of punishment required in the case of "ignorance," Aristotle says:

> ignorance itself is made a ground for punishment in cases where the offender is held to be responsible for his ignorance . . . and so in other cases where ignorance is held to be due to negligence, on the ground that the offender need not have been ignorant, as he could have taken the trouble to ascertain the facts.[88]

In this case then, the question would be, can anyone in today's mass media world of instant communications be unaware of the danger of exposure to certain risks, or at least of the necessity of finding information before acting (or failing to act) in ways that might place others at risk? This is probably simply a rhetorical question—the answer is obvious. And it is the very obviousness of the answer that prompts legislation supporting the public demand for "zero discharge," "sunset chemicals," and, in general, the quest for ecosystem integrity.[89]

Our chemical "dependence" stems from a consumerist life-style that ought to be reexamined in the light of the present discussion of "culpable negligence." Our responsibility then cashes out to more than the injunction to vote and speak out for environmental consciousness (on the positive side of our obligation) or to avoid deliberate or even "aware" acts of environmental "violence" and ecosabotage. Our responsibility will have to include a commitment to the quest for enough knowledge (compatible with our mental and educational capacities) to be aware of which activities (or omissions) might represent blameworthy negligence.

Like "R" in Sverdlik's example, one cannot continue to use technological tools and aids without ascertaining whether these "free choices" on our part correspond to "excessive risk" exposure for others. Once again, the *first* question the responsible moral agent must ask herself is: "Is the activity involving modern technology safe enough for others, whether I am the only one putting others at risk, or simply a contributory cause of their possible risk exposure?" If the answer is either "no" or "unsure," then abstinence is the only moral choice in the case of a possible grave risk; in the case of a low probability of miinor harms only, severe curtailment would be appropriate.

Another equally important question to ask oneself might be, "Is there anything I have neglected to do (or learn) in regard to anything I own, or operate, that might involve exposing others to excessive risks?" Once again, the answer will determine whether the agent ought to take some further action or undertake some reflection hitherto omitted, or neglected. This is not as easy as the last two paragraphs indicate. Some of the previous examples attest to the delicate balancing of rights and obligations that will be needed in order to move toward "integrity" as an ideal and goal.

An example from Chapter One could be brought back to mind. The body heat of a swimmer in a lake or river is sufficient to raise the temperature of that body of water enough to accelerate the life processes of some organisms and hasten their deaths. In cases like this, even a concerned environmentalist, not being aware of the facts, would see no need to abstain, curtail, or even investigate. Yet he might be disturbing a specific ecosystem only, not the basis of life on earth, so that the categorical imperatives of PI may not apply. On the other hand, a driver who needs to use her automobile, even in a good cause, to give talks about the environment, or teach environmental ethics for instance, will contribute significantly (particularly if the automobile is used regularly) to a serious, global threat. Is "abstinence" or even "severe curtailment" possible in today's Western and Northern urban societies? The answer is not obvious. Possibly some consideration of the least evil might be brought in at this point, although the "imperative" permits no consequentialist adjustments.

A number of difficult real life cases might be discussed. Difficulties about priorities are endemic to deontological moral systems, and a system that is based on admittedly imprecise life sciences at least in part, such as "integrity," will surely be no exception. But integrity is an ideal against which we need to measure our activity *first*. Ideals do not propose sets of precise rules; the work of reflection, respective weighing of alternatives, sincere self-examination for sufficient pertinent information (or the need to seek further knowledge), and many other such considerations, are left to the moral agent.

The agent's responsibility is clearly awe-inspiring, the difficulties monumental: the simplest, most basic imperative, that of environmental responsibility supported by PI, proposes an ideal or moral goal that is exceedingly difficult to attain and even to understand. It commands actions and omissions that might be intuitively or instinctively desirable or attractive, but in practice equally hard to define, analyze, and prescribe with any degree of precision.

The trouble is that if the argument of this work is accepted, we have no choice but to accept also the ideal of environmental "integrity," as the basis of obligation. We also need to strive somehow, continuing our pursuit of relevant knowledge and fostering an abiding concern for the persistence of life, to seek to support the harmonious functioning of life-support systems. This can be done not in one, specific, "guaranteed" manner only, but through actions and omissions in the conscious quest for a worthwhile but hard-to-define ideal.

When so articulated, this may appear to be a task capable of daunting even the most committed of persons. It might help to keep in mind that all ideals of morality, from Aristotle's "contemplation" as the "highest" form of activity, to Kantian "absolute good will" and through many variations through time, are all equally imprecise, incredibly difficult to achieve, and impose onerous demands on the ethically concerned moral agent. They all hold great promise of representing beauty, or truth, or the good, or a combination of some of these. "Integrity" has an additional aspect that renders it unique: it alone provides the basis of life and freedom for those capacities the agent needs in order to be moral. The next chapter will be devoted to a defense of the principle and of holism in general. The rest of the book will strive to make the principle operational, by answering the question: what sacrifices in environmental integrity can be made (if any) to gain or maintain "cultural advantages"?

Acknowledgment

I am very grateful to Evandro Agazzi, John M. Rist, Kenneth Schmitz, Thomas Hill, Jr., and Holmes Rolston III for their helpful critique of earlier drafts of this chapter.

Notes

1. A. Schweitzer, *Civilization and Ethics* (London: Adam and Charles Black, 1946), 255.

2. J. B. Callicott, "Intrinsic Value of Nonhuman Species," 138–172; Callicott also advocates "respect" although that is not the main point of his approach; see, for instance, "The Conceptual Foundations," in *In Defense of the Land Ethic* (New York: State University of New York Press, 1989), 93–94.

3. P. Taylor, *Respect for Nature*, 44–45. See also K. E. Goodpaster, "From Egoism to Environmentalism," in K. E. Goodpaster, and K. M. Sayre, eds., *Ethics Problems of the 21st Century* (Notre Dame, Indiana: University of Notre Dame Press, 1979, 21–35.

4. See Freya Matthews, *The Ecological Self* (Savage, Md.: Barnes and Noble Books, 1991); cp. Lawrence Johnson, *A Morally Deep World* (New York: Cambridge University Press, 1991).

5. Taylor, *Respect for Nature*, 29.

6. Ibid., 26.

7. Ibid., 79.

8. Ibid., 134.

9. Ibid., 172.

10. Ibid., 79.

11. V. and R. Routley, "Against the Inevitability of Human Chauvinism," in K. E. Goodpaster and K. M. Sayre, eds., *Ethics and Problems of the 21st Century* (Notre Dame, Ind.: University of Notre Dame, 1979), 36–59 is a good example of such a discussion.

12. Taylor, *Respect for Nature*, 53.

13. Ibid., 47.

14. Ibid., 41.

15. M. Midgley, "Duties Concerning Islands," in *People, Penguins and Plastic Trees*, 156–64.

16. Taylor, *Respect for Nature*, 209.

17. Ibid., 225–26.

18. Ibid., 241.

19. Ibid., 254.

20. D. Ehrenfeld, *The Arrogance of Humanism* (New York: Oxford University Press, 1978); this work brings out and argues in detail this point.

21. Taylor, *Respect for Nature*, 114; points (a) through (e) are argued on pp. 102–114.

22. Ibid., 101.

23. A. Schweitzer, 233.

24. Ibid.

25. Ibid.

26. Ibid., 234.

27. Ibid., 235.

28. Ibid., 236.

29. Ibid.

30. Ibid., 243.

31. Ibid., 240.

32. Ibid.

33. Ibid., 241.

34. Ibid.

35. Ibid., 243.

36. Ibid., 244.

37. Callicott, 153.

38. Ibid., 155.

39. K. E. Goodpaster, "From Egoism to Environmentalism," in *Ethics and Problems of the 21st Century*, 32.

40. Ibid.

41. Callicott, 155.

42. Ibid., 154.

43. Ibid., 158.

44. Christopher Stone, "Moral Pluralism and the Course of Environmental Ethics," *Environmental Ethics* 10 (1988): 139–54.

45. Ibid., 152.

46. Donald Brown, a private communication, December 29, 1992.

47. H. Rolston III, *Environmental Ethics* (Philadelphia: Temple Press, 1988), 79.

48. I am indebted to Professor Kenneth Schmitz, University of Toronto, for pointing out that "hostility," as such, has no place in wild nature. What occurs there is a combination of "ferocity" (on the part of the predator) and "fear" (on the part of the prey). Unlike two soldiers, meeting on the battlefield, no reciprocity and parity are present. Thus "hostility" is in some sense a misnomer. This, however, does not affect the point that any hostile relation may be coupled with respect, in the senses discussed, which is—after all—Nagel's point. I discuss this principle in Chapter Six.

49. Thomas Frankena, "Ethics and the Environment," in K. E. Goodpaster and K. M. Sayre, eds., *Ethics and Problems of the 21st Century*, 5.

50. Schweitzer, 245.

51. Ibid., 259.

52. Chapter Seven, Part B, this volume.

53. Rolston, *Environmental Ethics,* 79.

54. Chapter Seven, Part B, this volume.

55. Professor Arthur Schaefer of Manitoba reviewed a book by David Suzuki, for the *Globe and Mail*, newspaper, July 16, 1988, p. C19, Toronto, Ont.

56. Lucius Apuleius, *The Golden Ass (Metamorphoses)*, Book X, 18; Loeb Classical Library, W. Adlington Tr. (1566) revised by S. Geseln (London: Wm. Heinemann, 1965).

57. Fr. DK25 reads "Without effort he sets everything in motion by the thought of his mind," and Fr. DK26, "He always abides in the same place, not moving at all; it is not appropriate to his nature to be in different places at different times," in Philip Wheelwright, ed., *The Presocratics* (New York: Odyssey Press, 1966).

58. See Chapter Six, Part B, this volume.

59. Prof. Kwesi Wiredu of Ghana discussed this point in his paper, part of a symposium, "Are There Cultural Universals?" with John Passmore (Australia), S. Nasr (U.S.A.), and T. Oizerman (USSR), August 25, 1988 in Brighton, England, at the 18th World Congress of Philosophy.

60. Stone, *Moral Pluralism*, 140–46.

61. A. MacIntyre, "Corporate Modernity and Moral Judgment: Are They Mutually Exclusive?" in *Ethics and Problems of the 21st Century*, 122–35.

62. Stone, *Moral Pluralism*, 144.

63. Ibid., 145.
64. Arne Naess, *Ecology, Community and Lifestyle*, ed. and trans. by David Rothenberg (Cambridge, U.K.: Cambridge University Press, 1991), 23ff.
65. Ibid., 14.
66. Rothenberg, op. cit., 2–9.
67. Naess, ibid., 25.
68. Ibid., 20.
69. Lester Milbrath, in Naess, op. cit., 17.
70. Naess, particularly Chapters 4, 5 and 6.
71. John Rawls, *A Theory of Justice* (Cambridge, Mass.: Harvard University Press, 1971), 578.
72. Ibid., 579.
73. B. Gert, *Morality* (Oxford, U.K.: Oxford University Press, 1988), 8.
74. Ibid.
75. Ibid., 69.
76. Ibid., 67–68.
77. Ibid., 148.
78. R. F. Nash, *The Rights of Nature: A History of Environmental Ethics* (Madison: University of Wisconsin Press, 1989).
79. Gert, *Morality*, 225.
80. Steven Sverdlik, "Negligence and Responsibility," presented at the Central APA meeting in Chicago, April 29, 1990.
81. Ibid., 1–2.
82. Ibid., 3.
83. Ibid., 2–4.
84. Ibid., 8.
85. Ibid., 10.
86. M. Velasquez, *Business Ethics Concepts and Cases*, 2nd. ed. (Englewood Cliffs, N.J.: Prentice-Hall, 1988), 34–43.
87. Sverdlik, 10.
88. Aristotle, *Nicomachean Ethics*, III.V.8–9, Loeb Ed., H. Rockham, trans. (London: Cambridge University Press, 1975).
89. Paul Muldoon and M. Valiante, *Zero Discharge, A Strategy for the Regulation of Toxic Substance in The Great Lakes Basin Ecosystem.* (Toronto, Ont.: Canadian Environmental Law Research Foundation, 1988).

4

The Principle of Integrity and a Defense of Biocentric Holism and of Other Holistic Positions

Introduction: Individuals or Wholes?

The tension between individuals and wholes underlies much of today's environmental and animal ethics debate. A similar tension between individual persons and their societies exists in traditional human ethics. Further, the question of "individuals" and their rights affects not only ethical discourse but also the formulation of public policy, both in its long-term goals and in its strategic implementation.

In his analysis of "integrity," understood exclusively as a human virtue, Mark Halfon discusses the value of parts related to wholes in the context of Aristotelian thought. The connection between "virtue" and *eudaimonia* (well-being) is too close in Aristotle to permit a simple means-to-ends relation, because that would make the relation a contingent one. The entity possessing instrumental value (the means) could then have no intrinsic value at all, because means-to-ends relations do not always imply they are a necessary condition to the end (i.e., substitute means might do as well).

On the other hand, any part will be a necessary condition for the existence of a whole.[1] In fact the notion of teleology is most properly and primarily used in understanding a *living* organism.[2] Halfon concludes that "the theory of contributory value as integral–integrative is different from the theories of intrinsic and instrumental value."[3] This suggests a relation between individual and (extended) community that does not depreciate individuals while seeking to reintegrate them within the ecosystem. I shall return to Aristotle below.

For now, it is clear that if the whole can be termed "valuable," then a further "value" will be added, no less innate, additionally to human, specific values that an individual may possess—both innate and acquired. The value inherent in being part of a valuable and valued whole is seldom acknowledged, given the current emphasis on individual rights. Those who argue for the primacy of rights need to have recourse to a "theory of human nature,"[4] often to one that stresses human reasoning capacities, in order to defend this position. Of course, human rights can be defended on other bases, such as prudential grounds—viewing humans as bound by the social and legal norms within one's society[5]—or on consequential, intuitive, or Kantian grounds. Given the abundant critical literature available on this topic, it would be redundant to reproduce arguments here.[6] In Chapter Two, the metaphysical aspects of "integrity" were discussed.

We want rather to see whether "natural rights" has any possible relation to an ethic of environmental concern. It is important to focus on the aspects of "natural rights" of individuals that might have an impact on environmental considerations. Therefore, it is worth emphasizing that understanding a human being as part of a valuable whole adds objective value to human beings *precisely* as parts of ecosystems, a necessary premise for defending a biocentric environmental ethic. This value is dependent on neither contracts nor compacts; and it requires no specific definition of "human nature," not even the insertion of the value of rationality as *the* primary human characteristic, for its justification.

In this case, rather than viewing individuals as inappropriately "valueless" in respect to the whole, a biocentric, holistic position can add value to individuals independently of specific human characteristics. However, this line of argument, while eliminating one difficulty, substitutes two other serious problems. First of all, the value of the whole, or ecosystem, needs to be established beyond that of individuals, even human. Secondly, even if we have achieved a way of establishing this value, a moral doctrine needs to be universal and consistent in its application. But "organicist" theories of society are often cited as damaging counterexamples to biocentric environmental ethics positions. If the ecosystem as such is primary, thus superior, and the main locus of value, then—the argument goes—the value of all its components is merely instrumental. Like mosses or algae or any organism within an ecosystemic whole, persons too are reduced to being valuable merely as means; the end is the preservation and stable existence of the ecosystem of which they are a part.

Not only does this position lack respect for humans, because it no longer treats them as ends in themselves, but also it can no longer concern itself primarily with individual or even aggregated pain/pleasure. Conflicting, as it does, with both deontology and utilitarianism, as well as with contractarianism and considerations of fairness and justice, it is in fact environmental "fascism,"[7] as it requires us to pay homage to the good of the whole (or the whole of society) with little or no consideration being given to its human components.

The question then remains: is the acceptance of ecosystemic environmentalism similar to espousing totalitarianism in society, and, in fact, is the value of the whole even less capable of justification? In other words, can an ecosystemic environmental ethic be compared to the defense of a society such as Mussolini's Italy? Finally, is it even harder to justify the former than the latter cases as a "human good"? (Cf. Chapter Two for a discussion of "integrity" as a value in our sense.)

I have argued that the principle of "integrity" need not incur this criticism because it only operates as a *limitation* and basic first principle for all other interhuman ethics, which in turn stand or fall on their own merits. It only provides a basis from which to become aware of the human situation and of whatever role might fit the realities of our existence, but this might not be sufficient to exonerate our ecosystemic biocentric ethic from this damaging charge. But perhaps there is another way of viewing the relation between individuals and wholes that can avoid this problem. Before anything can be added to the ongoing discussion about "holism" and its alleged difficulties, one needs to examine the controversy in recent literature.

Biocentric Holism

What is "biocentric holism"? It is a philosophical position that takes life-support systems, and hence wholes, rather than individuals, to be primary. Yet, by taking life as a whole, and the specific environment (i.e., ecosystems) that support it as first in moral considerability, it *also* eliminates the conflict between individuals and wholes, at least at the purely biological level of existence. Ecosystems that are neither *willfully* nor *carelessly* stressed nor degraded tend in general to support *all* life within them. The "principle of integrity," as we saw in the previous chapter, does not propose a morality aimed at interpersonal relations, whether intraspecific (that is, among humans), or interspecific (that is, between humans and individuals of other, nonhuman, species).

The principle simply proposes as a first (or even as a preliminary) moral consideration, respect and noninterference with life in general, or life-supporting systems. In its extreme generality, the principle proposes no specific positive rule of conduct beyond the negative obligation not to degrade, attack, or destroy any natural system that may contribute directly or indirectly to the support of life. It deliberately does not discriminate between species, nor does it attempt to establish a possible hierarchy of intrinsic values for individual entities, in order to establish details of interspecific justice. The latter will be necessary as a further step to support second order principles, and to bridge the gap from the appeal to integrity (as I_1 and I_2, or structural and functional integrity) on the one hand, and specific problems that might require *positive* intervention on the other.

Now the principle of integrity (PI) permits *positive* intervention only in two sorts of cases. Interference with natural functioning and processes unfolding through time is required (a) when our activity has introduced an "injustice" that should be redressed. For example, the acid rain in Algonquin Park, a natural preserve in Northern Ontario, has harmed most of the vegetation, hence the deer need "hay drops" in order to survive the harsh winters. The second case requiring positive interference in the name of "integrity," would be (b) when the natural drive to preserve our species (see PI, Categorical Imperative 1b) might suggest interference with the spread of some other dangerous or threatening species in a shared environment, by ecologically sound means of course. An example of (b) might be the limiting of "killer bees," or "superbugs," or malaria-bearing mosquitoes; the first two examples also contravene structural integrity, because they have been introduced through previous human interference in ecosystems, as "exotics." The last example simply endangers the life of individuals of our species, though not species survival.

Hence "biocentric holism" in my formulation of PI is a position that recognizes intrinsic value in wholes which are life-supporting. It is also a position that proposes such value as the focus of moral considerability before all other individual considerations and before interpersonal morality. Through its support of the "strong right" to life, it leaves as an open question the valuation and comparison of all other "weaker" rights, beyond the basic life value it supports.

Now intrinsic value as such has been ably defended by many thinkers, including Paul Taylor, J. Baird Callicott, and Holmes Rolston III.[8] Many have also attacked it, particularly in its "holistic" mode. Yet although moral extensionism has had its critics, its similarity to the doctrines from which its various "applications" have originated (e.g., Taylor's or Regan's acknowledged Kantian roots), has perhaps served to make it more acceptable, and even "respectable" to some extent. It may also have contributed to the serious consideration it has received, even in attempted rebuttals. The same has not happened in the case of holistic theories of intrinsic value.

"Biocentric holism" may be understood in several ways. For instance, William Aiken uses a somewhat different expression. He says: "Ecocentrism is a nonanthropocentric position which places value on whole systems."[9] Arne Naess, as well, in his presentation of the "deep ecology" position (or approach) prefers the same expression, "ecocentrism." Although both Aiken's definition and the spirit of "ecocentrism" or "ecosophy" in Naess are close enough to the position I defend. I think "biocentric holism" captures the core sense of the doctrine in a better way. It is not meant to imply that "biocentric holism" advocates *absolute* respect for all life, as Albert Schweitzer, for instance, did. I find Schweitzer's position hard to adopt, though easy to admire.[10] I term "holism" "biocentric" because that seems to emphasize the centrality of life to the doctrine that is indeed "ecocentric." Whether we are speaking of "ecosystems" or "wholes," we are speaking essentially of life support, or what Holmes Rolston terms "appropriate survival units."[11]

In essence, the "whole" is not the same as the sum or aggregate of individuals, in that no single individual member of the biota (except humans of course) can affect life in a general way other than its own, or perhaps that of another organism that depends upon it. An ecosystem, however, does support life in a general sense. Hence, I believe it is appropriate to emphasize this function in the way we define holism. A question can be raised in turn, though: does this mean that landscapes or natural areas that are not life-supporting (such as moonscapes), lie outside the obligation of a biocentric holist?

The answer may be found in part in Aldo Leopold's work. "Beauty" is a component of the trilogy of value in the land ethic, the only component that is not necessarily connected with life. Technically then, a "biocentric holist" may count ecosystems that are not life-supporting secondary in value to those which are, whereas those who see beauty as primary (as Eugene Hargrove, for instance, does)[12] may not differentiate between the two. My own "principle of integrity" is based on a value that is partially structural, and that aspect would cover wholes that are not life-supporting as well, although priority would remain for life-support systems.[13]

Whatever definition is used, for many holists Leopold's "land ethic" has been a major source of inspiration, and there is no comparable major philosophical doctrine that can be traced back to intraspecific (human) ethics, as its starting point. In fact, the only possible human "analogy" is that of sociobiology, a paradigm so fraught with problems that it offers little help to anyone attempting to ground biocentric holism on an established moral doctrine. So, those who are inspired in varying degrees by Leopold's work, particularly his famous words,[14] are often dismissed in a cavalier fashion or, at the very least, viewed as upholding an undefensible position, one which—if accepted—would lead to conclusions that are "socially absurd" and "morally paradoxical."[15] The latter are only the latest in a long line of indignant but vastly predictable accusations that continue to be repeated monotonously. Detailed responses to these criticisms have been offered years back by both Callicott and Rolston.[16]

I consider their responses cogent and well supported. Nevertheless, the fact that their existence in print has not daunted the detractors of biocentric holism suggests that, perhaps, it might be worthwhile to reconsider the problems and add further counterarguments to the objections. Further, there is another line of attack, one based on the ecological claims that support ethical holism in the work of many (including myself). Is there scientific evidence for ecological claims about interrelatedness of all components of ecosystems, or about what actions are deleterious to wholes such as ecosystems, or even what exactly defines an ecosystem or its optimal state? If not, the critics insist, with some reason, biocentric holism cannot claim to be based on scientific information, nor to be clearly compatible with it (see Chapter Two, especially Sections (a), (d), and (d_1).

Scientific aspects of holism were discussed in Chapter Two. In this chapter, I will first summarize some of the major objections to biocentric holism and particularly to the "land ethic" to which the principle of integrity (PI) is conceptually closest.

Objections to Biocentric
Holism and the Land Ethic

A position of biocentric holism compatible with Leopold's "land ethic" is vulnerable to attack from several fronts. These attacks can be grouped under four major headings. The best known (and most frequently voiced) is (1) the one Tom Regan levies against the position. By making the biotic community, and hence the whole, the major focus of ethical concern, it is alleged that it correspondingly lowers the importance of the individual within the community. Hence, by analogy with other "totalitarian" ideologies, it is nothing but "environmental fascism."[17] In a similar vein, we hear it described as simply "social Darwinism," and thus open to all the objections the latter calls forth. Following upon (1) as a possible consequence, there is a second line of attack (2) which can be traced to, among others, William Aiken, who criticizes Taylor and Callicott. Aiken claims that "Eco-Holism" is misanthropy, pure and simple. Since the human contribution to ecosystems is minimal, their worth within these ecosystems is correspondingly small. Taylor reflects on the contrast between the fleeting quality of the human presence on Earth and the grave disturbances which that presence inflicts upon nature. He concludes that the termination of the human race "would most likely be greeted with a hearty 'good riddance!'"[18] Aiken concludes that "extreme eco-holism may not prescribe mass genocide or species suicide, but it comes close."[19]

Sergio Bartolommei claims that a holistic position supported by the "land ethic" leads to conclusions that are "morally paradoxical," as well as "socially absurd" as implied by Regan's objection.[20] Bartolommei claims that, while it appears extremely desirable to reduce the bias of the "judging" moral agent, a position evident in the common quest for an "impartial observer," a biocentric position "requires that the (human) agent be removed altogether from consideration." Should we decide to "dissolve" the judging moral agent, who will then have any "moral obligation" in regard to the land? Who will be capable of "respect for nature"? Bartolommei concludes:

> The land ethic, in its intent to demonstrate the limits of an ethic without environment, ends with an ethical theory of intrinsic value of the "biotic community," (by prescribing) an environmentalism without morality.[21] (My translation from Italian.)

In essence then, his claim is that the sharp reduction of the human "moral agent's" importance leaves one with an environment which "wins" by default, if at all, because there is no one left to judge competing claims, to approve or disapprove of standards, or to do the morally right thing with regard to nature. The human moral agent has lost the morality he is trying to defend. Finally, (4) an objection is raised that is intended to provide irrefutable evidence that biocentric holism is based on a fallacious argument. Those who launch this attack take David Hume's position on the "is/ought" dichotomy as the absolute refutation of any philosophical argument "from nature." This line of attack is so familiar that it needs no elaborate explanation at this time.

These are serious and important objections, and they merit equally serious response on the part of those who still defend biocentric holism. Yet, although some major thinkers have provided carefully argued counterclaims, it appears that no argument offered so far has succeeded in silencing the critics. And even if this lack of success is not due to any flaw within the proposed counterarguments, but to lack of open-mindedness or interest on the part of the critics, surely some remarshaling of those lines of defense, with the addition of some new "ammunition," might be of some use. From the perspective of bio-centric holism, supported by PI, defense from all four objections is possible. PI recognizes that the acceptance of the goal of "restoring integrity" will have social and political implications, but it is neither, as such, a specific interpersonal nor a social principle of morality. It simply requires the acknowledgment of both our unprecedented power and of that power's increasingly obvious limitations. The latter become perfectly clear when the true reach of our predictive powers is understood and accepted, in place of the present optimistic "faith."

In turn the *factual* conditions and limitations entail two logical and philosophical points: (1) the recognition of interdependence of all natural entities, supporting the adoption of an I–Thou rather than an I–it approach, as Naess suggests (citing Martin Buber);[22] (2) the somewhat paradoxical necessity to abstract, conceptually, from our total humanity, separating the inseparable: our purely biological existence from the rest of our human existence in all its complexity. The first point is fairly uncontroversial today, and it is based on a number of insights discussed in Chapter Two: it has been defended by Leopold, Naess, Rolston, and many others. The second point has been implicitly defended by many thinkers, although it is not often defended explicitly. For instance, Kant's categorical imperative entails the infinite value of life, a principle to which he appears to make only *one* major exception, in his defense of Cato's suicide, judged to be unique in the history of mankind. The Roman Cato committed suicide in order to escape being replaced as leader by the victorious Caesar, and this represented a "moral" suicide because it was meant to indicate to fellow citizens the absolute primary of freedom, even above that of one's life.

Kant envisions also the heroic cleaving to a principle, hence putting our own duty above bare subsistence in the rare cases when the two come into conflict, but that position does not describe the present difficulties and is no counterobjection to the present "primacy of life" stance. Neither our preferences nor our "self-fulfilment" could permit us to use others' lives as means to those ends; and that is precisely what policies that are not careful to prevent harm do, even while they purport to "better" our lives, or support our (other) rights to free choices. Again on the question of the primacy of life, virtue ethics considerations are at times somewhat ambiguous. Aristotle's thought, as we will see, provides the best support for the holistic position I defend. On the other hand, Plato's ideal of the "philosophical life" is somewhat paradoxical. Although it would be better *not* to be in a body, the philosopher's rational/moral life can only be *lived*, and any effort aimed at learning and eventually at self-improvement can only be pursued and achieved while alive. Stoic doctrine, and later that of Plotinus, permitted "reasoned dismissal," or the discarding of life, once the utmost capacity for learning, morality, and understanding had been reached and only decline loomed ahead. From this perspective, life could not be said to possess the "infinite value" Kant ascribed to it. Yet it persisted in its role as the highest enabling, or supporting value, the necessary (though not sufficient) condition for the achievement of any true "good." Hence it can be said the PI renders explicit a position entailed by most moral theories and positions in the history of philosophy.

The necessity for rendering explicit such a truism has been indicated by the present environmental crisis, and the need for a new starting point in morality was argued for in the first chapter. In fact, if the principle renders explicit an already existing, underlying tenet of much of moral theory, then what is required is a shift of emphasis, based on a changed mindset, rather than an entirely new moral position. The newness is retained, however, in the primacy and nonnegotiable status of the principle. Although Kant is probably correct in saying that in a very rare case putting our principles before our existence is a moral position worthy of admiration (it is also the position of martyrs, saints, and heroes, hence a superogatory one that remains, ideally, desirable) it loses its force when it is applied to others' lives or to the basis of life, globally.

Life itself does not represent our only goal; rather PI, because of its insistence of life's primacy, demands that we face the reality of the choices we make daily. It is not sufficient to speak of human goals of justice, peace, or equity and to obscure the possible conflicts between these and the preservation of life as such. We need to lay bare the choices we make in all their implications, rather than hide their true import under the cover of human development of fulfillment goals, which will certainly remain important, but which may become less meaningful if our life is threatened or even if its span is limited. A more prosperous, or freer, or more fulfilling life may be less appealing if its length or our health is affected by environmental hazards. Some individuals might object that they would prefer perhaps 20 prosperous years to 30 less prosperous ones, even though the latter might be less hazardous. This would be an entirely individual choice if it did not involve environmental risks that affect others whose choice would be different, as well as future generations and nonhuman animals.

Once again, the distinction between "strong rights" and "weak rights" becomes important (see below in this chapter for a discussion of Alan Gewirth's position on "rights"). PI does not eliminate individual rights, but by its very nature as an environmental life-protecting principle, it supports "strong rights" across the species barrier, while it reduces "weak rights" (e.g., all other rights, beyond the right to life), to secondary status. Arne Naess speaks of the "universal right to live and blossom," or "to unfold," avoiding judgments involving the relative merits of different entities, yet permitting one species to survive at the expense of others, according to the natural laws by which it is constrained.[23] Clearly this is not a very detailed guideline, but it is not meant to be. Naess for instance admits that, while suggesting "a guideline for behavior," deep ecology "does not tell anything about behavior."[24]

The principle of integrity, in contrast, suggests a somewhat clearer practical application, because the basic value that supports it is a practical notion, already used in legislation and regulation, hence at present, a basis for policy. What about the four objections posed at the beginning? From our standpoint, the "fascism" objection fails, as a category mistake, because PI only promotes and supports a general "good" without which no other good is possible, whether for individuals or groups. Hence, rather than impose totalitarianism, it demands respect, prima facie, for the freedom to unfold of all individuals, groups, species, and systemic wholes. The protected "unfolding" does not proceed according to the principle, but according to individual and specific capacities. Hence, but recognizing the distinction between human and nonhuman goals beyond the survival level, while strongly affirming their coincidence and mutuality at the level of survival, PI escapes both the "fascism" and the "misanthropy" charges.

The latter is also avoided through the acknowledgment of species primacy, in the face of conflict; this does no more than admit the existence of laws according to which various parts of the biota survive within an ecosystem. A principle that could not recognize such a basic fact, would do more than support "misanthropy": it would foster, within itself, the seeds of the elimination of all life on earth. If things could not survive at one another's expense, universal "anorexia" and death would ensue—clearly absurd, but worth noting nevertheless. Hence, the basis of life support made primary by PI *excludes* the possibility of hating any species, including our own.

In turn, the same aspect of the principle may be used to respond to the "disappearance of the moral agent" charge (3). There is no dispute, to my knowledge, about the fact that humankind is the only species we consider capable of moral agency. But the defense and protection of common life-support systems does nothing to diminish *either* the existence of *or* the stature of the moral agent. It simply ensures her sustained existence and reinforces both her commonality with and her difference from the rest of the biota. It is a non sequitur to assume that because humankind has the capacity for moral agency, in contrast with at least most of nonhuman nature (although I reserve judgment about ape, dolphin, and whale communities in this regard), *therefore* it follows that all aspects of their humanity are in marked contrast with the rest of nature. Hence, the existence of human "difference," even if it is viewed as a proof of their "superiority," says little or nothing about their biological requirements, which are neither markedly different from, nor in any way superior to those of the rest of the biota. On the contrary, the imperative following upon PI *supports* the persistence of the moral agent through sustaining her life, thus the necessary (though not sufficient) condition of moral agency.

Finally the fourth objection, which is the alleged improper passing from an "is" to an "ought," can be rejected from Holmes Rolston's response to the problem. Supported as it is by the limits that form the factual basis of our existence, the principle does no more than permit only commands and prescriptions within the parameter of what is physically possible and appropriate. The principle does not inappropriately use facts as values; it entails instead the careful study and consideration of facts, and it suggests a goal and ideal that are not incompatible with them. Rather than saying, "this is the way nature functions, therefore it is (morally) right," its claim is, "what we accept as morally right, must first of all *not* be something that conflicts with the way nature functions."

From the position of PI, then, we can generate answers to the four major objections to biocentric holism. Further, another distinctive aspect of PI is that it dissolves (at the level of life actualization) the conflict between individuals and wholes. It assumes (again, only at the survival level) the coincidence of "strong" interests (supporting strong rights) of individuals, species, and wholes. There may be cases when this coincidence cannot be assumed. In nonhuman nature, conflicts between individuals and wholes in general do not threaten the common life-support basis and are usually resolved in favor of the whole. Conflicts among individuals of different species are resolved with the strongest or most capable individual prevailing. In Chapter Six, Part B, I argue along similar lines in regard to our interaction with nonhuman animals. I also propose that, from the standpoint of PI, there is nothing unjust about supporting our own (individual and specific) life by "preying" on another's life, be it a carrot, a fruit, or a fish. Reintegrating such "preying" within its true province, that is, within natural processes, I once again separate the defense of "strong rights" from weaker ones and permit our own individuals (and our species) to "win" if they can against other individuals and species outside our own, but only in the preservation of life.

Returning now to the possible objections to the theory, it is fair to add that others have also responded to the objections mentioned at the outset and their respective defenses, arising as they do from different perspectives, marshal other arguments in support of holism. Notable among these are J. Baird Callicott and Holmes Rolston III.

Callicott's defense is primarily in support of Leopold, and it is based on Darwin's thought in conjunction with Hume's approach to morality. He advocates the development of a "sense of social integration with human and nonhuman nature," on the basis of which it is appropriate to "extend" one's "social instincts and sympathies."[25] This approach eliminates objections (1), (2), and (3), and a further appeal to Hume's requirement for factual input to foster a more enlightened "sympathy" offers also a response to (4).

Rolston's responses, based as they are on other principles, are somewhat closer to counterobjections based on PI. Objection (1) is once again eliminated as a "category mistake," given his explicit separation between "nature" and "culture." For Rolston, cultural and biotic communities are not alike, and that is why virtues that must be deployed in the former are not required in the latter. Further, in response to (2), "humans have duties at survival-unit levels,"[26] but even if their contribution to ecosystems is minimal, it does not follow that we have a duty to self-annihilation. As we are now speaking of human obligations, as an example, it might be appropriate to think of the prohibition against murder or rape. Even if one is desperately driven to commit these crimes by psychological forces one cannot resist, still it does not seem right to say that in that case one's moral obligation is to commit suicide. What might be required is to take medications reducing the level of certain chemicals, perhaps, or even to commit oneself to an institution that would make it impossible to pursue one's immoral inclinations.

In other words, the obligation would be to modify one's behavior by *any means* available, not to kill oneself. Thus Aiken's critique is not well taken. After citing Callicott's call to "discipline, sacrifice, retrenchment, and massive economic reforms,"[27] Aiken points out that this position has "astounding, staggering" implications for humans. He then concludes that this stance measures its worth "by the level of its misanthropy."[28]

This seems to confuse the behavior of the individual with the individual himself, a position parents, for instance, are often warned about. Parents are told not to manifest strong disapproval of a child, even while voicing strong (and appropriate) disapproval of unacceptable behavior. Telling a child, or even a convicted criminal for that matter, "what you are doing is wrong and don't ever do it again," is not tantamount to wishing for their death, much less demanding it as obligatory. Thus, even agreeing with Aiken that ecocentrism allows "no individual rights whatsoever" *within the ecosystem*, is not to embrace an inappropriate moral theory, even less a "retrogressive" one.[29] It is simply to recognize a factual situation that cannot be denied. No individual or species has the "right" to seriously disrupt an ecosystem and to expect to do it with impunity. In the final analysis, today's environmental crisis shows clearly that our "right" to freedom of choice does not carry much weight with ozone layers, toxic water supplies, or poisoned air. No law can be established, even by the most powerful leader on Earth, to permit us to use—say—nuclear weaponry somewhere and expect to still have the "right" to safe food/water/air. The "misanthropy" charge can thus be answered by Rolston as follows: "even for humans one cannot have a sound economy/culture on a sick environment."[30]

Even within the bounds of a different interpretation of Leopold, his claims about interdependence in the "land ethic" are not "dangerous nonsense," to cite one of the most superficial and vitriolic attacks on his principles.[31] Instead, it is indeed "dangerous nonsense" to insist on the "right" to ignore the realities Leopold uncovers. And although this point is not explicitly stated by Rolston, it appears perfectly compatible with his position.

Objections (3) and (4) can also be answered from the same theoretical stance. The "moral agent" must recognize (a) the "culture/nature" dichotomy and accept that while in interhuman moral quandaries an "is" is not an "ought," in environmental problems, as Rolston has it, the "is" represents the reality of the limits for any "ought" whatsoever."[32] Furthermore, an environmental ethic *must* be based on a metaphysic.[33] Our view of nature, Rolston argues, is "filtered" through our conceptual framework; yet, "perspectual though it is, what counts as value in nature is not just brought to and imposed on an ecosystem, it is discovered there."[34] What we have, then, is not ecology but "metaecology":

> Yet ecological description generates this valuing of nature, endorsing the systemic rightness. The transition from *is* to *good* and hence to *ought*

occurs here; we leave science to enter the domain of evaluation, from which an ethic follows. The injunction to maximize the ecosystem's excellence is ecologically derived but it is an evaluative transition.[35]

Thus, objection (3), claiming the "disappearance" of the moral agent, can be answered from this perspective. The agent is neither purely moral (in abstraction) nor merely prudential (in reality). It is simply the case that his *hubris* is reduced, his Cartesian bias eliminated at this stage. The moral agent *must* admit that his moral reasoning needs more than logical support; it needs the "scientific" test of fitting the reality which supports both his reasoning and, a fortiori, his existence. The full reach and implications of action will have to be understood in depth before a moral position can be developed.

In fact, it is not the "moral agent" that must be "removed," but the individual's belief in the right to theorize and prescribe without taking fully into consideration the factual realities of those actions which result from these prescriptions.[36] From the perspective of Rolston's theory, the charge of misanthropy is also based, like the one of "environmental fascism," on a category mistake.

An Argument from Aristotle in Support of Biocentric Holism

An examination of a different standpoint, that of Aristotle, will show that answers are possible to the objections noted, primarily to (1), (2), and (4), although an answer to (3) will emerge from the other answers as well. The answers in themselves may not appear to be too different from the ones already discussed, but they stem from a doctrinal foundation different in kind from the ones discussed thus far, and will therefore add to the unity of the philosophical underpinnings of PI.

We noted the several aspects of integrity which could be understood and explained through Aristotelian concepts and categories. For instance, several of these categories and concepts were used in Chapter Two (sections d and e); further, we argued that the concept of "optimum capacity" of an ecosystem was related to Aristotle's *ergon* argument, basic to his work, and particularly important for his understanding of human beings and their possible achievement of *eudaimonia* in *Nicomachean Ethics*, 3.7. Thus the question of the relation between individuals and wholes can also be fruitfully examined from the standpoint of Aristotelian doctrine.

What is the value of individuals and the value of wholes in Aristotle? In true Aristotelian fashion, the first thing to establish is the purpose or end toward which each living thing unfolds. This is not a conscious normative unfolding, in the sense of choosing one end among others, or one value among many. On the contrary; A. Gotthelf says, "Since a naturalistic account can . . . be given of the notion of the good within which Aristotle operates in his biology, it seems to me that the fundamental account of the final cause need not make use of that notion."[37] In Aristotle's biological account, all things move or change according to "locomotive natures" and "qualitative potentials" toward their "mature state" (*akme*). Therefore, it is clearly not an enterprise that needs philosophical defense in the sense that a moral doctrine does. Aristotle's is, rather, a doctrine which is "fundamentally empirical in character, and not an a priori doctrine brought to his investigation of nature."[38] In fact Aristotle uses *eidos* (species or form) as "norm" in his biology and his ethics, and metaphysics, although that is not a step that can be taken in this context, which is limited to interaction with nature.[39]

The "good" is identified as the achievement of the "mature state," which in turn "is identifiable in terms of the presence of maximal powers of self-maintenance without reference to independent normative criteria."[40] If, for "meta-ethical reasons the good is defined by reference to this same mature state," I think we have identified a "good" which remains valid outside the ambit of Aristotelian thought. This "good" may not impose on us a *positive* obligation, in the sense that moral agents will be obligated to bring about the mature, stable state of self-maintenance of such an entity. But it does bring a *negative* obligation, that is, an obligation on our part not to prevent that good through unwarranted interference with the various stages through which an entity may pass on its way to its own *telos*.

Even though the latter does not represent a normative value as such (for it or for the moral agent), the self-maintenance of an organic ecosystem is an indisputable value, the foundation of all other possible values for which one might want to argue. It is, moreover, a value for all life, not limited to humankind in scope, such that it may be valued by both anthropocentrists and biocentrists. Thus we have reached a foundational "good," "for the sake of which" action can be taken (or omitted) in a metaethical sense. We need not derive an "ought" from an "is"; we may simply observe and accept that this is a naturally unfolding "is," and that the *telos* appears to be valuable as such. It would be hard indeed to argue for a moral position requiring that there should be no life, hence, the existence of a stable foundation for all life appears to be an obvious "good" or value. Yet one might object that Aristotle's teleology appears to be confined to single organisms. However, this possible objection ignores the whole thrust of Aristotelian physics, ethics, and ultimately, even metaphysics. Individual *telos* is not viewed by him as the existential basis for individual self-fulfillment. Rather, what counts is *species* survival; hence, the further step introduced here, that is, the fact that ecosystems too transcend individuals and support species (as well as individuals), thus, that they foster and enhance biodiversity and life is in line with Aristotle's own thought.

The major "flaw" in Aristotelian science, is that he has no conception of evolutionary theory: for him, what exists has always existed, except perhaps for unusual coupling of animals producing unusual kinds (GA II.4.4.738b32). On the other hand, Anthony Preus has argued that, as species may be classified in terms of the character of the genetic information carried in the "chromosomes," Aristotelian science might be reconciled to modern findings, to some extent. He believes that Aristotle was indeed "groping for genotypic taxonomy," and some of what E. Mayr says, as we noted earlier, supports this position.[41]

What about the charge of environmental "fascism" as the inescapable consequence of accepting an organic teleology? Once again, an answer can be found in Aristotle: only in the case of "element potentials" actualizing their "irreducible potential for form" in the context of a *living* organism does such indisputable "value" accrue to the actualized nature, simpliciter.[42] Therefore, it is only when a living organism, that is, an interconnected organic whole, is under consideration or an interconnected system (and an ecosystem is often taken to be indeed such a whole), that we can most appropriately reason in this manner. On the other hand, the "naturalistic account" of the "good" *cannot* simply be transferred to a society or government. These are "artifacts," although they are, in a sense, made up of living parts, the citizens of that society. There is a vast difference between the relationship between the components of an organism or—for that matter— of an ecosystemic whole and the "parts" of a society or other social group. The former are diverse in themselves, but fitting only into fixed niches, playing specific roles according to an evolutionary established harmony, although some species may play a "substitute function" if required in some ecosystem (P. Colinvaux, 1990). This is not true of the latter, who may be optional parts of an optional whole, filling positions within it which are often interchangeable. This is only remotely analogous to a living organism: the variables are too numerous to permit an a priori decision about the possible value of any one element. Citizens may belong to one society or another; within that society they may move from role to role or not; and finally, the *akme* or finished "mature state" cannot be identified with ease, if at all, nor defended as foundational for value. An acorn can only become actualized as an oak tree, if favorable conditions prevail, but a group of citizens can form an almost infinite number of societies, both good and bad.

It is only within a stable, healthy natural environment that (a) individual roles are fixed with the exception noted on the previous page; (b) component parts as a whole identify (and can interact within) *that* environment and no other; (c) the "maturity" of the actualized state is potentially recognizable; and finally, (d) that and *no other whole*, when it posseses integrity (or at least health) and is naturally functioning, can sustain the very life of its component parts. The relationship between citizen and society is not at all like that: one can live in a socialistic state or a libertarian one. Within either, one might be a leader or a follower and fit (interchangeably with many others) a great variety of positions and roles. This is not true of natural systems: a plant cannot take the place of a fish, nor can it choose to live submerged any more than the fish can choose to root itself in the earth (although changes do occur, a switching of roles, change of prey, or movement into or out of the ecosystem, for example).

Humans have much more choice and can alter their habitat, but only to some limited extent, before they jeopardize both their habitat and their individual existence—precisely the problem that suggests the adoption of the "principle of integrity." Thus, the "natural" and the "man-made" are clearly different in kind. Therefore, it is inconsistent as well as incoherent to attempt to discredit natural teleology within the limits explained in Chapter Two, section (e), on the basis of possible undesirable consequences *outside* the natural realm. It is only within nature that the value of maintaining a stable ground for all life possibilities and potentialities is beyond dispute.[43] Therefore, it is inappropriate to attempt to treat ecosystemic biocentrism as analogous to organicist theories of society, and that particular objection to biocentric environmentalism fails as a faulty analogy.

The value of the organism when appropriately placed within a "live" (that is, a functioning, not degraded) ecosystem proceeds according to the notion of an "irreducible potential for form." This potential separates organisms from mere aggregates.[44]

Further, the seemingly inexorable movement toward a "better" or "superior" group or race, which is the core claim of social Darwinism, is totally foreign to the position of biocentric holism. G. Stein says, "The core idea of Darwinism was not evolution but selection."[45]

Nothing could be further from a holistic position, which seeks to re-integrate and restore to importance and value *all* parts of ecosystems, rather than exalt one group at the expense of others. Similarly, to establish so-called standards of "superiority," which are not only exclusively human but also (allegedly) specific to a circumscribed group, contradicts the principle of "integrity," which seeks to revalue all individuals of all species, through membership in ecosystems, not to emphasize arbitrary, imagined, or even so-called "scientific" hierarchies.

Stein classified the wrong-headed interpretation of Darwin's *Origin of the Species* by E. Haeckel, for instance, as aiming to "happiness as submission to the eternal laws of nature."[46] Yet the "laws of nature" are represented as nothing but an apology for *one* group within one species, at the expense of the rest, and *one* interpretation of "scientific and social progress," which is based on no eternal or divine *logos*. Instead of reintegrating humans into the ecosystems within which they have life, Social Darwinism emphasizes *hubris*, and that not even for all human beings, but only for certain individuals of a certain species, within a specific geographical and temporal milieu.

When Haeckel affirmed that "Man is not above nature, but in nature,"[47] and then went on to claim that "Civilization and the life of nations are governed by the same laws as prevail throughout organic life,"[48] he based this transposition from his interpretation of biology to social/political institutions on the very faulty analogy I indicated earlier. Therefore, his "analogy" would not work even if it had been based on true and unbiased scientific observation. Instead of restoring value to nonhuman parts of the environment as the biocentric holist is wont to do, he attempts to depreciate all in a vain attempt to glorify one single (human) group, the very contrary position to that for which biocentric holism strives.

Before leaving Aristotle, it might be useful to examine his "intrinsic value" argument (although not one he uses for an environmental ethic). The argument is to be found in the *Generation of Animals* and the *De Anima*. John Cooper summarizes Aristotle's position as follows:

> Living things are better than non-living things and existence than non-existence, so the continuous existence of living things is an important good; but since individual animals and plants are all perishable it is only by constant replenishment that this good can be achieved.[49]

Several interesting points emerge. The first and clearest is the ultimate value of existence and the belief that the continuing survival and "replenishment" of various life-forms in nature constitutes an indisputable good. The balance and stability of this continually changing and self-renewing existence are that "for the sake of which," the *telos* of all other natural entities develops, all movement from potentiality to actuality. Cooper adds:

> moreover, there appears to be an effective balance of nature, whereby no plant, or animal is so constituted by its nature to be permanently destructive of any other. Everything seems to fit together and the environment is such as is needed to support the kinds of plants and animals there actually are. . . . One observes in the world itself then, no internal disharmony or imbalance that could lead to its eventual destruction.[50]

It seems as though the principle of "integrity" might thus be defended on Aristotelian grounds. The difference, and it is an important one, is that Aristotle envisions no obligation, just the acknowledgment of natural ends and of natural processes unfolding in an orderly manner toward these aims. However, although no obligation appears to accrue to man in regard to this scenario, which is purely descriptive, if the goal represents not only a "good" but an ultimate value, then, as I argue, some obligation not to interfere with a naturally unfolding self-actualizing reality should be in order.

Although for Aristotle to speak of "obligation" in this regard would be incorrect and inappropriate, some recent work in environmental ethics not only describes natural processes in a similar manner, but also interjects the notion of "obligation" into individual organic development in a way that could be applied to organic wholes as well as individuals. Rolston says:

> Biological organisms . . . conserve an identity, an autonomy maintained over time by a functioning metabolism.[51]

Further, a possible counterpart to the Aristotelian "irreducible potential for form," both driven and driving toward a *telos* which exceeds "element potentials," can be found in Rolston's discussion of DNA: The DNA representing life is thus a *logical set* no less than a biological set. . . . The novel resourcefulness lies in the epistemic content conserved, developed, and thrown forward to make biological resources out of the physiochemical resources.[52]

The *descriptive* aspect here is not very different from Aristotle's account. Rolston adds:

> Even stronger still, the genetic set is a *normative set*; it distinguishes between what *is* and what *ought to be*. The organism has a biological obligation thrust upon it. This does not mean that the organism is a

moral system, for there are no moral agents in nature apart from persons. But the organism is an axiological system.[53]

The value is to be found in that *akme* or mature stable state we saw in Aristotle, in the works cited. We can therefore say that, "the physical state that the organism seeks, idealized as its programmatic form, is a valued state."[54] Aristotle could not conceive the possibility of individuals interfering with the achievement of natural ends, given the existence of satisfactory circumstances for their actualization. He viewed the natural unfolding of life as an obvious value, actualities pursuing their own internal ends without the need for human input. He also saw that stable, self-maintaining state as a source not only of value, but knowledge, thus doubly valuable.

Surely the organic interconnectedness of an ecosystem, of a natural "whole," possesses some of the same characteristics, so that it too can be described as an *axiological system*, when it is in a "stable, mature state," each of its equally valuable organic parts fulfilling their "biological obligation." As we saw in Chapter Two, it is not correct to envision a specific ideal "state" of an ecosystem and term it our goal or ideal. Nevertheless, in Aristotelian terms, "stable, mature state" can be translated in ecosystemic terms into a state capable of supporting the maintenance of diverse species of life, comparable to the reproductive function and role of simple individual organisms in their own "stable, mature state." Further, Aristotle's thrust toward a metaphysical understanding of the functioning of the whole physical universe can also be said to support the continued existence *telos* and "good" of the whole. Hence for Aristotle no conflict exists between the *telos* of individuals, species, and the whole, although we must exclude here the "Final Cause" (Prime Mover).

This may appear to be a rather sweeping statement; but recent Aristotelian scholarship moves in the direction of the position I defend, although to be fair, there has been controversy over the question of the possible extension of organic (individual) teleology. This represents a very important point in support of my position, hence it is worth analyzing in some detail. For instance, John M. Rist says:

> Nature always strives for the better . . . and Aristotle goes on to tell us what this means: being is better than non-being.[55]

All nature is "graded" and "that which is best is at the top of the hierarchy"; hence, "the principle of final causation comes from the top."[56] Hence, from the Aristotelian perspective, we can view the whole of nature as "motivated" by a series of final causes.

Insofar as each item in motion can "desire," it desires to be better, that is, it will desire being rather than non-being, life, rather than non-life, etc. . . .[57]

What is implied here is that not only can we speak of individual "natures," each with its immanent *telos* or principle of development, but that Nature as a whole (which "does nothing in vain") may have an immanent principle that "must work in a lawlike fashion," and this principle and *telos* transcend individual development.

Rist speculates whether this might be an "echo" of a "world-soul" concept. If the individual's "aspiration is to fulfill oneself," to achieve one's form or purpose, then a parallel "striving" or desire in all of *phusis* (nature) appears to be in line with Aristotle's thought and his doctrine of the Prime Mover. The latter cannot be said to provide a final cause for individuals only; in fact for Aristotle, as previously noted, it is fair to say that reaching one's physical *akme* or mature state, is primarily a *species* achievement, hence the fulfillment of one's nature in that sense is not primarily for our (individual) benefit, but for that of our species.

Further, in the *Physics* (192A 13–15), the "bold metaphor of matter desiring form" can be found. Once again, this applies to all of matter, not to individual parts of it. It represents a holistic "striving," not an individual one.[58] Hence, the world can be viewed as alive in some sense and as embodying a sense of overall (rather than individual) purpose, a good exceeding individual survival and flourishing. Aristotle says:

As in the universe (*en toi holoi*), so (in the soul), God moves everything.[59]

In conclusion, this interpretation of Aristotle is textually supported and defensible; as such, it supports biocentric holism as the ultimate value. Further, insofar as the persistence of being, species and life are "better" than the absence of these, it also supports the obligation to noninterference, as that might possibly "diminish" items that are good, or better and hence, make them "less" or "worse" in some sense. Nor is there a conflict between understanding that Aristotle's doctrine is fully teleological, incorporating a Final Cause and Prime Mover, and only accepting the usefulness, for our purpose, of most, but not all of his doctrine.

Yet even if we must leave aside that admittedly important aspect of Aristotle's thought, what remains and can be adopted is sufficient to add another perspective to show that minimally, and for the most part, in nature, the individual and the whole need not be in conflict at the survival level. Hence, if the Aristotelian thrust of this section is accepted, this approach to intrinsic value neither depreciates any of the individual living parts, nor does it render the moral agent obsolete.

Human Individuals and Environmental Wholes

The next two chapters will deal with the interhuman consequences of adopting PI, socially, politically, and internationally, as well as second order principles to render PI operational in relation to land uses. In this context, however, the question remains: What happens to *human* individuals when the primary consideration lies with a natural whole—does the principle of integrity give rise to conflicts?

Indeed, there can be conflicts between one's life and moral principles. However, if such conflicts are resolved in favor of principles, they tend to fall under the heading of supererogatory or heroic, rather than simply moral behavior. The Christian martyr Joan of Arc acted beyond the requirements of moral obligation. Aristotle draws a parallel distinction between the highest (moral) activity (i.e., contemplation), and his belief that a life of pure contemplation would go beyond human morality, but borders on a godlike life instead.

Leaving aside supererogatory action then, it seems as though a "strong right" of individuals, if such a thing exists, is surely the right to life. It is also clear that such a right is not in conflict with the requirements of either morality or rationality; the basic right then combines the two as *one* value. It is thus fair to state that the rationality that grounds all rights as well as the categorical imperative for Kant is not in conflict with the will to survive: "good will" is not and cannot be a will *not to survive*, as Kant makes abundantly clear in his treatment of suicide, as was argued earlier in this chapter.

Cato's act *can* be explained, *can* be defended, but it is not an act representative of a universalizable law. In most cases, the required "respect for humanity" in our person and in that of others precludes taking even our own life in the face of overwhelming difficulties or excruciating pain. In that case, it seems as though more comforts, or "technological advances," or any other present preference should not be sufficient to guarantee the universalizability of action that will result in environmental disintegrity, including endangered life-conditions for oneself and other humans.[60] In that case, even though rationality goes well beyond it, the desire for survival and the effort to ensure it represents a necessary first step, the basis of all other aspects and developments which make rationality worthy of respect. Earlier in this chapter, the charge of "environmental fascism" was refuted, and a defense offered for the value of constituent parts as well as the wholes they compose.[61] This led to the establishment of (a) a normative value for developed mature organisms and also for their community in natural ecosystems; and (b) a corollary prima facie duty not to interfere adversely with the achievement of such maturity, not to harm them, or disrupt their continued integrity and existential harmony.

Nor is this an inappropriate "obligation," given that both natural systems and natural organisms are open to harm, disruption, and adverse interference from entirely natural sources as well, and that even catastrophic happenings are not always triggered by human agency. A similar argument could be made for harm or interference with individual humans and it would be equally wrong. Humans too may be prey to diseases or harm from life-style choices that may prevent them from reaching maturity or maintaining their continued (organic) integrity, yet this neither permits nor excuses *our* possible interference with their health. Even if Mary were genetically disposed to die from cancer before puberty, for instance, it is not permissible, on that basis, to cause her death before or around that time from other causes, of my choosing. Gewirth, for instance, justly claims that, "Every person has a basic human right not to have cancer inflicted on him by the action of other persons"; further, and closely related to this right (Right to Non-Infliction of Cancer), "is a further right, which I shall call the right of informed control. Each person has a right to have informed control over the conditions relevant to the possible infliction of cancer on himself."[62] Therefore, a further argument can be offered from this perspective in support of PI. Not only is the absolute defense of "life," as supported by ecosystem integrity, representative of the strongest case for the adoption of PI, but another line of defense can be based on the general responsibility not to inflict cancer and other similar grave threats to health.

Aside from Gewirth's argument, which is limited to humankind, another parallel argument can be extended beyond our species, as degraded ecosystems and ecosystems polluted with carcinogens cause cancers to most forms of life, including fish, birds, and mammals; hence, the carcinogenic substances affect the functioning and the structure of ecosystems, as well as that of individuals of various species. Within this context these conclusions address only *one* aspect of human existence, that is, its biological stability and interaction with other natural entities.

Now, although PI defends an ethic of *respect*, not of individual or aggregate *rights*, still, it remains a deontological, absolute theory, in the sense that the possession of life and its collective support are viewed as primary. Hence, in a sense, it must view the *right* to life, or at least the right of the continued existence of a life-support system as absolute. Two questions remain: (1) does this entail that PI remains incurably anthropocentric? and (2) how can "absolute rights" of any kind be reconciled with any holistic position?

The answer to (1) emerges from the argument in Chapter Three, as well as the previous sections of this chapter. Unless we understand the whole Earth in an organismic way, it is hard to argue for an "interest" in life on the part of ecosystems. On the other hand, their functioning precisely as life support, on the whole, supports at least the possibility of teleology within their operation. From the Aristotelian standpoint, the worldwide commonality of both *telos* and "good" is sufficient to support the position that, at that level, no conflict exists between individual and whole that cannot simply be explained as part of the system's operation, the laws that govern it (and which include both mutuality and competition). Hence, all species, even while competing, appear to have access to a basis of support, and humans are not singled out by this perspective, except insofar as their peculiar capacities might render them—in some species-related way—fitter than others. The same, of course, could be said for other species, for instance, for cockroaches, who are certainly far more adaptable to changed or limited circumstances, and hence far fitter than humans for survival.

Hence PI is no more anthropocentric, from our standpoint, than it is "roach-centered" from the standpoint of roaches. On the question of the possibility of "absolute rights," indeed one may argue that a categorical principle is an absolute one and that even though it proposes an alternative to the present trend to traditional individual rights as understood within the Western tradition, it nonetheless covertly supports (different) absolute rights. An answer can be given to this objection, if "absolute rights" are understood against the background of the "concrete absolutism" defended by Gewirth.[63] His discussion assumes as the "supreme principle of morality," the "Principle of Generic Consistency." He says:

> this principle requires of every agent that he act in accord with the generic rights of his recipients, as well as of himself, i.e., that he fulfill these rights. The generic rights are rights to *the necessary conditions of action, freedom and well-being*, where the latter is defined in terms of the various substantive abilities and conditions needed for action and for successful action in general.[64] (my italics)

Surely the "necessary conditions of freedom and well-being" are bound to include *life* as their prerequisite. This appears obvious in the rest of the essay as well as the related discussion in another paper, mentioned earlier, "Human Rights and the Prevention of Cancer."[65] Gewirth's able discussion hinges on a case where an "absolute right," that a mother not be tortured to death by her son, is contrasted with the right to life of "countless innocents." In the example, terrorists demanded that the son perform a "superlatively evil," "monstrous" act (which Gewirth sees as lying at the end of the spectrum, in contrast with supererogatory or heroic acts, at the other end of the scale). If he will not, so the example goes, they will deploy nuclear weapons on a well-populated city, thus killing thousands in "retribution." Both the "rights" of innocents and that of the mother not to be tortured to death by her own son, appear to be absolute. What should be done? Are the son's refusal and the subsequent catastrophic occurrence simply "the heavy price exacted by moral absolutism"?[66]

Once the appeal to numbers (and consequentialism) is rejected, Gewirth appeals first to the doctrine of double effect, before rejecting it with an environmental counterexample. "Industrialists" and other polluters and users of carcinogenics and other food additives, he says, do not directly intend to cause death. Does this excuse their action? The entrepreneurs in question may even maintain that the enormous contribution they make to the gross national product outweigh the relatively few deaths that regrettably occur. Still, since they have good reason to believe that death will occur from causes within their control, the fact they do not directly intend the deaths, does not remove their causal and moral responsibility for them.[67]

Secondly, Gewirth appeals to the "principle of intervening action," to show that in the previous example the terrorists, rather than the son, remain primarily responsible for the ensuing catastrophe.[68] In essence then, even espousing the primacy of "absolute rights" does not commit one to morally implausible answers, provided that one's absolutism remains "concrete." Thus, it is from a "concrete" holistic position that one can consistently defend absolute rights to life, those which Gewirth would term "generic rights," or those rights that, minimally, permit an agent to be one. Such a moral agent could claim, "My freedom and well-being are necessary goods," because "certain general abilities and conditions are required for his purpose-fulfilling activity."[69]

In the same manner, at the level of basic or strong rights, PI gives rise to no conflict between human individuals and environmental wholes, because it defends the very conditions which are concretely necessary (though not sufficient) for any further activity an agent may want to pursue.

Integrity, an ideal based on natural/cultural harmony, suggests a better approach. Natural survival is viewed as basic, primary in the sense of underlying all other possible values. Such a holistic view does not conflict with individual survival of component parts. On the contrary, it supports and defends it.

Notes

1. Mark Halfon, *Integrity* (Philadelphia: Temple University Press, 1989), 150.
2. A. Gotthelf, "Aristotle's conception of final causality," in A. Gotthelf and James G. Lennox, eds., *Philosophical Issues in Aristotle's Biology* (Cambridge, U.K.: Cambridge University Press, 1987), 214.
3. Halfon, *Integrity*, 150.
4. T. Machan, *Individuals and Their Rights* (LaSalle, Illinois: Open Court, 1989), especially chapter 3, 63–100.
5. D. McKown, "Demythologizing National Human Rights," *The Humanist* (May–June 1989): 24–25.
6. T. Machan, "Are Human Rights Real?" *The Humanist* (November–December 1989): 24–25.
7. T. Regan, *The Case for Animal Rights* (Berkeley: University of California Press, 1983), 362.
8. See, for instance, Paul Taylor, *Respect for Nature*; J. Baird Callicott, *In Defense of the Land Ethic* (Albany: State University of New York Press, 1989); Holmes Rolston III, *Environmental Ethics*.
9. William Aiken, "Ethical Issues in Agriculture," in Tom Regan, ed., *Earthbound: New Introductory Essays in Environmental Ethics* (New York: Random House, 1984), 269.
10. L. Westra, "Respect, Dignity and Integrity: A New Proposal for Ethics," in *Epistemologia* 12 (1989): 91–124.
11. Rolston, op. cit., 160.
12. Eugene C. Hargrove, *Foundations of Environmental Ethics* (Englewood Cliffs, N.J.: Prentice-Hall, 1989); the centrality of "beauty" in arguments aimed to establish an environmental ethics is emphasized. For instance, Chapter Six argues for the existence and the "Superiority of Natural Beauty," the latter, pp. 185–98.
13. See Chapter Two, Sections (d) and (d$_1$).
14. Aldo Leopold, *A Sand County Almanac*. His most famous statement, the one Callicott terms the "summary moral maxim" of the land ethic, is: "A thing is right when it tends to preserve the integrity, stability and beauty of the biotic community. It is wrong when it tends otherwise," pp. 224–25.
15. Sergio Bartolommei, *Etica e Ambiente* (Milan: Edizioni Guerini and Associates, 1990), 55.

16. J. Baird Callicott, "The Conceptual Foundations of the Land Ethic," in *Companion to A Sand County Almanac,* 186–217; also his "Hume's *Is/Ought* Dichotomy and the Relation of Ecology to Leopold's *Land Ethic,*" *Environmental Ethics* 4 (1982): 163–74. See also Holmes Rolston III, "Is There an Ecological Ethic?" *Ethics* 85 (1975): 93–109; and "Values in Nature," *Environmental Ethics* 3 (1981): 113–28; "Are Values in Nature Objective or Subjective?" *Environmental Ethics* 4 (1982): 125–51.

17. Regan, 362.

18. Paul Taylor, "The Ethics of Respect for Nature," *Environmental Ethics* 3 (1981): 208–9.

19. Aiken, 269.

20. Bartolommei, 55.

21. Ibid., 56 (my translation from Italian).

22. Arne Naess, *Ecology, Community and Lifestyle,* 167, cp. 20–25.

23. Ibid., 168.

24. Ibid., 169.

25. Callicott "The Conceptual Foundations of the Land Ethic," 82–83.

26. Rolston, *Environmental Ethics,* 182, cp. 178, 180.

27. Callicott, op. cit., 34.

28. Aiken, 270.

29. Ibid.

30. Holmes Rolston III, personal communication, June 1991.

31. Wayne Sumner, "Review of Robin Attfield, *The Ethics of Environmental Concern,*" *Environmental Ethics* 8 (1986), 77.

32. Rolston, *Environmental Ethics,* 173.

33. Ibid., 230.

34. Ibid., 231.

35. Ibid.

36. Rolston says, "The gift of moral agency is just the capacity to evaluate others for their intrinsic value, putting the perspective of the moral self, self-interest of the agent in suspension, making a disinterested judgment of worth" (personal communication, June 1991).

37. A. Gotthelf, "Aristotle's Conception of Final Causality," in A. Gotthelf and James G. Lennox, eds., *Philosophical Issues in Aristotle's Biology* (Cambridge, U.K.: Cambridge University Press, 1987), 214. Gotthelf's understanding of Aristotle is not uncontroversial, but his is a solidly scholarly and well-respected position.

38. Ibid., 215.

39. Anthony Preus, "Eidos as Norm in Aristotle's Biology," in John P. Anton and Anthony Preus, eds., *Aristotle: Essays in Ancient Greek Philosophy* (Albany, New York: State University of New York Press, 1983), 340–63.

40. At this point many suggest the problem of terming a "value" the existence of a virus or bacterium. If the disappearance of one of these creatures would not bring out disintegrity for an ecosystem, then, according to the "principle of integrity" (of which more is below), interhuman (intraspecific) ethics of self-defense may prevail. For an illuminating discussion of "Society as

148   *Part One, Chapter Four*

an organism," see Holmes Rolston III, *Science and Religion* (New York: Random House, 1989), 202–3.

41. Preus, 344.

42. Gotthelf, 215.

43. G. Stein, "Biological Science and the Roots of Nazism," in *American Scientist* 76 (January–February 1988): 53.

44. John Cooper, "Hypothetical Necessity and Natural Teleology," in *Philosophical Issues in Aristotle's Biology*, op. cit., 247, fn. 7; cp. Aristotle, *De Generatione Animalium* 11.1731b24-732a3; *De Anima* II.4.415a25-b7.

45. Stein, 53.

46. Ibid., 54.

47. Ibid., 56; cp. E. Haeckel, *The Evolution of Man* (Jena: Appleton, 1903), 456.

48. Stein, op. cit., 56; cp. E. Haeckel, *Eternity: World War Thoughts on Life and Death, Region and the Theory of Evolution* (New York: Truth Seeker, 1916), 116.

49. Ernest Mayr, *Toward a New Philosophy of Biology* (Cambridge, Mass.: Harvard University Press, 1988), 45.

50. Cooper, 248.

51. Holmes Rolston III, "Biology Without Conservation: An Environmental Misfit and Contradition in Terms," in David Western and Mary C. Pearl, eds., *Conservation for the Twenty-first Century* (New York: Oxford University Press, 1989), 232.

52. Ibid., 233.

53. Ibid.

54. Ibid., 234.

55. John M. Rist, *The Mind of Aristotle* (Toronto: University of Toronto Press, 1989), 122; *De Generatione et Corruptione* (w.336B, 27ff); *De Caelo* (2.292 A22ff); and *De Generatione Animalium* (731 B24ff).

56. Rist, 122.

57. Ibid.

58. Ibid., 127.

59. Ibid., 129; cp. *Eudemian Ethics*, 8.1248 A25-6; A. Gotthelf, "Aristotle's Conception of Final Causation," in *Rev. Met.* 30 (1976), 226–54; for objections to this understanding of Aristotle, see R. Sorabji, *Necessity, Cause and Blame* (London, 1980), 164; W. Kullman, "Different Concepts of Final Cause in Aristotle," in *Aristotle on Nature*, ed. A. Gotthelf, 169–76.

60. I. Kant, *Lecture on Ethics*, Louis Infield, trans. (New York: Harper and Row, 1963), 147–54; cp. Thomas Hill, Jr. "Self-Regarding Suicide: A Modified Kantian View," in *Autonomy and Self-Respect* (Cambridge, U.K.: Cambridge University Press, 1991), 85–103, especially p. 93.

61. Rolston suggests a felicitous expression "puzzle pieces," as more than parts in the sense of the whole picture, but also that they are not interchangeable.

62. Alan Gewirth, "Human Rights and the Prevention of Cancer," in *Human Rights* (Chicago: University of Chicago Press, 1982), 181.

63. Alan Gewirth, "Are There Any Absolute Rights?" in *Human Rights*, 232.

64. Ibid., 219.

65. Gewirth, "Human Rights and the Prevention of Cancer," 181–96.

66. Gewirth, "Are There Any Absolute Rights?" 226.

67. Ibid., 220.

68. Ibid., 229–30.

69. Alan Gewirth, *Reason and Morality* (Chicago: University of Chicago Press, 1978), 60–61.

Part Two

Rendering the Principle Operational:
The Practice of Integrity

5

From Principles to Policy: Disintegrity as Violence

Today, we enthusiastically participate in what is in essence a massive and unprecedented experiment with the natural systems of the global environment, with little regard for the moral consequences.

Al Gore, *Earth in the Balance*

1. The Next Goal: Rendering the Principle of Integrity Operational

After explicating and defending "integrity's" value (Chapter Two), using the concept as the basis for an all-encompassing first moral principle (Chapter Three), and defending its holism from standard attacks using both defensive and "offensive" techniques (i.e., some new supporting arguments) (Chapter Four), much of the theoretical work has been done. The next step is to show that the principle of integrity (PI) is also capable of practical application to both morality and legislation.

Two major problems need to be addressed: (1) The idea of "pristine" integrity appears to exclude human culture as we know it, even in a reformed, reconsidered, reduced form; and (2) even if a response is possible to (1) since the principle is designed to exclude purely human interaction as defined in Chapter Three, from its normative reach, how can we proceed from it to also limit human culture as such in a way that is morally compatible with it? In essence if we cannot accept that human "good" must (and can) be limited exclusively to that which is biologically good, how do we proceed to a moral ideal that is harmonious with PI's requirements?

The next two chapters will be devoted to these questions. This chapter will consider briefly the meaning of individual integrity in contrast with "integrity" in our context (section 2), the different connotations of "disintegrity" in both ecosystem and social contexts, respectively (section 3), before turning to an example of these differences through the generally defensible social goals of feminism (section 4). This will be followed by a brief discussion of the human "good" that emerges (section 5), before concluding that "integrity," at least in its paradigm sense, is *not* a social goal (section 6). Finally, (section 7) I will show what is the true role of PI and of "integrity" in human culture and propose the first step required to render PI operational.

First, while "disintegrity" in biological systems is always a pejorative term, describing a state of affairs which is *always* bad, the parallel lack of integrated harmony in the realm of social practices and structures may not be. In fact, in the social realm, one might seek to make the system even more inharmonious or confrontational in order to achieve a new system embodying "integrity," as integrated, harmonious, and fair human interaction.

Thus, a dichotomy emerges: we demand the primacy of "integrity" as nonviolence in the ecological context, but permit violence, or at least hostile confrontation, as a means to "integrity" elsewhere. In the light of our earlier conclusions about the disanalogy between the biological and the cultural realm, this position manifests no inconsistency. Ecofeminism/feminism illustrates this point (see section 4 for a detailed discussion). While ecofeminism and the feminist peace movement exalt the Earth Mother metaphor, the reaffirmation of caring, nurturing, and nonviolent paradigms of interaction, they do not—at the same time—advocate passivity and compromise as a response to what they perceive as disharmony and oppression as existing in most (sexist) societies. Both gender-based unfairness and domination/victimization in all their aspects are viewed as impermissible, requiring rectification through assertiveness and confrontation, not compromise and accommodation. The goal remains one of *fair* harmony, or integrity, in contrast to the "harmony" of polarized extremes, and thus a different sort of "harmony," or "integrity."

Unlike ecological disintegrity, which does violence to the basis of all life within an ecosystem, its social (nonanalogous) counterpart may be acceptable and defensible, although the latter needs analysis and defense before it may be viewed either as a "good" or as an appropriate moral end (or even as a means to such an end). Sometimes focused, confrontational tactics may be used to restore fair harmony in society. The justification of this position lies in the fact that the violence is used in the upholding of a major ethical principle in society: it is a defense of personal integrity and a form of whistleblowing.[1]

Therefore, two questions need to be addressed:

(a) Is all disintegrity to be condemned as a form of violence and disharmony? and

(b) What—if anything—does PI suggest about the confrontational resolution of social (rather than ecological) disintegrity?

These questions will be addressed in turn, through various avenues, in the following sections.

2. Integrity and Disintegrity in the Individual

The PI outlined in Chapter Three was followed by two formulations of a "categorical imperative." The absolutism of the Kantian formulation was deliberately used to indicate the nonnegotiable quality of the principle, in direct contrast to the present state of affairs, whereby environmental questions are viewed as open to influence by pressure groups, economic adjustment, consumer (short-term) preferences, and the like. Grounded as it is in indisputable fact, the principle's assumption (the preferability of the continuance of life over its cessation) leads necessarily to the maxims commanded by the imperatives which follow from it. Any argument in the ambit of philosophy and morality generally assumes life's continuance. In the search for knowledge, or science, or goodness, arguments for life as such are usually considered unnecessary.

The same indisputable necessity for *categorical* imperatives, however, does not apply to any system or principle of interhuman morality. What does personal "integrity" mean? A brief review of the common language sense of the notion will help us discover whether the disanalogy indicated earlier between different forms of "holism" persists when the "wholeness" under consideration is that of a single human being. Integrity is viewed as very important in the individual sense, as Martin Benjamin notes:

> Internally, it provides the structure for a unified whole, and unalienated life. Those who through good fortune and personal effort are able to lead reasonably integrated lives generally enjoy a strong sense of personal identity.[2]

Further, Benjamin notes, those who choose the integrity of their moral convictions over the possibility of a longer life, "like Socrates and Sir Thomas More," are objects of great admiration. However, the strong conviction or commitment implied by the phrases "integrated lives" and "a strong sense of personal identity" is not necessarily connected with goodness. Another definition of "individual integrity," says Benjamin, yields

> A conception of the person as an integrated triad, consisting of: 1) a reasonably coherent, relatively stable set of highly cherished values and principles; 2) verbal behaviour expressing these values and principles; and 3) conduct embodying one's values and principles and consistent with what one says. These are the elements of integrity.[3]

Unfortunately, if we substitute Hitler's "values and principles," and "consistent behaviour" for that of Socrates, we still have strong identity and even integrity perhaps, but with a total loss of the admirable, heroic component.

Once again then, although "integrity" as pristine or recovered harmony is intrinsically and indisputably good and desirable in the case of biotic communities and ecosystems, as well as individual organisms (viewed from a purely biological standpoint), a case needs to be made for the desirability and goodness of individual integrity as such, if it is meant to transcend its biological meaning. Like animals, and plants, whose integrity is essentially genetic and ecological and which excludes optional choices, humans "do not gain their integrity by genetic expression alone."[4] Benjamin adds; "Nonetheless, integrity is not sufficient for morality, nor does it always provide clear and straightforward direction."[5]

John Rawls too argues that being "virtues of form," the virtues of integrity are "in a sense secondary."[6] The disanalogy that clearly distinguishes the primacy of ecosystem integrity from the debatable position of social systems "integrity," is retained at the individual level. In its morally "good" sense, it is an extremely desirable trait, particularly for highly "interdependent" institutions and organizations, where the constancy and reliability of individual integrity represent the necessary basis for trust, confidence, and consistent results.

Yet a preoccupation with maintaining a commitment to a previously chosen and cherished principle, or with retaining one's consistency above all else, may be a rather mixed "good." The principles that guide our life, even if reflectively chosen and deeply held, cannot be such that they preclude reexamination for all time. Benjamin rightly cites Socrates in this regard:

> I value and respect the same principles as before, and if we have no better arguments to bring up at this moment, be sure that I shall not agree with you, nor even if the power of the majority were to frighten us.[7]

That which is admirable in individual integrity—beyond its biological application—lies in its steadfastness, in its refusal to yield to persuasion or threats, once specific moral principles are accepted. Plato also argues in this manner in his discussion of the Guardians in the *Republic*.[8] However, these attributes are not sufficient for true virtue at the philosopher's level, as philosophers need to exercise their *own* rationality today, as in Plato's time. Onora O'Neill, for instance, says of Kantian practical reason:

> The maxim of abrogating one's own capacity for autonomy, of choosing not to choose—is a somewhat special case: such a maxim of deference

cannot be universalized because it is in the first place self-defeating. A life in which the capacity for autonomy is successfully abrogated is no longer a life led on maxims and hence no longer a life in which morally worthy maxims can be adopted.[9]

Thus, not only in an ethics of virtue such as Plato's, but also in Kantian ethics, the reflective, free exercise of reason is the prerequisite of morally correct action, in fact of all action that can be termed moral. This general requirement is equally present in utilitarian and contractarian reasoning. John Stuart Mill, for instance, in his defense of "liberty," argues against the pressures of majority opinion. Thus, "integrity" in this sense is a worthwhile goal if, and only if, it is both (a) steadfast, and (b) open to further principled evaluation, a somewhat self-contradictory requirement.[10]

What emerges from this brief discussion is the clear difference between (a) ecosystem integrity, and (b) individual integrity as far as their normative reach is concerned. In order for the latter (b) to be considered a true "good," content must be added to its formal character. This in turn entails that in certain social or individual cases disintegrity may be morally preferable to integrity, so that departure from a specific action-guiding principle or set of rules, might be preferable to cleaving to it. Unlike biological ecosystem integrity, individual integrity can be set aside when it is found to be wanting in the light of reexamined principles or of a different or new factual basis.

Now what about the concept used in the social–political context? We saw earlier the disanalogy between "integrity" as applied to an ecosystem or a social system. This section traced the same disanalogy for the concept's application to an individual, and we saw that disintegrity might be morally preferable to integrity in certain circumstances. All disintegrity appears to involve some violence to an existing "whole"; whether violence can have some morally desirable aspects in the social sense, that is, when applied to a social–political system governed by firmly held world views, will be the question considered in the next section.

3. Disintegrity Beyond Biology: Violence or Compromise?

The argument of Chapter Four clearly distances that which is appropriate for the biotic community from that which is appropriate outside it. In general this is a dangerous position to hold. Environmental degradation and abuse as well as all manner of careless and inappropriate action have been supported by claiming that human morality stops at the species barrier. However, adopting PI as our first consideration poses a clear limit to this line of reasoning. Instead of taking the position that the difference between the two realms justifies lack of concern for the biotic community, the adoption of PI forces one to make the latter primary instead.

Thus, for the most part, interference by humans with the functioning of biotic communities and ecosystems is—prima facie—suspect: such interference needs defending with evidence that it is demonstrably neither harmful nor damaging. Too often even minor acts of interference cause disruptions that do violence to an ecosystem's integrity.[11] One might say that what ought to be done in the ecological context is the reverse of what represents justice in the case of human activity; the latter is judged nonharmful and the agent is taken to be innocent until proven guilty. The converse ought to hold in the case of human interference in the functioning and processes of ecosystems, and in some cases this indeed takes place. For instance, in the well-known case of *Just* v. *Marinette County* (WI), the family was forbidden to build on their own lands on the grounds that these were wetlands, a fragile ecosystem whose integrity and stability needed protection on behalf of future generations. This was done without the immediate need to prove specific harm, as in tort cases.[12] Further, the regulation preventing fill on the Just property was not considered a taking, and thus not compensable under the Constitutional Fifth Amendment. The court order forbidding fill and building on wetlands was, rather, based on a police power to prevent harm.[13]

This position, while severely limiting human enterprise at times, is both desirable and appropriate given the incapacity of science to make truly accurate predictions about long-term effects of human actions.[14] In many cases we can equate interference with violence, which brings disintegrity to biotic communities, and which is, therefore, morally inappropriate action from an ecological standpoint. The same would not necessarily be true of similar actions within social communities.

To begin, let us reconsider the basic reason why a fundamental disanalogy between biotic and social communities exists. The former's "stability," "integrity," and continued existence are deemed to be an indisputable good, if we assume the desirability (and the objective "goodness") of the persistence of life on earth. No further argument is required to prove that any violence to continued ecosystem health and integrity is—prima facie—wrong. Social systems, by contrast, are diverse embodiments of various interpretations and conceptions of the "good"; thus their continued health and integrity is not an absolute good. And if the "good" members of a social system perceive as a necessary determinant of social policy and interaction is not such an absolute, then an argument or reasons will be required to establish such "good's" primacy and defensibility. There is nothing new about this: it is simply an acknowledgment of the difference between positive and critical morality, about what "is" and what "ought to be" the case.[15]

If we can show a present social system to be unjust, or not respectful of individuals, or otherwise unfair in its treatment of its constituents, then we have no obligation to respect the system's integrity or protect and ensure its present or future existence. Even Thomas Aquinas in the thirteenth century held a similar position. A law that was not in line with and respectful of "divine law" was no law at all, it was simply a "form of violence" (*violentiam cuiusdam*), and citizens not only had no obligation to obey it, but even had a clear obligation to disobey it.[16]

How far Aquinas would permit one to go in rejecting this form of "violence" is not immediately clear. But as he permits repelling harm aimed at our own biological existence—even when it involves the (regretful) killing of a murderous assailant[17]—violence might even be appropriate in this context, provided other avenues have been tried and failed and that, as the doctrine of double-effect requires, no primarily evil intent (in regard to the lawgivers) may be present. If those who formulate the laws constrain us to do actions that militate against the prescriptions of "natural law (in the legal sense)," then our first obligation to the latter, and to what is divinely prescribed for human beings, prevails.

The problem is conflict in obligations and the quest for ethical guidance in cases of moral disagreement. Benjamin cites Richard Rorty as deploring the "Platonic Quest" for absolutes, to which philosophers appear to be driven by the fear of relativism.[18] Ethical doctrine must be capable of dealing with real "moral conflict and disagreement" and should not be the "clone" of abstract logical theories. In order to be a real and valuable guide, it needs to avoid the Scylla of idealism and abstraction, without foundering on the Charybdis of relativism. In order to do that, however, it must be more than an ad hoc acceptance of limited "rules" agreed upon by a select group, and embodying a limited and limiting form of "means to ends" rationality.

It is not only Aquinas or Plotinus who view humankind as possessed of spirituality and deriving their essential being—if such a thing exists—from the understanding of their place within the universe. As we saw earlier, other thinkers whose philosophy is not committed to a

First Principle, also recognize "man-as-a-valuable-and-valuing being," rather than simply as a bundle of (largely consumerist) preferences.[19] And it is not even necessary to opt for *one* or the *other* of these two choices, that is either (a) permanent, absolute ethical standards, by definition "Platonic," in the sense of being removed from the reality of human activities they are meant to direct, or (b) cultural or historical "contingent" ones, too limited within a specific reality to be philosophically respectable or useful to anyone *outside* their confines.

Rorty critiques both the tendency to reify moral concepts and the tendency to design principles that are "transcendent."[20] The flaw shared by the only two possibilities he appears to envision seems to be their distance from actuality, and their common desire to seek precisely what can be so distanced, and thus to correspondingly depreciate existing reality. When we are guided by this desire, we approach problems by "sending out bulldozers" to reshape the earth when it does not conform to our carefully designed "maps," as in Renford Bambrough's example.[21]

When PI is adopted, the problem of remoteness from reality is no longer present, as the starting point for all ethical considerations is the recognition of our real position in the universe. In fact, all further choices we might make intraspecifically, in order to *remain* moral choices, must not conflict with this original recognition of our position. In essence then, we cannot claim that the "good" or a "system" should be taken as univocal concepts when applied to both, hence their respective preservation is not equally desirable and violence cannot be automatically condemned. "Integrity" is an ecological goal, and it can be a personal and social goal only with qualifications, explanations, and clarifications. The impermissibility of "violence" in the sense of "ecoviolence" or even deliberate "ecosabotage," however, must not be confused with a requirement to diminish or alter the natural, *violent* functioning of ecosystems in wilderness areas. Rolston, for instance says: "Wilderness is a gigantic food pyramid, and this sets value in a grim deathbound jungle. Earth is a slaughterhouse, with life a miasma rising over the stench." Even John Stuart Mill, he adds, lamented that nature is "an odious scene of violence."[22] PI, in contrast, is a principle for humans and for their interaction with natural entities and ecosystems, not for individual components of these ecosystems, an absurd conceit.

A clear example of this dichotomy can be found in a special sort of environmentalism, that is, in ecofeminism, or the purported unification of ecology and feminism, and that will be the topic of the next section.

4. Feminism and Ecofeminism

In a recent presentation to the "Concerned Philosophers for Peace," Mary Mahowald responded to a panel's question about the "connection between concern for the environment, feminism, and peace," basing her answer on the concepts of life and equality: she views these as "implicitly addressed in a discussion of environment and feminism."[23] After touching upon the basic value of life, she describes "equality" not as sameness, but as a "flowing of each one's potential . . ." through relationships with all in the world. Thus,

> Concern about promoting these relationships necessitates concern for life and the environment and rejection of whatever is divisive, such as war.[24]

The position of ecofeminism also stresses the "feminine" connection to earth, the promotion and nurturing of life, women's role in agriculture, the intimate connection between women and the earth's life cycles, females in ancient earth rites and mythologies, and the Gaia hypothesis. In all cases the emphasis is on the contrast between male and female. The male approach is associated with patriarchal "domination" and subjugation of women and everything that is deemed to be "lower," including the rest of the earth. The "female" approach is viewed as open to reciprocity, equality, and acceptance of interdependence and nurturing.[25]

The basis for this dichotomy is found in traditional patriarchal social practices, which are in turn grounded on the conceptual patterns that support and legitimize them. Karen Warren, on the other hand, focuses on the concept of power:

> Violence is a sort of "power play" whereby one attempts to dominate, conquer, manipulate, master or otherwise exercise control over others or one's environment.[26]

She suggests that there are "important connections between violence, power and systems of domination"[27] and that "patriarchalism" is at the very root of these connections. "Power" itself can be viewed in "four important senses": (a) "power-over," (b) "power-with," (c) "power-within," and (d) "power-against." It is the last, "power-against," that will be important for my argument. In general, Warren's position is well-defended in its feminist background and interpretation of social conditions. No doubt the "patriarchal" conceptual framework helps to isolate "problems" as well as "solutions," to mediate what is or is not "right," or "acceptable," just as the paradigm of "scientism" does. "Scientism" (the adoption of a rigorous scientific methodology as the model of all epistemological and metaphysical reasoning) or "scientific objectivity" is often taken to be the goal and model of all sciences and disciplines; it also works to contextualize and conceptualize all ethical dilemmas, particularly in regard to environmental issues.

Any prevailing ideology (as the example of patriarchalism indicates) fulfills pretty much the same function: it tends to color, mediate, and interpret circumstances, happenings, and events by placing them against a framework of interpretation or worldview that guarantees meaning and is thus explained and validated through the reigning "gestalt." Thus, although I have no problem with identifying "patriarchalism" as *one of the factors* within this paradigm of objectification, I *do* have a problem in viewing it as *the* root of the problem, or its primary (and main?) cause. It is clear that with the Renaissance and the triumph of human reason, the "scientific" model of knowledge prevailed as the only legitimate one.[28]

Further, scientism, with all the concept implies, is certainly not in conflict with "patriarchalism": no doubt the two can coexist peacefully, and in fact do (Warren's notion of "power-with" comes to mind). On the other hand, there is another point that conflicts with Warren's assessment.

An objection can be raised at this point. Is "scientism" not associated with the very same detached, manipulative, reductionist, and controlling attitude we find in "patriarchalism"? In other words, should "scientism" be viewed as yet another manifestation of "machismo" and—ultimately—"patriarchalism"? A lot has been written on whether a "value-free or autonomous science is methodologically possible."[29] As far as "constitutive values" are concerned, for instance, Kristin Shrader-Frechette shows clearly that not only moral values but also cognitive and methodological values are involved in each step of a scientific procedure. The idea of "value-neutrality" in science has, in fact, been rejected by many. For instance, Evelyn Fox Keller "has argued that the language of mainstream science is permeated by an ideology of domination created in the very processes of personal psychological development and individualism characteristic of modern European and North American societies."[30]

Thus, science can be shown not to be value-free in two different ways: the first pertains to what Helen Longino calls "constitutive" values, the second, to "contextual" values.[31] Further, we might rephrase this by asking to what extent societal values influence the direction and aims of scientific research, and vice-versa. The claims for the "autonomy" and the "integrity" of science might also be questioned.[32] The former claim is hard to defend because science is most often dependent on "corporate and/or government funding."[33] The latter claim cannot be defended either, if one perceived "integrity" in this context as internal cohesiveness, impervious to the intrusion of individual and group beliefs, values, and interests.[34] Rather than insisting on an autonomy and a purity that are hard to find in today's scientific enterprise, Longino argues that scientific knowledge is, ipso facto, social knowledge. Hence, both science and society are understood far more clearly if we accept and admit their symbiotic relationship to one another rather than attempting to separate violently and arbitrarily a two-headed entity, rather like a set of Siamese twins. The "objectivity" we might reach by such a bloody operation is not real. Longino says:

> The transformation of an idea into scientific knowledge, has the effect of purging it of idiosyncratic features of its initial proponents. This gives it an impersonality often misinterpreted as objectivity. It is not the impersonality, however, but the collaborative social process of transformative interrogation that makes it objective. And while the marks of individuals may be eliminated by this process, the marks of culture are not.[35]

This is extremely relevant to the environmental concern that represents our primary quest. Longino adds that since "science-based technologies play an increasing role in our lives," we must depend on complex scientific methods of inquiry in order to discover the harmful effects and dangers we are exposed to. Thus, we need to understand the input of interests and values in what we learn:

> It is crucial to understand the technical—biological, chemical, statistical—dimensions of such inquiry, but unless we also understand the ways in which contextual interests shape inquiry, we will be unable to be properly critical of studies purporting to blame or exonerate these concomitants of modern industrial life.[36]

Thus, we must accept the "patriarchal" input into "scientism" as a given and as contributing to the problems we confront: neither is compatible with an ethic of respect. Yet another component is also present in the goal and the practice of science, that is "reductionism"; "reductionism" is both a methodological practice and a metaphysical view. Methodologically, reductionism is the practice of characterizing a system or process in terms of its smallest "functional units. Metaphysical ontological reductionism argues that those smallest functional units are what is real. . . ."[37]

Reductionist science is everyday science, and although it is, ultimately, as decisive and controlling as "patriarchalism," I do not think it can be argued to be entirely gender-specific, though many have taken that position. For instance, Vandana Shiva argues that way, citing Sandra Harding and Evelyn Fox Keller.[38] The former terms science a "western, bourgeois, masculine project," and even sees "bad science or misused science" as a "distinctively masculinist science."[39]

I find this rigid "apartheid" of the sexes unacceptable. For instance, pragmatically, there are many women, as well as men, who take a reductionist positivist approach in philosophy. There are also many women in science or politics who take precisely the approach Harding describes as "masculinist." To say they take it because they perceive it to be the most acceptable, "dominant" paradigm, is to beg the question by deliberately ignoring the possibility that these women might indeed have a mind of their own (as much as this is possible for either men or women within a society), and that they do perceive this approach as correct. I doubt that hormones rule us to the extent that all women who do reductionist science are necessarily hypocritical, frustrated "Mother Earth" followers instead. We should allow that they may be moved by autonomous choice, not merely by "patriarchal" pressure or a self-serving adoption of the "accepted" modes of scientific inquiry.

Therefore, even though many feminist writers have analyzed "science" as an expression and a mode of "patriarchalism," it seems as though the two should be kept discrete, rather than conflated into one. In the absence of a more convincing argument, it seems preferable in principle not to insist on polarizing masculine and feminine to the extent of making the dichotomy an indisputable "fact." This approach does not represent the "truth," and it could be misused by the proponents of a "ghetto" mentality, who even now defend a twisted "vive la différence" position, and use it to justify stereotyping and discrimination.

Another point conflicts with Warren's assessment of the primacy of "patriarchalism" for environmental problems. Disrespect for nature is not a necessary component of "patriarchalism": many less developed countries' social systems, where women are depreciated and subjugated and their work marginalized and trivialized in ways no longer visible in Western democracies, are nevertheless *very* respectful of nature and view it as imbued with religious meaning and even "divine power."[40] For instance, some small African villages are clearly strongholds of patriarchalism, where gender roles are strongly demarcated and defined.

A recent television program (Canadian "Visions" channel) showed a female agricultural expert showing the television reporter and other scientists environmental degradation and agricultural/forestry problems in her native region, including a remote village. The translator/voice-over explained that, traditionally, gathering firewood for the village needs had always been women's work. However, recent inroads into readily available sources put what little wood was left and available so far away that gathering had to be done by men. "They were the only ones with access to means of transport (that is, mules and a cart)." The commentator added, "In this way environmental problems affect social mores in the villages." No question was raised about women being given access to transportation, and only the general convenience of villagers succeeded in introducing a change in women's traditional roles. On the other hand these same villagers were shown to be concerned about environmental problems. They strongly objected to allowing market factors to influence the introduction of nonindigenous trees and crops which would have an unfavorable impact upon the land. Speaking of the same sort of society, C. K. Omari says:

> In traditional African societies, religious taboos and restrictions took the place of reforestation campaigns. . . . People knew their responsibility towards natural resources. . . . Positive values towards the use of natural resources were inculcated from generation to generation.[41]

In a similar vein, Islamic societies, where women are routinely considered unequal to men,[42] strongly defend environmentalism and foster an attitude of awe and respect for all nonhuman entities with and within which we live, on religious grounds. These entities are viewed as created by God, made as He willed them, and therefore must be respected as we respect their Source.

Thus, the practice of "patriarchalism" is not a sufficient condition for a position combining disrespect and domination of the environment: in many societies the former flourishes, while the latter does not.

Nevertheless, we can accept that in present-day Western democracies, the conceptual framework of "patriarchalism," combined with scientism/technologism, represents an integral part of an ideology that does not recognize environmental respect as primary, and which accepts and glorifies violence.[43] Thus, the attitude that combines "power" (in the first three senses which Warren analyzes) with a hierarchical view of all that exists, whereby some entities are "higher" and "better," others "lower" or "worse," is a component of a worldview that permits and even encourages environmental disintegrity. Scientism is equally in conflict with holism and the nonconfrontational stance advocated by PI, as it views all things (including humans) other than the cool, remote, impartial "expert," as available for manipulation, analysis, and—ultimately—control.

There is another argument that can be advanced against identifying feminism with environmental concern aiming at "integrity." The most important practical point about "integrity" in regard to policy-making is the recognition of the urgency of the goal. "Integrity" represents a goal that requires immediacy in (a) a change of perspective or different world view, and (b) priority action, rather than graded, long-term plans. Correctly assessing the prevailing modes of interaction with nonhuman nature as violent, confrontational, and divisive, the goal of "integrity" demands that (a) we acknowledge promptly our true position within the universe, and (b) we fit our actions to that reality, through a quest for harmony and the immediate abandonment of violence, confrontational divisiveness, and atomism, the characteristics of present interaction.

On the other hand, social and political ideologies espousing a vision beyond the present status quo, necessarily need a transitional period, often including a more or less violent overthrow of the present power structure. Marxism, for instance, comes to mind. Whether or not one believes in the ideal of a "Renaissance" man, living the good life in a nonexploitive, classless society, this socialist "heaven" has to be preceded by a period of more or less "bloody" dismantling of the prevailing social structures.

It seems to me that the ultimate triumph of feminism presents a similar scenario. Women *cannot* seek harmony as the immediate priority on their agenda: that course of action would lead to adjustment and ultimately to compromise (of which more in the next section), rather than to the overcoming of patriarchal, sexist structures. Warren, for instance, says:

A use of power is appropriate or morally permissible when it is exercised to produce needed or desired change without creating or maintaining oppressive relationships per situations of dominance and subordination.[44]

Two questions need to be raised here: (1) Can this sort of power be exercised (and viewed) as nonviolent and nonconfrontational? and (2) Is "power-against," in Warren's sense, significantly different from the sort of confrontation one needs to practice in order to turn around the present mode of perception in regard to the environment? We will examine both in turn. First of all, "violence" need not assume physical connotations of harmful behavior to be such. Most feminists, to my knowledge, do not espouse and defend a bloody revolution, even if it appears necessary in order to reverse the status quo. Warren certainly does not:

> Lacking the requisite resources and options of Up groups, whatever power is exercised by Downs against Ups is exercised in the larger context of oppressive Up-Down hierarchies of power (i.e., power-over power of Ups) and privilege.[45]

The "standard for assessing" the legitimacy of uses of "power against" is "the same as for power-over relationships":

> [T]hey cannot be used to perpetuate, maintain, or justify oppression or oppressive relationships.[46]

Yet this position, while it is a logical and defensible one in many ways, appears less than clear as a guide to action. After the presentations of the recent panel referred to at the beginning of this section, not one of the many feminist voices heard suggested accommodation or compromise as suitable options. What remains is, of course, confrontation, in the hope of eventually reaching a plateau (the year 2090 was suggested), where any sort of "power" relation would be both inappropriate and unnecessary. And perhaps it *is* possible to reach one's (legitimate) social goals without bloodshed, war, or violence.

If our goal requires an attack on the present power structure, on the other hand, confrontation, disruption, and interference with the smooth functioning of the present social system must go through a period of disintegrity, and must bear the burden of disruptive interference, if the goal can be reached at all. A case in point might be the injustice in the system of South Africa, perhaps, even without citing the killing and general violence heralding the demise of Nazi Germany.

Therefore, the feminist agenda must include disintegrity first and now, if only so that the hope of harmonious integrity in the future might be fulfilled. But this is not and cannot be the position of those seeking integrity in the ecosystemic sense. The subject matter, the target of our harmony-restoring practices, needs neither destruction nor further disruption before it can be reconstituted. It is the social system we need to turn around, even when seeking *environmental* harmony, and whether the former will immediately be "harmonious" is not a primary concern. The primary physical harmony we need to restore can flourish and even coexist with less than perfect human societies, as the previous discussion of the separation of patriarchal values and ecosystemic values in many Third World countries indicated. Of course, it would be vastly preferable to have a harmonious and just social system existing with (and as part of) a harmonious and healthy "natural" system, but the former needs ethical argumentation separate and beyond PI and its imperatives.

To tie an agenda which is desperately needed to maintain all life on earth to any other goal, however worthwhile, particularly when it is a long-range one, is to misunderstand the urgency of the former. An attempt is made to enhance one goal by associating it with a goal generally supported by all rational people. It is also—implicity—to accept, as Kai Nielsen does in another context, that socialism—for instance—provides the "only hope" for environmentalism, because environmental degradation appears to be unavoidable within the capitalist framework of a work ethic that upholds material values, "growth" as success, and the necessity of waste (a position, we now know, is totally incorrect on factual grounds). It follows that, given the "plight of the workers," environmentalism must (temporarily!) be put on "the back burner."

In essence, this is to negate the assumption and starting point behind the first principle I have advocated, that is the ultimate value of life on earth as a whole, and substitute for it a feminist version of the familiar "I'd rather be dead than Red," an illogical and unacceptable position. It is only while we are alive that we can continue to fight for intraspecific rights, be they religious, racial, or gender-based. And those of us who have lived under some kind of dictatorship (as I have, as a child under Mussolini), can probably testify that it is better to be alive, even if it entails having been oppressed, tyrannized, and demeaned for a time.

The answer to the second question I raised (2) emerges to some extent from the answer to the first. In a sense we must enter into a confrontation with the power structures that direct human societies in order to demand a much saner approach to environmental problems. But our principle of action is directed at the environment, and the harmony and integrity it demands is that of ecosystems, not that of human society. By the same token, our confrontational stance is directed at society's present power structure, not the ecosystem we inhabit. Perhaps the difference I am trying to clarify is that between two sorts of urban reform: (a) rebuilding, and (b) restoration. The former, rebuilding, takes a "bad" area, unsound structures, an unsafe insanitary neighborhood perhaps, and the decision is made that it is beyond modification or "patch-up" solutions: it must be torn down and rebuilt from scratch. That is the way dictatorships and other blatantly unjust social systems are viewed; the oppressed do not accept "band-aid" solutions or concessions. They want a revamping of the system, preferably by peaceful means, but if necessary through violent over-throw followed by a fresh start.

On the other hand, restoration requires a totally different approach. The grand old downtown building and the historically valuable (but dilapidated) mansion are carefully "saved," their facades cleaned and restored, their soundness painstakingly reconstructed through a care-ful study of their former, pristine glory, which must be returned to the structure or even the whole area (as in a reclaimed waterfront for instance). In the latter then, destruction and rebuilding are not even considered: we do not employ a two-step plan, the first of which de-mands (justified) violence. For restoration, gentle but thorough assis-tance aimed at restoring as accurately as possible what was originally there is the aim, not a "better" or "newer" state of affairs.

The difference is thus laid bare: unlike social reform (i.e., violent or at least confrontational activity aimed at bringing about an ideal, *new* situation), the restoration of integrity starts from an ideal that *is* or at least *was* already there, as a reality, and attempts to redress pre-vious mistakes and correct previous problems, as one would try to restore a sick patient's organism to the health she previously enjoyed. This is *not* done by destroying the "flawed" organism in order to re-build a "better" one.

In essence, the "treatment" of disintegrity is careful, nurturing, re-storing activity aimed at something that is alive. The recipient of our activity, the moral "patient," is an organic whole (an ecosystem). By contrast, in social ethics the target is an ideology or a power struc-ture. Human beings are indeed involved in each area, but in very dif-ferent ways. We must conclude that, even if violence is avoided, if oppression and dominance are no longer acceptable, then feminism, at least in the present tense, is uncompromisingly confrontational and rightly so.

Environmental concern, guided by PI, on the other hand, is uncom-promisingly caring and nurturing. It is concerned with something orig-inally healthy and strong, that is now stressed and severely affected. It is restoring, not tearing down, even temporarily, in the effort to rebuild. One may wonder at my choice of example to show the dif-ference between a social and an ecological principle. I have chosen "ecofeminism," because it purports to combine under one "flag" what I take to be the first concern of morality, that is the pursuit and defense of integrity, with one of the most worthwhile examples of a defensible cause in purely interhuman morality. The tension that arises is the general one discussed in Chapter Four, that is, the conflict between individuals and wholes, further aggravated by the human urgency of that concern. It is also particularly difficult for me personally, because it is a cause to which I am entirely sympathetic.

What this discussion has indicated is that (a) we must not be drawn even by our own gender concerns, to limit or thwart the *universality* of the principle of integrity and its absolute primacy, as women, like all live creatures, need life support/protection before any other rights; (b) other powerful, all-pervasive ideologies beyond "patriarchalism," and concomitantly with it have brought us to the present environmental impasse; (c) we need to acknowledge that feminism, whatever its particular aspect, is inescapably and undeniably *individualistic*, hence, at least prima facie, in conflict with *any* holist primacy. Hence, combining feminism with an ecocentric position renders it somewhat self-contradictory.

The bottom line remains that whatever worthy (social) cause one may put forth for consideration, the defense of life-support systems for all the biota remains primary. Further, many issues remain purely ecological (such as choices involving species treatment within ecosystems) without any social or right component whatever. Hence combining such a rights-based cause with a holistic one which is purely ecological, is to paper over a vast difference between two disparate moral approaches. Similarly, to speak of "holistic rights" or "ecorights" for animals, would be equally problematic. Tom Regan, as we saw, is neither a "holist" nor a "deep" ecologist, as he would be the first to admit.

5. The "Principle of Integrity" and the "Good" (Social and Individual)

The previous section addressed the role of confrontation, violence, and disintegrity in ecofeminism. Accepting the causal role of "patriarchalism" in the present depreciation of the environment and its routine acceptance of violence and control on those viewed as "lesser," still leaves the question of patriarchalism unanswered. To say it is not the *only* cause or answer to the problem, and to cite scientism/technologism as equal contributors, commits one to attempting to assess their respective proportions, as components of a powerful structure of domination. My present enterprise—overall the examination and defense of PI and, in this particular chapter, "disintegrity" and "violence" in social and natural systems—does not permit me to explore that question at this time. It is, however, an interesting and needed research issue; tracing the historical, ideological, social, and psychological background to the present status quo and the relative proportions of all contributing factors, would no doubt provide evidence confirming and expanding on my contention. Many others have emphasized in their writing *either* one *or* the other factor, broadly speaking. A balanced view, assessing their proportionate contribution, would contribute to an understanding of their role.

Nevertheless, I am in full agreement with the contention that many "feminist" issues may be seen as interweaving with environmental issues in a number of areas. An example may be the need for ecologically sound increases in food production and changes in agricultural practice, particularly in less developed countries where a woman's role is largely traditional and subordinate.[47] At any rate, what emerged from the previous section is that the establishment of a better (more integrated) social structure may require—minimally—a period of confrontation, and possibly one of upheaval or even violence. Some level of disintegrity must in consequence prevail at some point in the present or immediate future, before society can reach the desired new state. This is not the case for ecosystems, where the *cessation* of violent, confrontational practices toward nature is both (partial) means and goal, and where disintegrity and human violence are *always* viewed as undesirable, never as a desirable means to a desired end. In natural systems in a state of integrity, "harmony" in community and "unstressed ecosystems" go hand-in-hand because there is no question of a forced, coerced, or unfair harmony within natural structures. Hierarchies do indeed exist there, but they are "natural" and therefore beyond questioning; each part contributes appropriately to the ecosystem and its harmony. Thus, the question of whether "harmony" is bought at the price of unfairness or domination simply does not arise.

It is clear that there are major differences between social and ecosystem structures. One is the ideal goal (and the real existence at least in principle) of some "standard" of harmony, of biotic integrity, that is factual, at least in its basic form, to each ecosystem in time and space. Their social counterpart, by contrast, may suggest a standard such as a "fair" or "just" society. However, neither "fair" nor "just" are univocal terms: as Alasdair MacIntyre, for instance, argues, neither "justice," nor "rationality" even, have been consistent in meaning through time, colored as they are by the traditions within which they are viewed.[48]

Nor can they be shown to be available for study at a specific location or in a specific time, even in principle. Hence, while one must argue for and defend a particular vision of the "just" or "fair" society, this is not required, at least in a general way, for ecosystems. Unfortunately no IBIs (indices of biotic integrity) exist for societies; at least not one that can be factually demonstrated and accepted across time and place. Perhaps the inclusion of humankind in the ecosystem's biota, thus their reintegration (at least in *one* aspect of their existence) within the rest of live organisms, will suggest models that might be applied to establish an intraspecific "standard" that will capture all aspects of purely human interaction.

On the other hand, the argument of the previous section showed that "integrity" (as harmony within and with the ecosystem) might be sought, prized, and even lived by human groups and societies which *also* live with and accept social unfairness and injustice. Many societies live with and accept unwarranted coercion and domination of subgroups and minorities. If these societies decided to pursue the goal of fair "harmony" and internal "integrity" they would need to aim for goals and an optimal state hitherto nonexistent in their own social and ideological histories. Neither their respective roles within the whole nor their view of what is "good" will be fixed ones.

Therefore "integrity" and even "fairness" may be necessary but not sufficient components of the optimal state sought: "integrity," as we saw, may reflect an undesirable component in the core beliefs of any individuals or groups who "cannot be swayed": "fairness" may in turn be understood in different ways and may involve assigning burdens and benefits according to what is perceived as "fitting" in a specific society (i.e., women not using means of transport that are only allowed to men). Perceptions of this sort may vary with times and societies' locations, whereas moral doctrine attempts to seek reasonably defensible absolutes, while making a conscious effort to uncover the different senses of both "rationality" and "fairness" as "justice" in different traditions.

It is because of these difficulties and the complexity of our quest that interhuman ethics and politics need to view "integrity" in context, and its adoption as a variable, rather than an unchanging, unmixed good. It is also for these reasons that Benjamin sees both "integrity" and "compromise" as having important roles in both ethics and politics. Compromise may at times be desirable from a moral standpoint and even preferable to "integrity," although it needs careful formulation and fine tuning, rather than being used as a device for "splitting the difference." One of Benjamin's examples uses the case of the Jehovah's Witness parents, who holding on to *their* beliefs, *their* convictions, and *their* "integrity," forbid a transfusion for their dying child.

In this case, the absolute of integrity may be deemed less than admirable, and even rough compromise (such as splitting the difference), would be a bad choice.[49]

And if all interests are perceived as equally legitimate, then—in the interest of minimizing conflict—we might seek solutions which replace moral discourse with "the language of nonmoral interests," another inappropriate choice.[50] Benjamin's argument starts from the powerlessness of even great and sound abstract ethical principles to suggest a definite solution to difficult existential problems. Questions such as the continuance/cessation of life-support systems, the possible use of embryos, or perinatal medicine in connection with various recent technologies, or even abortion itself, can be argued from either the principle of utility or from a Kantian position of "equal respect," he says, and earnest, moral persons will perceive one or the other approach as the most significant one. Thus, he claims, choosing one position over another may be hard to defend.

Yet, paradoxically, it is the very existence and general acceptance of the legitimacy of these principles that is "sufficient to refute wholesale scepticism and relativism." He adds:

> It is simply false that general, rationally justifiable principles have no role to play in regulating our moral judgements and choices, and that morality is, at bottom, nothing more than a matter of personal preference of cultural mores.[51]

The latter, however, reenters the arena of ethical decision-making, through his concept of (human) integrity. To say that "we should do whatever produces the most good," is an "empty platitude," unless we provide at least a partial context for such "good."

Another example Benjamin offers shows how some "good" may be contextualized, though not all of it. For instance, some actions that might be viewed as "means to the good" within the ambit of an Amish community, we might not recognize as such. However, "both the Amish and the non-Amish can agree on utilitarian grounds that the ravages of a preventable disease would be a bad thing and then join forces to combat it."[52]

The contextuality of all "rationality" (including moral reasoning) has been argued for by MacIntyre. Benjamin adds another dimension. He views one's thought-out and deeply held "world views," the source of our determined and definable character, as the basis of our identity and integrity (that which "give(s) shape and meaning to one's life"), as something that should be accorded respect and consideration in moral decision-making. His one qualification, our "integrity" should not be based on "a world view and a way of life that . . . clearly violate(s) widely shared, rationally justified principles."[53]

While this appears to be a reasonable and practical approach, there is a clear element of circularity in an argument that demands an appeal to principles, then asks that individual integrity (based on specific, well-entrenched worldviews) be used as a "tie-breaker" when principles alone cannot solve controversies—only to add the proviso that such a worldview must not conflict with "widely accepted traditionally held principles." Integrity is here given a strong role in inter-human ethics, but its formal character may not be sufficient to bear the weight of responsibility cast upon it. If integrity represents an individually held set of principles that defines one as a specific human being, the general question of what constitutes the "good" in the name of which we must cling unshakeably to our principles, is still left open.

6. "Integrity" in Its Paradigm Sense Is Not a Social (Intraspecies) Goal

As we saw, "integrity" per se cannot represent a purely human, social ideal or goal; its pursuit, as such, cannot be commanded or rationally chosen. On the other hand, we can (and must) pursue singly and collectively the goal of respecting and restoring harmony to ecosystems. This requires that as societies, groups, and individuals, we abandon hostile and confrontational interaction with nonhuman entities. This requires the adoption of PI and the categorical imperatives that follow upon it. We noted that putting the ecosystem (a "whole") first, does not turn a biocentric environmentalist into a "fascist" or totalitarian in the social sense, because of the basic disanalogy between the structure of natural and social systems. In the former, the indisputable primacy of the "good" of natural systems (i.e., its continued, healthy existence), eliminates the requirement for separate arguments to support a conception of the "good." In the latter, in contrast, such arguments are unavoidable if we want to claim the existence of a communal "good."

A further disanalogy between natural and social systems emerged from our discussion, in regard to integrity as a goal and principle of action. That difference hinges on the negative: disintegrity and disharmony as confrontation and violence must be assessed differently in the two contexts. Previous sections in this chapter were devoted to that topic. As far as the natural environment and human interaction with it is concerned, the absolute prescriptions of "integrity," the restoration of harmony starts with the realization and acceptance of our position and role within ecosystems and is sustained by them. However, even that recognition and that role are not an exhaustive definition of what or who we are. Human beings are first of all human animals, but after that we do have, individually and collectively, interests other than that of survival. Some of these are simply preferences while others are deeply held values. The "common good" in the sense of the "good" of the community beyond the conditions of healthy survival and stability, must embody those values and those interests, provided their pursuit does not involve environmental or interspecific violence. This "common good" is much harder to define, as is the extent of the necessary limits between individual and common goals. Thus, absolute imperative, if appropriate, needs to be qualified and adapted, carefully formulated and defended. Although this aspect of the ethical standpoint I suggest has not yet been thoroughly examined or researched, it seems as though the Kantian position (perhaps as defended by Onora O'Neill, Thomas Hill, Alan Donagan, and others), may well be compatible and "harmonious" with PI.

At any rate, whatever interhuman "ideals" we deem appropriate to pursue, we do not have the convenience of observing them in operation before attempting to reproduce them. For instance, peace and harmony are considered to be great social goods, easily defended because they represent cherished values. It would be hard to imagine a society having, as its goal, hostility among its members, disharmony, and confrontation, in a Hobbesian "war of all against all." Yet no society exists presently that embodies the goal of complete peace and harmony, particularly as a true ideal, that is coupled with fairness and justice. A society which operates harmoniously by allowing oppression and dominance of certain groups and individuals is still not an ideal society.

The case is different, when the starting point is environmental concern. PI starts with an unequivocal rejection of violence: that is a general concern which it shares with all ethics of respect for nature. In fact, all forms of interference with nature are—prima facie—suspect, until "proven innocent" of damaging effects. In a history entitled *Ecology in the 20th Century*, Anna Bramwell says:

> [T]he call to deny all dominant or potentially dominant relationships—including affection—is as dramatic and novel a moral ideal as earlier was chastity.[54]

She adds,

> [T]he belief that any alteration of another being is wrong even if inspired by care and affection may or may not be true. But an awareness of the potentially sadistic aspects of being object to subject, once stated, lingers . . . .[55]

She sees aspects of this sadism in many relationships, hitherto unsuspected and unexamined, such as that of parent/child, siblings, sexual partners, and that with the "old."[56]

Earlier, I argued that many changes in social structures and institutions demand a period of violence or confrontation before "utopia" can be reached (even aside from questions about whether such utopias are desirable, or even possible). Bramwell believes that even a *peaceful* change from the prevailing paradigms of domination would manifest violence:

> To cease from dominant-inspired relationships would be as violent a social and familiar change as the attempt to refrain from sexual congress was at the turn of the century. . . .[57]

Thus, neither "integrity" nor "disintegrity" is a univocal concept when used in the biological and ethical/social senses, respectively. Once again, the facile connection with "fascism" is negated, whereas the negative connotations of interference, confrontation, hostility, and even violence, acquire vastly different meanings in the two contexts.

This reinforces the PI and reiterates the validity of the categorical imperatives I propose. This analysis also shows that the principle, which appears to advance grandiose and sweeping universal claims, does so only in a largely noncontroversial context and has a much humbler reach and effect in regard to interhuman normative theories, where it is willing to concede the supremacy of other ethics, such as the Kantian deontology, provided such ethics are interpreted in a way which does not conflict with the principle described here.

Finally, by laying bare a number of disanalogies between the environmental and social ethical realms, the principle also shows—ipso facto—why (and how) the latter are not entirely successful in stretching beyond the species barrier. In this manner, the "principle of integrity" validates and justifies its own existence and—one hopes—the present enterprise.

7. The Role of Integrity and of the Principle of Integrity in Human Society

In Chapter Two, in an effort to understand biotic "integrity" from as many perspectives as possible, the concept was viewed in its two aspects, structural and functional, as I_1 and I_2. In the context of human society, some further distinctions must be introduced. Integrity's protection and restoration, as the primary goal of the categorical imperative following upon PI, suggest that only human interaction with wilderness or "undeveloped" areas need to be considered. In that case, the dwindling size of our pristine areas globally would indicate that the target of our morally concerned activities is so small that most of us will only have the chance for remote interaction with it, through environmentally sound activities, but no direct interaction at all.

On the other hand, three points militate against such a limited understanding of PI. First, having distinguished PI from doctrines which extend respect so far that our own survival is at stake (such as that of Albert Schweitzer), clearly some interaction with natural systems, viewed now as *instrumentally* valuable, must be required. Second, even the phrasing of the Great Lakes Water Quality Agreement of 1978, which prompted and inspired this work, seeks to direct human activities in the Great Lakes Basin ecosystem, an area far from pristine, as we have seen. That agreement also counsels reintegration of human kind as part of the biota of that ecosystem, rather than simply as "protectors" and "defenders" of the pristine portions or areas, wherever these might be. Finally, even those who aim at restoration of a pristine habitat, not only question the *physical size* of the wilderness ecosystem required, in order to support specific habitats, but also recognize the necessity for a "buffer zone" beyond the required "core" area.[58]

All these reasons indicate the need for extending the requirements of integrity. But how can the first principle and its ensuing categorical imperatives be extended? It is clear that although the concept of integrity can be approached through the abstractions suggested by I_1 and I_2, (that is, structural and functional integrity) the way to render both concept and principle operational is through a further conceptual division of integrity into I_a and I_b (that is, as "pristine" and "buffer" zone integrity). The absolute value of integrity, both as ideal and as paradigm as it emerges in Chapter Two, is the necessary primary sense of the concept. It is beyond dispute that integrity needs to be preserved, respected, and if possible restored over much of the Earth. How much of it we need is another question and one which, unfortunately, does not afford clear answers at this time, although some studies, specific to certain ecosystems, offer equally specific answers. Some scientists, when pressed for an answer, say, "perhaps 15 percent of all the Earth might be all right, for safety, but 25 percent may be safer and better, and 95 percent much safer." *The Wildlands Project*, for instance "calls for 23.4 percent of the land to be returned to wilderness, and another 26.2 percent to be severely restricted in terms of human use."[59]

In the light of three points listed above, an answer to this question is absolutely vital, and its pursuit appears to represent an urgent goal of scientific inquiry. What we must do is reserve the primary sense of integrity we have discussed so far, for the targeted areas (as I_a), and apply to the "buffer" zones and specific areas in culture, the goal and obligation of I_b. Examples of the latter might be an organically functioning farm, managed through low-input agriculture, a carefully monitored free-range farm, or whole communities such as those of the Mennonites (although even these may pursue unsafe environmental practices) and others whose lifestyle is not highly technological. In these instances, humans are *using* the Earth, rather than *preserving* it, but they are doing so in ways that do not conflict with whatever percentage of the Earth's pristiness they are duty-bound to preserve and respect. Rural development, light (nontoxic) industry areas, where health/treatment/ research/teaching facilities are located, would fall under this heading.

What of urban centers, not-so-light industries, and the rest that are normally taken for granted in today's technological society? Even the secondary sense of integrity (I_b) does not apply to these areas: neither pristineness nor even environmental health (as *present* acceptable functioning of ecosystems) exists here. For these areas, our guidelines would indicate that activity pursued here must be limited by the absolute prohibition to interfere with I_a (including both structural and functional aspects), and I_b, as healthy functioning of instrumental landscapes, beyond the pristine. When areas where purely human culture prevails are guided by the twofold obligation of I_a and I_b, then integrity will prevail, but only analogically, as citizens consciously refrain from causing severe environmental damage, while still pursuing carefully limited activities that transcend the purely ecological dimensions of their area (such as building roads, city/shopping complexes and the like).

In purely urban centers, which cannot be eliminated completely, when we are guided by the principle of integrity, our activities will need to consider (1) our *place* within the universe (see Chapter One), hence the ethical dimensions and qualitative limits of specific forms of interaction with our environment (e.g., the interactions peculiar to human "culture"); and (2) the *scale* within which we must operate in order for this interaction to be *quantitatively* morally defensible. Condition (1) demands that the *kind* of activity we engage in, should not conflict with the requirements of I_a as well as I_b, as such. Hence, it prohibits the manufacture and use of herbicides, pesticides, toxic chemical products that affect the ozone layer, nuclear power by-products, and so on. It is the *quality* of these activities, whatever their *quantity*, that is hazardous to life-supporting systems and all life in general including all humans, but also extending beyond the species barrier. Condition (2) demands serious consideration of the *scale* (or quantity) of these activities. In Chapter One, we saw the example of a nature-loving swimmer in a lake, raising the temperature of the water, hence accelerating the lifecycle of smaller parts of the ecosystem's biota and causing their premature death. Does that mean that it is *always* impermissible to raise the temperature of water bodies? The answer is that, although that might be true for areas where I_a should prevail, it would not be automatically true for areas governed by I_b, but that both in I_b-controlled areas and in other culture milieus, the specific *scale* or *size*, as well as quality (i.e., how much heat) of the disturbance need to be considered.

Hence the human being in "culture" needs to ask herself not whether or not to have a distinctive human culture, but to have one that is harmonious with the biological/ecological realities of our existence. The second formulation of the categorical imperative in Chapter Three is emphasized by this position. Only by understanding properly as much as possible about the functioning of ecosystems and their temporal and geographical scale will we know what safe role culture may play. Not enough scientific work has been done on the importance and the function of "buffer" zones, or, in our sense, of areas governed by and exhibiting I_b, especially at the biospheric level.

Therefore, we are not in a position to be precise about how much limited interference, or interference that is carefully controlled and, therefore, may be less harmonious with ecosystem functioning, yet still attempts to preserve some natural "health," may be permissible. Once again the warning of *Beyond the Limits* by D. Meadows et al. must be heeded: "drive" as you would in a vehicle without certified, guaranteed brakes, in bad weather, with fogged windows, and uncertain roads. Thus any acceleration, sudden move or even continuation of driving patterns evolved against the background of technical certainties must be avoided until *proven* safe. This suggests that the principle of integrity can generate second-order principles that are as specific as the current scientific understanding of ecosystem/biospheric functioning can make them. In essence, we can tell what we ought to do, if such-and-such were the case, as it appears to be from the standpoint of scientific understanding and predictability, limited though both of these might be. It also recommends extreme caution from the standpoint of morality, just as much of today's science recommends caution from the point of view of prudence.

Keeping in mind that second-order principles are still principles, not particular "solutions" to specific problems, we are now better equipped to view interhuman activities from the standpoint of PI. We will consider these in the next chapter, keeping in mind the distinction between I_a and I_b discussed here. Thus the next step, or target, is to see how PI performs when operating at the level of interhuman transactions, at the level of interaction with animals, and with the sort of "instrumental landscapes" envisioned as "buffer" areas governed by I_b.

Notes

1. Laura Westra, "Terrorism, Self-Defense, and Whistleblowing," *Journal of Social Philosophy* 20 no. 3 (Winter 1989):46–58.
2. Martin Benjamin, *Splitting the Difference Compromise and Integrity in Ethics and Politics* (Lawrence: University Press of Kansas, 1990), 53.
3. Ibid., 51.
4. Holmes Rolston III, personal communication.
5. Benjamin, 53.
6. John Rawls, *A Theory of Justice,* 519; cp. Benjamin, 46.
7. Plato, "Crito," in *The Trial and Death of Socrates*, trans. by G. M. A. Grube (Indianapolis: Hackett, 1988), 43–54; cp. Benjamin, 46.
8. Francis MacDonald Cornford, trans., *The Republic of Plato* (New York: Oxford University Press, 1945). Plato carefully distinguishes the "guardians" from the "philosopher": Their respective epistemic capacities dictate and circumscribe the limits of their moral economy.
9. Onora O'Neill, *Constructions of Reason: Explorations of Kant's Practical Philosophy* (Cambridge, U.K.: Cambridge University Press, 1989), 156–57.
10. Martin Benjamin's study has already been noted. Mark Halfon's work, *Integrity*, focuses on personal integrity.
11. Bryan G. Norton, *Why Preserve Natural Variety?* (Princeton, N.J.: Princeton University Press, 1987), esp. 77–84.
12. Chief Justice E. Harold Hallows. "Just vs. Marinette County, Supreme Court of Wisconsin, 1972, 56 Wis. 2d 7, 201 N.W. 2d 761'" in Donald Scherer and T. Attig, *Ethics and the Environment* (Englewood Cliffs, N.J.: Prentice-Hall, 1983), 132.
13. Mark Sagoff, "Takings, Just Compensation and the Environment," in *Upstream/Downstream*, 160–61; cp. Holmes Rolston III, "Endangered Species and Private Property," in *University of Colorado Law Review*; cp. discussion in Chapter Two, section b, "Legal Aspects of Integrity."
14. Both Aldo Leopold, in *A Sand County Almanac*, and David Ehrenfeld in *The Arrogance of Humanism* present conclusive arguments for this contention; cp. discussion of "integrity" in Chapter Two.
15. H. L. A. Hart and Lord Patrick Devlin debate the difference between the two forms of morality and the state's obligations in that respect, in their

respective monographs, H. L. A. Hart, *Law, Liberty and Morality* (Stanford Calif.: Stanford University Press, 1963); and Lord P. Devlin in *The Enforcement of Morals* (London: Oxford University Press, 1965).

16. Thomas Aquinas, *Summa Theologica*: II-II.Q.67.art.7. Augustine took a similar position as well.

17. Aquinas clearly states that the violence used in repelling the assailant must be proportionate to the violence he is attempting to do to us. Further, according to the doctrine of "double effect," our only intention must be to keep ourselves alive, we must bear no malice to our attacker and have no desire to destroy him.

18. Benjamin, 79–80.

19. Ibid. Also the arguments against "consumers' preferences" as guides to public policy in Mark Sagoff, *The Economy of the Earth*.

20. R. Rorty, "Pragmatism, Relativism Irrationalism," in *Consequences of Pragmatism* (Minneapolis: University of Minnesota Press, 1982), 165; cp. Benjamin, 78.

21. Renford Bambrough once cited the example of a construction crew being sent to map an area for construction. Returning after some time and after some natural events that somewhat changed the landscape, the crew decided to even things up by sending out bulldozers to change the landscape back to their previous observations, as reflected on the earlier maps.

22. Rolston, *Environmental Ethics*, 218; cp. John Stuart Mill, "Nature" (1874), in Jean O'Grady and John M. Robson, eds., *Collected Works* (Toronto: University of Toronto Press, 1963–77), vol. 10, p. 398.

23. Mary Mahowald, "What is the Connection Between Concern for the Environment, Feminism and Peace?" presented at the Central APA, New Orleans, April 26, 1990, p. 1.

24. Ibid.

25. Karen Warren, "Towards a Feminist Peace Politics," *Peace and Justice* 3 (1991): 87–102.

26. Ibid., 2.

27. Ibid., 3.

28. Helen Longino, *Science as Social Knowledge* (Princeton, N.J.: Princeton University Press, 1990). The latest addition to that literature is Kristin Shrader-Frechette, *Risk and Rationality* (Berkeley: University of California Press, 1991) particularly Chapters 2 and 3.

29. Longino, 96.

30. Ibid., 10; cp. B. Barnes and D. Edge, eds., *Science in Context* (Cambridge, Mass.: MIT Press, 1982); B. Barnes and D. Bloor, "Relativism, Rationalism and the Sociology of Knowledge," in Martin Hollis and Steven Lukes, eds., *Rationality and Relativism*, (Cambridge Mass.: MIT Press, 1982), 21–47.

31. Longino, 4 ff.

32. Ibid., 5; ethical, as well as epistemological problems may arise in the context of "property rights" in regard to results of scientific enquiry. A classic case is the "DBCP Case," in M. Velasquez, *Business Ethics, Concepts and Cases*, 2nd ed. (Englewood Cliffs, N.J.: Prentice-Hall, 1988), 398–401.

33. Longino, 7–12.
34. Ibid., 224.
35. Ibid., 225.
36. Ibid., 226.
37. Ibid.
38. Vandana Shiva, *Staying Alive* (London: 2nd Books, 1983), 15–31.
39. Sandra Harding, *The Science Question in Feminism* (Ithaca, N.Y.: Cornell University Press, 1986), 81; cp. 102.
40. L. Westra, Kira Bowen, and Bridget Behe, "Agricultural Practices, Ecology and Ethics in the Third World," *Journal of Agricultural Ethics* 4 no. 1 (1991) 60–77; cp. Shiva, *Staying Alive.*
41. C. K. Omari, "Traditional African Land Ethics," in R. Engel and J. Engel, eds., *Ethics of Environment and Development* (Tucson: University of Arizona Press, 1990), 165–75.
42. L. Westra and J. Harris, "Business Ethics: A Perspective from Islam," unpublished paper, presented at the European Business Ethics Network Conference, Milan, Italy, October 3, 1990.
43. A. Baier, "Violent Demonstrations," in R. Freyt and C. Morris, eds., *Violence, Terrorism and Justice* (Cambridge, U.K.: Cambridge University Press, 1991), 33–58.
44. Warren, 4.
45. Ibid.
46. Ibid., 8.
47. Westra, et al., "Agricultural Practices," 60–77.
48. A. MacIntyre, *Whose Justice? Whose Rationality?* (Notre Dame, Ind.: University of Notre Dame Press, 1988).
49. Benjamin, 18.
50. Ibid.
51. Ibid., 102.
52. Ibid., 103.
53. Ibid., 105.
54. A. Bramwell, *Ecology in the 20th Century: A History* (London: Yale University Press, 1989), 62–63.
55. Ibid.
56. Ibid., 63.
57. Ibid., cp. 256, fn. 74.
58. Reed F. Noss, "Sustainability and Wilderness" in *Conservation Biology* 5, no. 1 (1991): 120–22; "Wilderness Recovery: Thinking Big in Restoration Ecology," *The Environmental Professional* 13 (1991): 225–34; "Can We Maintain Biological and Ecological Integrity?" *Conservation Biology* 4, no. 3 (1990): 241–43; "The Wildlands Project," *Wild Earth* (Special Issue), 1993.
59. R. O'Neill, personal communication, January 30, 1993, Oak Ridge, Tenn.; cp. Charles C. Mann and Mark Plummer, "The High Cost of Biodiversity," in *Science* 260 (1993): 1868–71. The passage cited refers to the Oregon coast.

6

Some Consequences of Adopting the Principle of Integrity

PART A: INTRASPECIFIC CONSIDERATIONS:
INDIVIDUAL, SOCIAL, AND INTERNATIONAL
IMPLICATIONS FOR PEOPLE

1. Introduction

The title of this work promises an "environmental proposal for *ethics*," hence some consequences ought to follow for human ethics, that is, ethics within the species *Homo sapiens* or intraspecific ethics, although the principle proposes first and foremost an all-encompassing environmental morality, one relating to all species. Let us say, for the sake of argument, that the foregoing has been convincing: we have adopted the "principle of integrity" (PI) and are convinced that no action can be moral that does not foster environmental or ecosystem integrity. Unfortunately, there is no assurance that only one choice of action or policy would ensue or fit our requirement. The principle has no clear "second-order" principles that evidently follow from it and this presents a difficulty. A lot of deep thinking and analysis is left to the moral agent, becauses no "user's rules" come with it.

At the end of the previous chapter we noted that even the adoption of PI is simply not enough. Even if integrity is a defensible value, strong enough to support a principle of moral obligation, the *extent* of our obligation (or the scale of integrity required) is not specified. Further, the necessity for areas where the primary sense of integrity must prevail (I_a) *also* demands the further setting up of boundaries for "buffer" zones where a less-demanding sense of integrity is necessary (I_b). Present restoration efforts already address the two-way requirement of a "core zone" and a "buffer zone." The "conceptual core restoration zone" required to provide a "functional landscape mosaic of adequate extent" can be defined and specified, provided there exists a target community or communities whose habitat is to be restored.[1]

Unfortunately the same scientific support is not available when more general principles are sought; and when our target is a country or, worse yet, the biosphere, the problems of scale criteria multiply. Ontario (Canada) has proposed a goal of 15 percent of pristine (or "integrity") corridors. Costa Rica presently has 20 percent of its area that is protected and preserved. Monte Hummel of World Wildlife Fund (Canada) argues for preserving wilderness, in his recent collection of papers, *Endangered Spaces*:

> The 1982 World Parks Congress in Bali called for 10 percent as a target for protection. This guideline has since been endorsed by the United Nations Environment Program, which noted a call for a tripling of protected areas.[2]

Some other figures he offers are from the United States (excluding Alaska): 1.7 percent of the country is "wilderness," and an "additional 5.4 percent is roadless. Alaska has 24 percent of its land protected, and the Wilderness Society (U.S.) would like to see it raised to 50 percent." But the *Wildlands Project*, mentioned in the previous chapter, goes beyond wilderness protection, to demand (a) additional corridors, and (b) buffer zones, and as we saw, many are dismayed about the possible impact of such projects.[3] Other possibilities are either goal-specific or vague, because there is not enough scientific evidence to support any precise figures in a defensible manner.

Nevertheless, even if it is not fully determined, what emerges from this discussion is conceptually valid. There is an urgent need to go even beyond defining integrity; the further question is, how much of it is absolutely necessary? Consequently, the definition and extent of buffer zones to protect it is equally vital for an ethic of environmental respect and concern. But if our ethic's goal is already the target of public policy, and it must be rendered operational, the problem remains both at the theoretical and at the practical level: it is not possible to have an ethic whose "ought" is limited by the factual reality that "is," and to expect it to produce practical applications of its principle, when science itself cannot be precise about what is *prudentially* right and appropriate.

Hence our discussion in this chapter will be based on the hypothesis that, although we may not know what it is exactly at this time, there is an optimum percentage, relative to the ecosystem of the biome, which should be preserved in (or restored to) a state of integrity

(I_a).[4] There is also a further area to be considered, a "buffer" area (I_b), which is necessary to ensure the proper functioning and preservation of I_a. The scale of both I_a and I_b and their proportion, relative to the area and ecosystem considered, will lie in the specific percentages present science can support. What remains consistent is the necessity for the highest possible percentage of integrity in a core area, comprising I_1 and I_2 (that is, as I_a), and an appropriate buffer zone, or I_b, where ecosystem health is present and, as argued in the previous chapter, the ecosystem will be used respectfully in such a way that human uses will not conflict with the goals of I_a. It is for this reason that buffer zones (I_b) can still claim to have integrity, because the preservation of primary integrity in the core area represents the criterion and standard of what is permissible in the "buffer." This must remain a "universal but flexible norm," in the sense that the scale must remain relative to the requirements of specific ecosystems (while holding universally against specific human goals or preferences that might conflict with integrity).

The scale of urban spread that might be acceptable is also unclear. Several points must be taken into consideration from the standpoint of humankind ideally or in principle: (1) we need *food production* that is sufficient for the needs of *all* the world's population and that is equitably distributed; (2) *"equitable distribution"* implies that present and future humans have access to the food produced, hence *sustainability* is mandatory; (3) sustainability is to be generally understood as pertaining not only to agriculture and forestry, but to *lifestyle* as such (which must be clearly sustainable), so that not only food, but also shelter and energy use fall under this heading. Hence, "cultural" centers must be harmonious with I_a and I_b, rather than in conflict with them.

The difficulties facing us when we attempt to approximate this "balance" of scales and interactions are immense. An example might suffice to indicate the uncertainties and conflicts we are facing. In order to change from the reliance of fossil fuels (which are rapidly becoming exhausted or are environmentally hazardous) to solar energy, we *also* need land, not concrete or paved areas. An estimate of land requirements suggests we will need a 750,000-hectare flooded reservoir to provide energy at the present level for an average city.[5] Hence, even though the principle pertains to our interaction with the ecosystems of which we are a part, there are clear implications for our conduct in "culture," singly and collectively.

What, if anything, does the principle suggest about interhuman ethics? The first point to note is that PI is holistic; therefore the compatible choices it might support will have to be correspondingly holistic. As indicated earlier, PI tells us nothing specific about interpersonal relations: its input might suggest holistic applications, but only in regard to the support of life. The "principle" is based on "integrity" as a multifaceted value so that, minimally, the valuable aspects of integrity will have to be preserved in interhuman morality by those who wish to consistently support the principle. In other words, if PI is acceptable after serious consideration of the values grounding our obligation, then a commitment to those values must also govern our choice of interpersonal morality.

As far as possible "holistic" applications are concerned, someone might object that both Chapters Four and Five (as well as portions of Chapter One) argue strenuously *against* making claims that transcend ecology and move into the social realm. These claims were said to represent "category mistakes"; in fact, the whole defense of biocentric holism from the standpoint of integrity was largely based on this clear division between the biotic and the social realms. That division and perspective still stand in the context of any specific "society." Yet there is one context within which PI can be legitimately translated into social/political action, and that is in an international, global context.

To be sure, the principle cannot tell us which social system is preferable; yet it can prescribe negatively, showing where and why international relations might be contravening its tenets. The "good" or goal to be implemented is to be understood purely in biological terms, consistent with the restoration of integrity in both its related aspects (I_1 and I_2) as defined in Chapter Two. Hence, in Part A of this chapter, interhuman and interpersonal choices based on *negative* prescriptions from the standpoint of PI will be discussed (section 2), followed by the goal of "integrity" in the context of national democracies (section 3). We will then turn to PI and international equity considerations (section 4); and finally to a concluding section (5) on a possible solution: "environmental triage." In Part B the implications of PI for relationships between human and nonhuman animals will be examined. Part C will examine general considerations in other interaction with instrumental landscapes, buffer zones, areas in culture, and sustainable agriculture.

2. The Value and Method of the Principle of Integrity: Does It Suggest Any Specific Approach to Interpersonal Ethics?

Some negative conclusions follow from PI in regard to personal morality. Although the principle as such is not capable of prescribing anything specific, in the sense that we cannot simply state an interhuman counterpart, such as "virtue ethics" or "deontology," the principle *does* gain support from certain values, absolutely and categorically. Therefore its acceptance will entail that, for the sake of consistency, neither those values, nor that approach be dismissed when we make the transition from the holistic to the individual mode. To switch allegiance from previously accepted values, or to demand a different normative framework altogether, would manifest an unacceptable eclecticism. Although Chapter Three offered the suggestion of "fitting ethics" like a set of Russian dolls, the general "shape" of the dolls must be coordinated, if they are to fit inside one another.

Hence, the most important aspect of an interhuman ethics must be its "fit" with PI. The most important tenet it must exhibit is that of "respect for life," in the sense that life (and the systems that support it) has to be viewed as a "good" possessed of infinite value, or prima facie incommensurable, in the Kantian sense. Thus, the first aspect of "integrity" (as the goal of biocentric holism) manifests a value that must stand as such even in intraspecific interaction (at least prima facie it must not be violated even within human ethics). Consequentialist considerations of any sort, no matter how desirable the purely human "good" they might bring about, would not suffice to set aside the absolute respect for life. It would be clearly inconsistent to make life-support systems primary in the main principle, then fail to consider life in the same light, intraspecifically. Just as natural integrity is intended—at least prima facie—to be absolutely primary, hence to override all "cultural" goods that might conflict with it, so too the absolute value of life should remain primary in interhuman ethics.

It is appropriate, in the context of interhuman relations, to return to the ten values of integrity listed at the end of Chapter Two, which I will now list again for the reader's convenience.

Integrity's value may be based on the following intrinsic aspects:
1. It is a *universal value, global* in a sense different from both peace and health, the only other values that may compare in relevance with it.
2. It is a *revolutionary concept*, a catalyst for the necessity of rethinking both *national* basic beliefs about just human interaction and human rights, and accepted standards of previous *international* interaction.
3. It emphasizes the meaning of its paradigm case, organic unity, and the *value of freedom in its two senses*, negative and positive, in that regard. Negative freedom requires no interference with the organism's biological identity; positive freedom re-

quires that the organism's conditions be such that it may continue in its capacity to develop and change while retaining identity.

4. It includes the *value of health* in a nonanthropocentric sense.
5. It indicates and supports the *value of the whole*, while correspondingly emphasizing the reduced role and status of individuals including humankind. This emphasis is *only* applied to biological interaction, *not* to social or cultural activities.
6. It supports the *value of harmony*, including that between individuals and whole, and structure and function, once again, *only* in the biological sense indicated in (5) above.
7. It encompasses the *value of biodiversity*, and (a) the *life-support functions* and (b) the information/communication it supports.
8. It subsumes the value of *sustainability*, hence *stability*. In fact, it is absolutely necessary in some proportion, for the sustainability of all other parts of the landscape.
9. It emphasizes the *value of life/existence* as such (that is, for *all* individuals and wholes).
10. It shows the *congruence of morality, science/empirical reality, and metaphysics*, in integrity as an environmental value.

In Chapter Two, the ten aspects of integrity's value were listed in the order in which they arose in the several sections of the chapter. Rather than list them again in another order, they will be discussed (using the original numbers assigned) this time in regard to human interaction when appropriate, to understand the meaning each aspect might acquire in this changed context. We noted the value of respect for life (9) above: it remains the focal "absolute" in human ethics as well. Next, we can consider the global, universal value of integrity (1). A consistent interhuman moral doctrine will have to be universal as well. No light is shed by this requirement, as all morality is taken to prescribe universally. Nevertheless, "integrity's" principle prescribes categorically, hence, only doctrines based on Kantian thought, or virtue ethics perhaps, will show a suitable "fit." These are based on principle, rather than prescribing action on the basis of agreement (or contracts), or consequences based on aggregate preferences (or utility).

Possibly this is one of the reasons why "integrity" is to be viewed as a revolutionary concept (2). It is revolutionary not only in the environmental sense, by recommending subverting (and inverting) the usual order between interhuman and interspecies or environmental ethics, but also in at least two other senses. The insistence on (a) categorical principles that are nonnegotiable or amenable to majoritarian choices, is revolutionary in itself in today's moral climate. Equally "revolutionary" is its holistic thrust (b). Holism is not favored in today's moral debate: the thrust of moral doctrine has been increasingly individualistic, seeking to extend moral consideration to minorities, marginals, and animals.[6] Another point needs to be made in regard to the difference between individualism and holism. Some holists who defend Aldo Leopold's "Land Ethic" do so by an appeal to the concept of "community," as Baird Callicott for instance does, speaking of many "communities" to which we belong and to which various degrees of "pull" should apply through moral "sympathy." The use of "community," however, while it is appropriate in social and political philosophy, is somewhat question-begging in the context of an environmental ethic which purports to be holistic. As we saw in Chapter Two when ecology was discussed, the "community" approach was *contrasted* with the "ecosystem" approach, and the latter, not the former, is taken to be holistic.

To coopt the concept of "community" to defend a *holistic* approach in environmental ethics, is to paper over a vast chasm between two ecological camps, and some recognition of this problem should be shown. I tend to think of communities as "aggregates" not wholes, at least as far as natural entities are concerned. And the problem persists even in the social category, hence it is relevant here, when human ethics compatible with integrity are discussed. For instance, the present terrible conflict in the Balkan States is that of three *communities*, Serbs, Croats, and Muslims, within one *whole*: clearly one concept cannot serve in each case.

Hence, should we wish to use the notion of "communities," we must start by clarifying the sense in which it could be used in a holistic ethic. Leopold was working within earlier paradigms in ecology, and I have avoided using the concept because of these difficulties. Because holism, as such, has been defended in Chapter Four, I will not repeat those arguments here, and move on to the next listed value instead.

We are on somewhat firmer ground from the interhuman standpoint when we consider the value of "freedom" (3). Freedom is viewed as a major value in the context of most ethical doctrines. This apparent agreement, however, is only superficial. When "freedom" is understood as primary in the modern sense of fostering largely unrestricted choices (provided they do not infringe upon the equal freedom of others), then rather than finding an environmental "fit," we face a "value" in direct conflict with environmental integrity. To understand the meaning of freedom in our context, one needs to ensure that the two senses noted earlier are taken into consideration. For single organisms and ecosystems, both negative and positive senses of "freedom" from the ecological to the interhuman context, the biological sense of the term must be preserved. "Freedom" in the biological sense is intended as freedom to flourish, to be free of outside interference, *not* in the sense of "freedom of choice." This leads to a sort of "biological only" formulation of Kant's imperative (in its second sense): one must be prepared to adopt an ethical approach that forbids merely using humans' biological "personae," or preventing in any way their free maximum development, or diminishing in any way their natural capacity to withstand stress, to recover after change, or to "retain their identity" in the physical sense.

Hence, in the interhuman value of "freedom," one finds "health" (4) subsumed, although even in this case, structural interference with an individual's identity (through diminished or altered "integrity") should also be inadmissible, even if health were to be, somehow, preserved. Since most moral doctrines would also count physical integrity and the retention of one's physical capacities as a great value, neither the adoption of (3) nor that of (4) would represent a problem or obstacle in the choice of a moral doctrine, provided "freedom" is consistently understood.

The next four points (5, 6, 7, and 8) are purely environmental and holistic, and they are not relevant to interhuman relations. Because (9) was discussed at the beginning of this section, only (10) remains, and it groups together some complex values for moral consideration. First of all, how necessary is the input from metaphysics? Such an addition would no doubt be considered revolutionary. Yet, whether or not we wish to consider metaphysical or even theological support for PI, a metaphysical understanding of the value of "integrity" is unavoidable. "Integrity" proposes as a goal the "optimal" structure of an entity, or its "excellence"; it raises questions of "origins" as well as "ends" or goals; both of these aspects of integrity demand metaphysical analysis.

If a metaphysical component is accepted, then it should remain as an accepted part of the framework of ethical decisions in interhuman morality, and this may create a serious obstacle for some who prefer to keep ethics and metaphysics separate. If it is not accepted, I believe the principle can stand without the support of metaphysics, but the choices available from compatible interhuman ethical systems appear to be limited to those that either explicitly or implicitly accept a metaphysical component. In essence, then, some might be persuaded by the need for a holistic environmental ethic and even accept PI in that context, yet find that the coherence requirements demand the embracing of interhuman ethical positions they find, unacceptable.

For now, although this section inevitably suffers from imprecision endemic, I believe, whenever an ethics is used *beyond* the context and the "clientele" for which it was designed, some suggestions have emerged about the sort of doctrine that may be compatible with PI. These indications for the choice of a possible compatible ethic are necessary, because no one should find acceptable a principle and a goal which—if held consistently—would yield unacceptable consequences for human interactions. Hence, a clear statement of the values and conditions of an eventual position on interhuman ethics is absolutely necessary for anyone demanding coherence of beliefs. No attempt is made at this time to either design a new interhuman ethical system, or select as most compatible, one that has been already established in the history of moral philosophy. However, the earlier discussion of the several aspects of value in integrity, coupled with this brief section, ought to suggest at least the direction of one's quest for a compatible moral theory of interhuman interaction.

3. Some Social and Political Consequences: The Goal of "Integrity" in the Context of Democracy

The principle of integrity counsels biocentric holism, thus creating special problems for possible applications to sociopolitical goals. In Chapter Four, the latter were carefully separated from the biological and environmental goals the principle supports. This in turn raises some questions about any possibility of applications of the principle to the sociopolitical realm. We must start by eliminating the quest for any specific social order: the principle's universality (except for the ecosystem approach it counsels, with its somewhat limited biological goals) precludes using the principle for anything other than the ecological realm.

On the other hand its very universality makes the principle politically revolutionary. I have suggested elsewhere that when dealing with policy options governed by the guideline of "integrity," we might want to choose two additional principles to direct our action, the "Harm Principle" and the "Equity Principle," which are compatible with the goal of integrity and offer second order principles for specific problems and policies.

The Harm Principle indicates that (a) direct harm to persons, (b) harm to persons through ecosystem damage, and (c) harm to ecosystems as such, are not permissible.

The Equity Principle requires that such rights as those to "equal protection" (U.S. Constitutional Amendments 5 and 14), or "rights to the security of persons" (Canada Charter of Rights), or other human rights as set out by the United Nations Declaration, be equally available to all without consideration of gender, age, or other differences among humans. Further, it mandates that our actions also be governed by the principle of intergenerational equity, as specified by Edith Brown Weiss.[7] Neither of these additional "principles" suggests a specific social order or ideology.

Nevertheless, we assume that democracy represents the best possible system of government, the only one capable of supporting and defending the civil liberties we believe represent the ultimate value in nation states. Further, we believe that democratic nation states possess the right to self-determination. Yet the belief in the right to self-determination of autonomous democratic states is open to several counterclaims, two of which are particularly damaging. First of all, "Self-determination is a means to the end of social justice."[8] As a means to an end, it cannot be viewed as an end in itself; even less as an unchanging state, beyond criticism. Second, self-determination implies a group's decision to act as a unit and to be viewed as a separate, autonomous entity. If this decision is based on consent by the people, the question remains, "Who are the people?"[9] This leads to an even harder question: "Who decides who are the people?" Paul Gilbert raised a similar question in the context of terrorism. If democracies can, at best, vote about what happens within their own territory, how can disputes about borders be resolved. No peaceful, democratic resolution of territorial disputes is possible.

Several implications for democracy arise from the Harm Principle and the Equity Principle quoted above. Based on these principles, which embody commonly held values, our approaches to correct environmental (and agricultural practices) need modification. Some changes suggested by the principles and compatible with PI are:

(a) economic factors should not be used to arbitrate issues of human mortality or morbidity;

(b) economic, industrial, and agricultural activity must be brought into harmony with the limits of sustainability of the ecosystem we inhabit;

(c) governments should view environmental contamination as demanding priority action rather than simply requiring ongoing research;[10]

(d) divisive regional and even national policies which are now "ecologically blind" in their conception, funding and implementation, must be given "ecological eyes."[11]

Point (d) raises some questions which are also discussed in the final chapter of Eugene Hargrove's *Foundations of Environmental Eth-*

ics. In his "Afterword," Hargrove talks about moving toward a "balanced view system." His starting point is John Passmore's worry about all attempts to define an environmental ethic; Passmore not only sees environmental ethics, as such, as pointless, since the problems they address require political/social, not individual action, but also sees them as verging on the subversive, as constituting a first step toward "the overthrow of Western democratic institutions."[12] Hargrove, however, disagrees with Passmore's position. He argues for the need to reemphasize tradition, intrinsic and aesthetic values, so that the aim of "complementary action at both levels" (that is, ethical and political) can ensue.

In this sense, then, Passmore's worry can be laid to rest. Yet, I think that Hargrove's confidence in the desirability and effectiveness of the "complementarity" of ethics and politics within the present Western democratic scenario is somewhat premature, given his own concerns. Hargrove is correct in insisting on the primacy of intrinsic/aesthetic value, beyond economic and even instrumental considerations. On the other hand, it then seems necessary to question and qualify the endorsement of both "democracy" as such and, even more, the existence of separate, nation states with absolute power within their borders.

Although the authors of *Food 2000*, for instance, do not recognize the implications of their conclusions, the problem is implicitly present within their assessment. That "laws" must be given "ecological eyes" is essentially correct, but it is a claim that needs serious consideration. It entails that (a) laws and regulations be chosen according to an ideal goal, or "good," rather than represent the haphazard implementation of voters' preferences, however popular, or those of specific interest groups; and (b) individual states ought not to be the ultimate arbiters of which laws and regulations are chosen.

Now, at the risk of impugning the "sacred cow" of democracy, I see a direct conflict between it and the above position, and Hargrove also addresses to some extent the problem of the environmental viability of the status quo. He says, "The democratic state must educate its citizens so that they have the environment-values needed for both ethical and political action."[13]

The question of whether to teach values is still controversial, as Hargrove himself admits. Also, until these are learned, is it right to leave questions that might affect all life on earth in the hands of voters who lack education on these subjects? Furthermore, voters are, at best, limited to questions within their own political borders. How can one design and implement policies that cross national boundaries within the present divisive and atomistic political reality?

Hargrove recognizes the "pragmatic" aspect of utilitarianism. He says:

Utilitarianism may most appropriately be thought of as the democratization of ethical values. Unfortunately in order to speak to everyone, the utilitarian converted all good into degrees of pleasure, a good that is not a higher good but has the merit of being a good everyone can understand.[14]

Hargrove, I believe, is right. But just as his argument indicts utilitarianism, so too, by the same token, it pinpoints a parallel problem with democracy. The discipline of economics may not have actually defended its own values, but too many people are now convinced by its unproven assumptions: "[the] inordinate emphasis on money and getting good value, considered despicable in the last century, is now the standard in our own."[15] The recent conversion of "pleasure," or economic advantages, to preferences, is of little use to save utilitarianism from these problems.

But if utilitarianism based on economics is not the best way to approach environmental problems, and if the majority is nevertheless convinced of the soundness of that approach, then it seems to follow that majority rule, in its present (as yet uneducated) state, is inimical to environmental values. The majority can only vote to support its own preferences and, Hargrove says, "In summary, the instrumental resource value of nature, expressed in economic terms, will always, in principle, outweigh its aesthetic and intrinsic value."[16]

We may need, therefore, to return to Passmore's point, not to agree with him and dismiss everything that may conflict with "Western democracies" as a given but, rather, having recognized and admitted the primacy of environmental concerns, in order to stop and take a hard look at the impact of both "democracy" as it currently exists, and of fragmented and divisive nation states. The worldwide study, *Food 2000*, cited earlier, correctly pointed out the necessity of transcending the latter yet failed to draw out the spirit and implications of its position. I believe this "spirit" can be found to some extent in Hargrove's "Afterword."

The practical implications and difficulties of the adoption of this position are staggering, and the theoretical and ideological ones no less extreme, but I am not sure that the alternative can be moral— that is, the continued reliance on institutions and practices which are insufficient to cope with the present acute problems. A simple example will suffice to show the difficulty. In the lower area of the boreal forest, north of Thunder Bay in Northern Ontario, there is a small community, Atikokan. Its inhabitants are mainly, though not exclusively, Canadian Natives. It is isolated, has extremely harsh, long winters, high unemployment, and no prospects for economic improvement.

In 1985 a nuclear facility in Manitoba decided that the rocky Canadian Shield in that particular area would make an excellent radwaste disposal site. They immediately started sending around their public relations people, who even gave lectures to faculty and students at nearby Lakehead University, explaining how *utterly safe* everything would be and how there was no need for "hysteria." Pointed questions from the audience (primarily from this philosopher) disclosed that they certainly had no new answers to the familiar problems, endemic to that industry, which Kristin Shrader-Frechette had detailed and attacked many years ago.[17]

Had there been a referendum, no doubt the majority in Atikokan would have voted in favor of the disposal site. Would that have been the morally correct decision, since if the consequences included effects on the health, not only of the voting community, but also of persons too removed from that location to be allowed to vote, their children and even their children's children? People clearly have the right to have their autonomy respected and to decide about their own lives, and even to make their own mistakes. Yet, just as the right to drive a car does not extend to driving when drunk because of the possible harm to the public, so too, I believe, the individual and collective right to self-governance does not include the right to make choices that might undermine others' rights to life and freedom from harm. Current legislation and regulatory expressions of environmental policy support the rights of future generations, even in cases of possible harm. That is the position of any environmental Bill of Rights (such as the one presently sought by the New Democratic government of Ontario).

In fact, a serious commitment to the public interest should force us to undertake a *moral* rather than simply a *social* audit of our activities and policies. The difference is that a majority of people will often prefer short-term gain over long-term safety, especially since the trade-offs are never clearly explained or publicly discussed in the media. Clearly governments, professionals, and institutions have an obligation, as Hargrove pointed out, to "educate," to clarify, and to be candid about issues involving risk. Even during this process, however, they have an obligation to be paternalistic, that is, to implement the less dangerous choices as *morally right*, even if (temporarily) unpopular, and thus not perceived as a social "good" by "informed" citizens. Their obligation appears to parallel that of other professionals in positions of trust. A doctor's obligation arises from both the patient's trust and the doctor's superior knowledge and understanding of problems and consequences. The doctor must prescribe in order to bring about the physical "good" of the patient, and to minimize harm, not according to the most popular choice.

Now some, for instance Kristin Shrader-Frechette, have argued against the absolute power of "expert opinion" in deciding public policy issues. She has recently advocated allowing populist expression to balance the perceived "absolutes" of the experts. This clearly contradicts my own position, at least in practical terms. The reconciliation can be found, I believe, in her book *Nuclear Power and Public Policy*.[18] She suggests a modified "jury system" as the best solution for difficult policy decisions. This approach has the merit of incorporating the "education" requirement proposed by Hargrove. Juries must be presented with *all* expert evidence and the best possible "case" from both sides. Nor can a jury's deliberations be dismissed in favor of majoritarian decisions. In this manner, a more balanced decision might be reached, avoiding both the dangers of exclusive reliance on "scientists" and "experts" and that of an unprepared or uneducated public.

Clearly, the practical side of my position requires working out in more detail than can be attempted in this brief presentation. I offer a broad sketch, rather than a detailed proposal. However, generally speaking, the only other form of governance I can suggest as an alternative would be the return to some sort of Platonic philosopher–queen instead, in order to support the primacy of PI, for which I have argued.

This conflict indicates one of the most revolutionary aspects of the goal and principle of integrity. In the next section the relationship between integrity, international relations, and international equity will be discussed.

4. The Principle of Integrity and International Equity

Being foundational for environmental ethics at a *global* level, PI understandably raises serious questions about national democracies in general (in addition to the questions raised in the previous section in regard to democracy as such, within a national order). The argument of the last section showed that if (a) all serious environmental concerns are global; and if (b) laws, policies, and regulations must therefore be given "ecological eyes"; then (c) no uninformed, limited, national democratic vote can serve to deal appropriately with the problems we face. Even if it were possible to ensure that information were made available to a specific national group, that might not be sufficient to ensure that an international ecological policy would be chosen.

What militates against that possibility is the very existence of nationalism, that dictates the centrality of ourselves and our next of kin and our interest, over and above those we perceive as "others." In the *Republic*, Plato makes a similar point in his outline of the "best society." Not only did Plato deem it necessary to ensure that all decisions be made in the light of the "good," and that only someone competent to understand the "good" (i.e., the philosopher king/queen) could be leader, but he also designed a specific training for the guardians to ensure that the "good" would be understood and chosen.

Guardians, from whom the philosopher–king was chosen, were not allowed to own property or even to have families. In a move far more radical even than present-day Rawlsian requirements for a "veil of ignorance" and the "original position," the Platonic requirement for almost monastic distance from the "normal" citizenry of their time suggested vividly the corruptive force not only of the financial motive but also of "clan" membership.

If you knew who "yours" were, Plato thought, it would be natural to want to favor them, a practice that can even be observed in the wild, as discussed in Part B of this chapter. Wolf, bear, or bee would also recognize and prefer their own species to others. Plato's point was clearly not taken from scientific observation, but its force remains today. Pushed to an extreme which today's ethical discourse would not accept, Plato's position is also a holistic one, albeit one suffering from the very "fascism" flaw we were at some pains to reject in Chapter Five. But the environmental ethics enterprise *forces* us to look beyond specific interests of any sort, whether family, group, national, or even purely human. It also requires that we not view ourselves as absolute owners of our territory (unlike other species in the wild), a position the Athenian Plato would never have accepted.

Still, if our lifestyle is such that it affects life on earth, then, unlike wild species whose lifestyle cannot have that consequence, as far as we know, we need to pursue a universal goal. In turn a universal goal, a global "good," may well involve a group sacrifice of some sort, or at least a ranking of priorities arranged so that our preferences rank below the primary goal. It seems as though nationalism should be obsolete on those grounds, and that competitive, divisive laws and regulations should no longer be supported. But in that case some of the very bases of international relations may be brought into question.

Once again, what about state autonomy, the principle of nonintervention and its relationship to respect and tolerance for cultural and group differences? How would these fare in regard to questions of global justice, for instance? In essence, does nationalism still have a role to play in today's global moral difficulties? PI suggests a standpoint from which to examine this problem. First, "integrity" as a goal is based on the value of survival. If states and nations are viewed as discrete, individual entities, then their status as autonomous entities is based, as some claim, on the "moral principle of national survival."[19] Yet "national survival," as Charles Beitz notes, is an ambiguous notion. It is only fully defensible in the sense of "survival of the nation's citizens" but not otherwise:

> When "national survival" extends further (for example, to preservation of forms of cultural life or to the defense of economic interests) the view's prima facie acceptability dissipates precisely because the survival of persons is no longer at issue. In such cases the invocation of the national interest does not necessarily justify disregard of other moral standards.[20]

Hence the "autonomy of states" is not sufficient to justify immoral action, nor is the argument that no moral principle of international justice exists. Currently, the "sanctity" almost of individual nations and states is perceived as the only "just" political form of government, and their "autonomy" is seen as almost on a par with individual autonomy and equally hard to impugn on any grounds, including moral ones. Beitz points out that in earlier times states were not perceived as "self-sufficient" units. Rather:

> Previously a different conception of international order had been ascendant; in that conception, exemplified by Grotius, states were regarded as elements of a larger moral order and their boundaries were not viewed as barriers to external moral assessment or political interference.[21]

Of course, in Grotius's time the analogous "inviolability" of individual autonomy *within* a state was not accepted either, whereas a universal metaphysical and theological order was accepted without question. Beitz's argument appears to parallel the one supported, in a different context, through PI. It was argued that there is nothing sacred about any social order, thus prima facie there is nothing immoral about interfering with it when it appears to contravene universal moral principles. In fact, it is easier to support a principle that simply has as its basis universal survival, than to attempt to decide what constitutes an "immoral activity" in a state from other standpoints.

Therefore, if citizens' survival, rather than the survival of the social order, is at stake, then interference with national autonomy is permissible, regardless of the wishes of the national government in power.[22] Intervention with national governments *does* require serious justification, but ensuring the survival of citizens is enough to justify interfering. In other words, the analogy between individual, autonomous persons and discrete, self-sufficient autonomous states does not hold. Nor may a state legitimately resist intervention aimed at ensuring citizens' survival purely on the grounds that the government exists by consent and was democratically chosen. We noted earlier, in section 3, problems with democratic majority decisions, and with consent. Further, it is obvious that groups can join together by consent or for the "pursuit of common ends,"[23] without thereby being exempt from the moral judgment of the human community beyond their borders, or confines. For instance, a group such as the Ku Klux Klan, even if unanimous in the pursuit of its goal, could not justify its goals as "moral" on those grounds. Such unanimity would be rare in nation states, where a narrow or at best comfortable majority supports it leadership.

Even in the case of independent states, Beitz argues, "the weakness of the argument from consent to legitimacy also undermines the argument from consent to autonomy,"[24] thus the state is not immune from moral criticism.

Individuals are thought to retain the right to autonomy no matter what their moral status, provided their activity does not harm or affect the rights of others negatively. States, however, "can legitimately demand to be respected as autonomous sources of ends," only if their "institutions satisfy appropriate principles of justice."[25] S. I. Benn and R. S. Peters, in their classical treatment of international relations in *The Principles of Political Thought*, state: "In the end, moral duties are owed to men; they are owed to states only insofar as they are organizations which serve men."[26]

These authors speculate about the validity of international laws, without the validating authority of a state: "Is international law 'law'?" At the time when their work was published, most international law had to do with war, although they cite Henry Sidgwick on another international problem: "Sidgwick for instance denied that a particular community had an exclusive and unqualified right to the 'utilities from any portion of the Earth's surface.'"[27]

Yet the problem is not solved by such statements: even if a "state of states" or an international "superstate" could be summoned, somewhat like a United Nations, such a body would still have no great power other than the use of sanctions or other nonviolent means. Worse yet, "There is no wide consensus on moral standards for the settlement of claims."[28] Hence, the establishment of a "world-order" institution *requires* as its basis the existence of some categorical, universal principles on the basis of which it could legitimately intervene.

PI, I suggest, is just such a principle, as it both *demands* the existence of an institutional body powerful enough to support and even enforce the policies it requires and *also provides* the objective "moral standard" about which wide consensus is not only possible but existing and actual.

Like the "neutral nonintervention standard governing intervention in international law," the "virtue" of integrity as a standard is that "it is impartial between competing conceptions of the political good."[29] This is because the "good" proposed by PI is indeed an international, global goal, universally acceptable.

For instance, in the 1991 Gulf crisis and war, Iraq's action of deliberate sabotage of the earth (that is spilling immense quantities of oil into the sea), which can only be termed "ecosabotage," was universally deplored. Whatever one's position in regard to the Arab/Western politics involved, the act of ecosabotage was condemned by all.[30] It is worth noting that even if both the oil and the area of the spill were in Hussein's own domain, and the former were his state's property, this would not help him deflect universal moral censure.

Beitz, in his illuminating discussion of Rawlsian doctrine shows that, unlike persons' "natural talents," "natural resources" are not such that anyone can have a "natural" or prior claim to them. No special rights attach to the soil under our feet, or the air above us, whereas one's ability to compose poetry or to sing, belongs to one in a very special way.[31] Following the "social contract" model, as Rawls does, for instance, will not yield a solution that is morally acceptable, as he perceived "a greater symmetry to the domestic and international contracts than is in fact appropriate."[32] Beitz emphasizes that, at the international level at least, it is necessary to distinguish "natural and social contributions to the society's level of well-being."[33]

The holistic approach thus required emphasizes the basic tenet underlying his critique, the question of interdependence. It is not the case that autonomous, self-sufficient states voluntarily come together to agree on conditions for interaction. On the contrary, their interdependence as coexisting entities on the same planet and, hence, as individuals who are totally dependent on the same life-support system, is *primary*. This basic fact must be taken into consideration in the area of international justice, and PI is appropriately foundational for that task. Still, as Beitz points out:

It is easier to demonstrate that a pattern of global interdependence exists—and that it yields substantial aggregate benefits, than to say with certainty how these benefits are distributed under existing institutions and practices.[34]

It is even harder, no doubt, to quantify details of harms arising to groups and nations from overuse of "joint" resources, such as air, water, and soils, by other groups or states. The most recent World Bank findings, for instance, clearly indicate that continued overuse and overconsumption of meat, well beyond the necessity for protein, by richer Western nations impose harm and serious deprivation on less developed countries.

Other instances of political "inequalities" connected with a resource might be seen in the participation in world trade of oil-exporting countries, in contrast with those that are not so blessed.[35] Power, engendered by the "possession" of natural resources, dictates who enjoys most benefits and who is left with disproportionate burdens. International equity, therefore, does not direct the allocation of benefits and burdens.

Some feel that a changed social order is necessary to ensure international equity. For instance, Kai Nielsen contends that capitalism must be overturned so that equitable redistribution of benefits and resources between the "haves" and the "have-nots" can take place, or, as he puts it, between "North and South."[36] Yet this view remains atomistic and individualistic. For instance, he sees as primary the individual interest to "bodily and moral integrity," so that "to require a person to give up her religion or political convictions to enhance social harmony or even peace is another intolerable intrusion in that person's life—it simply runs roughshod over her civil liberties."[37]

Nielsen appears to believe that switching political systems would not represent an "intolerable intrusion" in a person's life. Yet he sees "political convictions" as constituting part of an inviolable core of a person, their "integrity," a somewhat self-contradictory position. There are possible objections to his position. There are possible "switches" that might serve as well, or better, to redress "North–South" inequalities. One possibility might be the adoption of a serious religious belief in our role as "stewards," interacting respectfully with all entities on earth, as the Christian farmers of *Earthkeeping (A Christian Journal of Faith and Agriculture)*, for instance, recommend.[38] Another possibility is the adoption of an ecologically conscious moral stance, such as PI, which would be effective in two separate ways. First, it proposes a goal that is universally acceptable from the environmental standpoint. It mandates, ipso facto, the implementation of laws and regulations to limit the "capitalistic license," which presently permits freedom of enterprise and the pursuit of purely economic goals, unchecked by global, communal goals. Secondly, it counsels respect for the basis of life as well as for all entities living within ecosystems, including animals, which would involve the abolition of agribusiness, factory farming, and all other wasteful, exploitative practices.

This in turn would free immense areas of the world for growing sources of protein other than meat, such as grains, beans, and other legumes. This would help feed large numbers of inhabitants of the "South" as new practices and the abandonment of our present wasteful consumer preferences increased the availability of food. This result is independent of any specific social organization; I am not aware of any study linking political beliefs to meat consumption, or any specific ideology such as socialism, to vegetarianism.[39]

A possible objection which emerges centers on the persistence of an individualistic, rather than holistic, standpoint. When the two "goods," that is, the "good" of the individual and that of the ecological whole, coincide, as they do at the survival level advocated by PI, then no problem arises. On the other hand, if one perceives one's "civil liberties" as ultimate, no matter what one's preference in social ideology, then ecological harmony or integrity cannot be *the* primary concern, as was noted in the discussion of "ecofeminism" in the previous chapter.

There is nothing to prevent an individual in a less developed country from wanting desperately to enjoy not only freedom from famine and deprivation, but also parity with the lifestyle of more developed countries, with all their wasteful and unsafe practices. Would Nielsen be prepared to accept some mechanism for preventing such a scenario from unfolding? If so, on what grounds, if "civil liberties" of the individual are primary? As serious concern with universal survival ought to come before individual preferences, even in political ideologies, the PI's ecological goal ought to govern international relations, before all other preferences. Once again, "strong (or basic) rights" ought to prevail before "weak rights" are considered. Given our entrenched beliefs in the primacy of individual or, at best, of democratically chosen preferences over all else, this remains a major stumbling block to the practical acceptance of PI.

5. A Possible Solution: The Approach of Environmental Triage

We have noted that while PI makes no specific recommendation about further principles for governing interhuman relations, the consistent adoption of the foundational values and formal method of the principle do. Thus some guidance might be available, at least negatively. The categorical approach demanded by the principle suggests that equally principled or categorically prescriptive universal moral theories should be chosen, in preference to those based on (a) contracts or (b) aggregate preferences. Further, the possibility of a metaphysical component, compatible with PI, suggests that a doctrine permitting, or compatible with, such a component might be preferable, although not absolutely necessary.

From the sociopolitical standpoint, PI raises serious difficulties, although it supports no specific recommendations. Some of these problems are (1) the conflict between democracy and the ethics of environmental concern; and (2) the elimination of *all* social causes as primary (both necessary and implicit, given the primacy of environmentalism) although some social/political organizations would make an important contribution to explaining and analyzing the causes of existing environmental crises. These causes (such as ecofeminist concerns with the importance of the affirmation of feminism in this context) could remain as *secondary* targets for environmental action and policy, after policies intended to protect the life-support system had been implemented.

What is required is the practice of a sort of environmental "triage." For example, if an international body such as the United Nations were endowed with a large grant to attempt to redress several serious problems, such as (a) ecosabotage, (b) racism, and (c) sexism, PI would counsel spending those resources *first* on safeguarding life on earth for all (that is, all parts of the biota, including humans of all races and both genders), before even attempting to gauge the relative merits of the two remaining causes and the severity of their respective problems. Like all "triage" practices, this entails adopting a ruthless "bottom line" mentality, as in all cases of limited resources and multiple threats and perils.

This approach does not, however, indicate a lack of concern or respect for the two other causes. Similarly, two paramedics who would be called to a multiple vehicle accident where several victims *all* appeared to require immediate intervention and care would *have* to choose the two worst cases from the standpoint of life threatening conditions, and perhaps even allocate the most serious case to the more experienced paramedic of the two. This is not to say that they would not consider the others seriously or view them as unworthy of respect and care. It would simply indicate that they would perform "triage," i.e., they would assess priorities until further help arrived.

In essence then, the priority of life-support systems would dictate no specific choices in the social or political realms other than the selection of a governing body, institution, or other mechanism most likely to accept and implement the priorities which PI dictates. The same approach would be taken in international relations. While still respecting individual cultural differences, viewpoints and groupings as embodied in separate nation-states, from the standpoint of PI, one would be required to take a universal moral stance that accepted global survival as primary. This stand, of course, would only be taken when global "threats to life-support systems" emerged and would not encourage a general interference with civil liberties, lifestyle preferences, and the like, in other cases.

For instance, accepting for argument's sake the World Watch predictions and their concern with Western-style meat consumption, an international legislative body empowered to uphold PI could bring sanctions to bear against Western capitalist nations to discourage excessive meat consumption demanding either the dismantling of McDonalds or their conversion to the sale of soyburgers, and so on. It could not, however, interfere with the Inuits' dietary habits, even if these included the consumption of deer or elk, which are equally "meat." The crucial difference is in whether or not the practices interfere with life-support systems that support international equity. The goal in the first case would represent an implementation of PI, the second, related one, the fostering of an interhuman goal (that of restoring justice) compatible with the first one, and the principle. In other words, Inuit dietary choices impose no unjust hardships on less developed countries.

Hence, the principle, once accepted, suggests negative applications as well as some general positive ones. It recommends that neither individual nor group choices or preferences be considered primary in the face of an attack on systems that support life when the threat to life is a serious possibility. The principle acknowledges the lack of precision endemic to ecology and possible to all life sciences, but it does not permit this "argument from ignorance"[40] to lead us to ignore serious possibilities, as it is within the capacity of present science to predict these. The principle does not demand that one return to absolute reliance on "experts" and risk assessment procedures: while we acknowledge the careful critiques of these already in print, they need no duplication at this time.[41]

The principle suggests that a globally enlightened public should be permitted, and in fact encouraged, to speak out on global issues beyond the reach of the democracy or other political system within which they reside. The justification for placing such power in the hands of a United Nations-style organization and in persons far removed from the geographical location of the possible life-threatening problem, lies both in the gravity of the threat and the fact that the reach of the threat far exceeds its national borders. Even without detailing specific examples of the problems, such as Chernobyl or the destruction of the rain forests, the existence of which manifest a global rather than national or geographically specific threat, the *definition* of the *only* sort of grave issue that ought to be handled in this manner underlies its justification.

The principle of integrity only issues a categorical imperative when life-sustaining systems are in peril; it does not arrogate to itself the "right" to dictate in other cases. Just as it is deemed fair and just that a whole nation participate in a vote the result of which will affect all citizens, so too, all educated and aware cosmic citizens ought to have a voice in environmental questions that will affect them, no matter what their *other* citizenship, race, or political ideology. The problems are both grave and holistic. The recommended response is correspondingly categorical and holistic. In conclusion, a stance that is compatible with the principle emerges from a consideration of international distributive justice as such. Beitz says:

> When as now national boundaries do not set off discrete self-sufficient societies, we may not regard them as morally decisive features of the Earth's social geography. For purposes of moral choice, we must instead, regard the world from the perspective of an original position from which matters of national citizenship are excluded by an extended veil of ignorance.[42]

PART B: INTERSPECIFIC CONSIDERATIONS: ECOLOGY AND ANIMALS

1. Introduction

The conflict between holistic and nonholistic positions reemerges when one considers the relation between human and nonhuman animals. It would appear that a principle that makes environmental considerations primary ought to suggest a possible reconciliation between animal ethics and the ethics of the environment, a possibility of which J. Baird Callicott, for instance, despaired in his earlier work. How could one go about constructing such an ethic of reconciliation? Is Callicott's "sympathy in community" the answer?

2. Callicott's Position
(Sympathy in Community)

As biocentric holism is essentially a position based on intrinsic value, holistic ethics in general need not be incompatible with a view based on "inherent worth" for individual organisms, and prescribing duties of respect on our part. And in that case, while it might be difficult, it should not be impossible to generate a compatible position on the question of our obligations to animals, from the standpoint of an ethic that is environmentally inclusive.

Paul Taylor has argued that these holistic views only suggest certain ways for humans to act in accordance with the "ecological niche" they occupy, and in fact include no conception of moral agents as having duties to individual organisms, "each of which is viewed as possessing inherent worth."[43] I argue that even if this is true, holistic ethics need not be incompatible with such a view, and "duties to individual organisms" may indeed be the best approach for our purpose, as Taylor argues.

Even if we seriously consider animals as individual bearers of rights just like humans, it is not necessarily true that we have—ipso facto—to abandon ecological ethics any more than we have to do so if we consider humans to be bearers of such rights. It is, in both cases, a question of carefully examining our principles as well as their specific application in order to establish priorities in each case.

In contrast, Callicott's argument for a joint ethic is based on sympathy, natural among humanity, as he claims citing David Hume, and not necessarily terminated at the species barrier.[44] This sympathy exists primarily in biosocial groups which are entirely composed of individuals of one species, such as humans, elephants, or bees, but also persists in mixed communities, comprising both animals and humans, who have historically lived together for a long time. He prefers to talk in terms of communities and sympathy rather than the sentience of animals, as Peter Singer does, or their "rich subjective life," which grounds animal rights in Regan's view. Nor does he mention Taylor's approach, that is, respect, because it is severely limited in its application by his exclusion of all but wild animals from consideration. At any rate—if I understand him correctly—Callicott holds that our existence as social beings entails that altruism is as natural to us as being part of a group is. But could someone deny perhaps the very existence of interspecific sympathy? I am not sure that even intraspecific sympathy as such is totally indisputable, although it appears to be better grounded than the former. In its defense, Callicott cites not only Hume but Mary Midgley, as he speaks of a community formed of both humans and the animals they have traditionally worked with.[45]

It is probable that, at a minimum, instrumental value has always been ascribed to those animals which have contributed in some way to the human community down through the ages. In fact, this is probably the source of our feeling of modified "kinship": our horses or cats or hens may have aroused the same sort of possessive feeling that servants have elicited, though probably to a lesser degree. Still, it is possible to raise doubts about sympathy, as many claim to have no such feeling, including such animal defenders as Singer. Nevertheless, it is not possible to doubt certain other facts about animals in the wild, in relation (a) to each other (within the same species), (b) to the environment in general, and (c) to those belonging to other species.

Facts are not ipso facto ethical prescriptions; in applied philosophy, however, the "factual realm" suggests the limit of norms and establishes the background and context of such normative judgments.[46] What are the "facts" governing wild animals and the environment? In ecological terms, as Leopold puts it, "an ethic . . . is a limitation of the freedom of action in the struggle for existence."[47] Callicott, citing Charles Darwin, says that "the natural in the world as actually constituted is one in which one being lives at the expense of the other."[48] Finally, Holmes Rolston suggests "what *is* in nature may not always imply an *ought* (and it may seldom do so in interhuman ethics), but *ought* in environmental ethics seldom negates wild nature."[49] If we accept the fact of survival at the expense of one another, we can then minimally establish the limits within which we can put philosophical argument or intuition to work. The reality of animal/environmental intercourse (aside from intraspecific behavior, for the moment) is characterized not by sympathy, but by controlled and limited hostility; it is needed for survival, just as Heraclitus noted in 600 B.C. when he wrote, "It should be understood that war is the common condition, that strife is justice, and that all things come to pass through compulsion of strife."[50]

Yet the reality of constant strife existing in nature appears to grate on our moral sensitivity; it is far easier to tolerate the birth, growth, decay, and death of grasses, trees, and insects than of sentient creatures, who are perhaps too much "like us" for comfort, and it is even harder to see ourselves as an integral part of this cycle. Pain, in our mind, requires some sort of justification: Why should innocent creatures suffer? Might it be possible to train predators to be vegetarians? Since we "know better," should we not at least lead the way by relinquishing our carnivorous bent, thus avoiding some of the pain and suffering of sentient beings?

I believe this view to be wrongheaded in two senses. First, it leads to an unavoidable polarization between animal and ecological ethics, torn asunder by the criterion of sentience and capped even by the possible requirement of sympathy. It seems to me that a defense based on either sympathy or sentience can only be supported by paternalistic disrespect for the realities that govern all life. As Rolston points out, predation is a fact of life, as is the interdependence of feeding upon one another. Nor is this to be viewed as "bad." "But the burden of proof is on a human evaluator to say why any natural kind is a bad thing and ought not to call forth admiring respect."[51] If what is right includes ecosystemic patterns, organisms generating sustaining environments, as Rolston maintains, it is nonsense to respect lions and call jungles "bad."[52] If we propose rights for animals, we show a sort of consideration for them which, at the same time, finds their ways and the processes according to which they function and have their being to be inferior to our "enlightened" ways. For instance, we could probably avoid a lot of anxiety and suffering to all human beings by introducing some mild tranquilizers into cities' water supplies. Yet few of us would find this action to be either moral or enlightened; it would be a paternalistic action, demonstrating no respect for our individual way of being and our autonomy.

Note that so far we are dealing primarily with reconciliation of (wild) animal ethics and environmental ethics, admittedly the easier position to achieve and defend. The question that arises now is: If the grounding assumptions for this position, such as either individual rights or sympathy, are at least open to criticism, what else can be put in its place? I suggest an ethic that accepts both the inescapable facts of natural hostility and instrumental interdependence and the respect due to all of nature, including animals. How these two standpoints can be combined is the topic of the next section.

3. Respect in Hostility: A Possible Foundation for a Joint Ethic

I spoke about "facts" concerning animals, environment, and humans in the previous section. How do they relate to one another? Respect appears to be the predominant virtue, but it is coupled with either hostility (in quest for possible food sources, or in competition for them) or indifference (toward other species which are not relevant to survival for the specific individual animal). It is only in the case of intraspecific relations that notions such as kinship or perhaps even sympathy surface. As in human societies, both kinship and sympathy become stronger when a familiar relation exists among some of the animals, but—perhaps in contrast with human animals—they do not, even then, transcend the established "pecking order" of the group. A wolf is loyal and devoted to its mate and cubs, and cooperative within the established order, with other members of the group. He interacts with others according to his needs: with hostility, to kill prey required by himself and by those to whom he is responsible; with indifference to all others, but without the intent to destroy carelessly or for any purpose other than individual or group survival. The component of respect is present in the manner in which the kill is accomplished: what is taken is just what is required. There is no killing for decoration, sport, fun, or even curiosity (science), although some atypical behavior has been noted on the part of animals on occasion. Thus, simply from a consideration of the "ecological niche," as Taylor suggests, we can argue neither for a total lack of sympathy nor for its existence. What we see is behavior appropriate to that niche, and that is simply *not* all-of-a-kind.

In all natural entities it is behavior which is differentiated according to its target. In general, it is governed (1) by hostility, based on the primacy of survival (individual, familial, and specific, in that order), and (2) by indifferent respect for interspecific dealings not covered under (1). For example, no wolf decides to rip up grasses or wild flowers or to kill animals which do not threaten him and he does not need to eat. Once again, neither sport nor scientific curiosity stimulates hostility or careless destruction. Finally, (3), with a specific kin group, animals exhibit varying degrees of solicitude and sympathy, but cases of interspecific sympathy are—to say the least—rare.

If we are intent on reducing our arrogance and reducing or moderating our belief in human superiority, it might be best to accept ethical principles which do not start from the premise that every form of behavior which differs from intraspecific human intercourse is "inferior," in fact so much so that animals ought to be persuaded, if possible, to act upon our principles. What might serve us better instead is a less Protagorean position, an admission that man is not the measure of all things, and perhaps a further admission that an understanding of the rational laws of the universe might afford us a better ethical basis for both human and nonhuman entities, singly and collectively.

Although my position is far from being a utilitarian one, I agree with Singer on one point at least: feelings toward animals, such as I might recognize in myself and many others, are useful and pleasant, but not necessary. A qualified defense of the natural ends and interests of animals requires neither sympathy nor emotions, although these do enrich one's judgments and make them more complete. In the same manner, I may respect my neighbor and treat him in a morally correct way without necessarily feeling sympathy or affection of any sort for him. Singer takes the same position with regard to our duties to persons in the Third World on the grounds that they are too far removed from us in space, lifestyles, and worldviews for us to feel more for them than a very generalized recognition of their plight and our duty toward them.

In contrast, Thomas Nagel argues convincingly not only for the possibility, but also for the necessity of respect, even in the most hostile of all human endeavors, war. If there can be such a thing as a just war (something neither Nagel nor his utilitarian opponent in the argument, R. M. Hare, takes for granted),[53] then we can retain our morality even in hostile situations, through the exercise of limited, nontorturing, and discriminate weaponry, and—even more importantly—through the conscious separation in our minds of the existence of the human being from that of the attacking soldier. In the case of the former, our respect must never falter, even in the face of our justified hostility. We must be able to see him as one single human being: "our conflict with the soldier is not with his existence as a human being."[54] In essence, even enemies require "that minimal respect which is owed to them as a human being."[55] A simple attempt to translate this doctrine into one applicable to animals and other nonhuman parts of the environment might be seen as question-begging. Nothing allows us, without argument, to assume that "minimal respect" is owed to nonhuman entities, at this point. I have argued for respect and intrinsic value in earlier chapters and will not rehash those arguments now.[56] What this argument can prove, however, without other defense, is that even in a situation in which specific, discriminate, nontorturing killing might be morally acceptable on absolutist (deontological) grounds, such killing, though the ultimate expression of hostility, can retain the element of respect.

Now how can this argument help in the reconciliation of animal ethics and holistic, biocentric environmental ethics? It shows that it is possible to admit to no sympathy for an individual, even one of the same species (another human being) and still retain respect. Thus, if the "brute fact" of nature is hostile interdependence among the species (and I know some defenders of animal rights will disagree with this to some extent), then our respect not only for individual entities, but also for the processes and laws which govern them, and according to which they interact, allows us to admit to interspecies indifference and even to the possibility of killing on occasion, provided that the same interspecific respect that animals manifest in their dealings with one another governs us as well.

My argument aims to show that it is possible to conceive of respectful interaction with *individuals*, even in conjunction with a biocentric environmental ethic. This is, after all, what the animals themselves practice, according to their place within the ecosystem, and an ethic of respect does not necessarily force vegetarianism upon us; although on ecological grounds alone vegetarianism may not be the best alternative, a severely limited consumption of meat might be preferable, as Callicott argues.[57]

The real difficulty, however, remains untouched: how can this approach help us cope with the problem of existing practices concerning domestic animals, laboratory animals, and agribusiness in general?

4. Nonhuman Entities Beyond the Wild: Can an Ethic of Respect Be Extended?

Nagel bases his *absolutism*, as he calls the deontological approach he uses in war morality, on retaining a Kantian respect for humanity even in the face of (justly?) hostile relations. Can this respect be understood in more than human terms and extended to the far reaches of a land ethic, primarily concerned with respect for wholes, not parts, and certainly not parts that have been removed from or have never been in their natural habitat? Rolston speaks of "two cultures," and this permits him to differentiate the behavior of and approaches toward individual entities in terms of where they belong. In contrast, I take the main thrust of any ecological ethic to be that it refuses to accept different sets of values, one for an isolated community of human beings and another reigning only in the wilds, because such an approach implies that whatever "rights" the animals have acquired in their wild community are lost when their descendants or mutations have "adapted" to (and have been adopted by) human communities. The inability of an anthropocentric ethic to work in both communities is one of the major sources of environmental problems. Are "two different but equal cultures" not the expression of a ghetto mentality based on the premise that we are different (and superior) and thus—ipso facto—can share neither an ethic nor ultimately an environmental community with the rest of the world? No matter how good two parallel educational systems may be, it seems to me basically wrong to decide that—for instance—children of a different class, color, or ethnic background ought to have "the best," but that we ought not to share ours, whatever it might be.

The conceptual problems engendered by this approach spur me to argue that we *can* have *one* extremely broad ethic. If it is capable of covering all other entities, I want to argue, there is no reason why it could not cover humans, as well as their mode of interaction with others of their own species. Just as an ethic of environmental respect on our part does not preclude the possibility of an animal group having and abiding by their own rules within their own community, so too, as long as no conflict arises with the larger ethic, we can also have our preferred rules, principles, and ethical doctrines to govern our own interaction, and these can be as restrictive and intraspecific as we like. In this sense, then, the question is not whether an environmental ethic can supersede or replace, say, the Kantian categorical imperative, but rather whether the latter is compatible with our wider ethical concerns.

Thus, rather than start with a "humans only" ethical perspective and then strive to broaden its basis to cover other entities, or perhaps decide to take the "different but equally good route," it seems preferable to start with an all-encompassing ethic, and agree that other, more specific (perhaps stricter) sets of ethical principles may well govern each group's interaction (including our own), *provided* that (in our case) no conflict arises with the broader principles. Rolston sharply separates human from environmental ethics:

> In an environmental ethic, what humans want to value is not compassion, charity, rights, personality, justice, fairness, or even pleasure and the pursuit of happiness. Those values belong in interhuman ethics, in culture, not nature, and to look for them here is to make a category mistake.[58]

I have tried instead to suggest broader principles which encompass both intraspecific dealings (i.e., those involving other humans) and interspecific ones (i.e., those involving other natural entities), thus allowing for the existence of both sets of principles in harmony, without any attempt at forcing one set upon another, but allowing the broader, environmental ones to be prior, all-encompassing, and binding on all. How can we apply these principles to the problem posed in this section? When speaking of domestic animals, Rolston affirms that "it is not merely the pain, but the indignity of domestication that is deplorable."[59] Yet, while he feels, as I do, that "pain is not the only value," he separates pain from affliction, because the latter can only be felt by humans who would experience this "heightened, cognitively based pain, distinct from physical pain, that humans would if bred to be eaten." Still—he claims—we have "no strong duty to deny their natural ecology, and only a weaker duty to make their life better by avoiding pointless pain."[60]

The passages cited appear to embody two principles: (a) the "indignity of domestication" and (b) the (weaker) "duty to avoid pointless pain." If these are joined, we can reach a position that does not conflict with my ethic of respect, based on the realities of the ecological norms that govern their existence. For Rolston, however, domestic animals fall in the crack—so to speak—because they are "in the peripheral rural world," neither in nature nor "in culture." He raises the question whether industrial farming introduces suffering in excess of ecological norms, but postpones the quest for possible answers.

From my standpoint, meat eating is not inadmissible, provided it does not (1) harm ecosystems (seriously), (2) introduce disrespect for nonhuman animals, or (3) cause pain in excess of "what is in wild nature."[61] Rolston supports, to some extent, (1) and (3), as we have seen. It is important, however, to distinguish the intraspecific right to life that humans have vis-à-vis other humans, but which loses force if the human wanders into a jungle and is confronted by a hungry tiger. Within that habitat it is *right* for him to be a source of food, and similarly with the rabbit that he encounters in turn if lost in the woods. So far, perhaps no great disagreement exists with Rolston. On the other hand, I strongly disagree with his position that domestic animals are "artifacts"; their connection with the wild (albeit remote), their sentience, the existence of their own projects and goals (albeit limited ones), within the enforced limitations of their environment, all combine to preclude this characterization. I do agree with Regan, however, that being responsible for some entity's life does not entail a total lack of moral responsibility toward that entity; even if we deliberately bring children into the world, this does not absolve us from the duty of respect. On the contrary,

> Voluntarily to arrange for the coming to be of farm animals is voluntarily to acquire duties to these animals one would not otherwise have, whether that was one's intention or motive for arranging for their coming to be or not.[62]

In this sense, our requirement of respect is increased in proportion to the responsibility we acquire for their coming to be. A similar case is normally made for duties to all human beings; however, we also have specific duties of responsibility owed to family and friends, such as clan members, that sometimes supersede these other more general duties. The latter become our responsibility in a sense that does apply to the rest of humankind.

I cannot reconcile in any way either generic respect or specific responsibility with the indignities, de-individualization, and disrespect implicit in agribusiness practices. Therefore, such practices fail to meet the requirements of (2) and (3) above. Further, and even more damning from the standpoint of (1), possible harm to ecosystems, the whole practice of meat eating, based on growing "meat," fails in all these respects, and therefore cannot be condoned on the basis of a joint ethic of respect. If vegetable protein is an environmental "better bet," and more might then also be available for starving humans (thus also fitting better with our intraspecific duties), then on all counts, all forms of wholesale "meat business" are immoral and should be discontinued (or phased out at least).[63] McDonald's may have to serve up soy or veggie burgers, and our whole mind-set may need to be revised. In fact, on the question of meat eating, Callicott's "three best alternatives," in order, appear to be eminently satisfactory and in line with the joint ethic of respect I suggest. These are (1) living "within the parameters of the aboriginal human ecological niche," through hunting and gathering "wild plant foods," (2) eating from one's own orchard, garden, henhouse, and so on, and (3) buying or bartering organic foods from one's neighbors and friends.[64]

What about laboratory animals? If we permit use of animals to sustain other life, as in modified "predation," limited, respectful meat eating, careful of inflicting as little pain as compatible with loss of life (to individuals belonging to other species), then the same principles ought to be implemented in the scientific use of animals. It is environmentally appropriate to attempt to save the lives of innocents in our species at the expense of individuals in other species; however, it is not appropriate to breed, use, and destroy rats carelessly for trivial experiments such as those performed by psychology freshmen.[65] Nor is it appropriate to trap for furs when artificial furs and other products do a commendable job of keeping us warm and protected (provided, of course, that the production of these artifacts does not cause irreparable or unpreventable environmental damage).

Not all uses so obviously belong in either one camp or the other, for it may not always be easy to differentiate between the life-saving and life-enhancing. Nevertheless, keeping firmly in mind the "principle of integrity" and interspecific duties which are at least harmonious with environmental realities, and not in conflict with them, it ought to be possible to decide on individual cases. It might help to repeat here Rolston's position:

> What is in nature may not always imply ought (and it may seldom do so in interhuman ethics), but *ought* in environmental ethics seldom negates what *is* in wild nature.[66]

When this position's *is* is unpacked in terms of general ecosystemic respect, taking into account hostility and limited interspecific interference (based primarily on the requirement for life sustenance), and when it is further enriched by the addition of more stringent intraspecific duties (which include duties engendered by acquired responsibility for domestic animals), then it is, at one and the same time, an "is" which can support both a holistic environmental ethic of animal respect and an ethics of purely human concern, under the umbrella of the principle of integrity.

PART C: General Considerations: Buffer Zones, Areas in "Culture," and Sustainable Agriculture

1. Introduction

This work was intended as an exploratory journey into the meaning/role/application of the concept of integrity. The question posed at the outset was, *why* is the restoration/protection of integrity a mandate of legislation and a goal of mission statements and other important documents? An answer was provided in Chapter Two in which the meaning of the concept and its value was outlined and defended. Another question followed: Even if integrity is a value and a defensible goal of public policy and legislation, is it sufficient to support not only prudential, but also moral considerations? The theoretical response to that second question was taken up in Chapters Three and Four.

But a principle as basic as the principle of integrity, and one which expresses an urgent need, must be (a) rendered operational and (b) shown to be functionally and operationally better and clearer than other "deep" or holistic positions, in order to be viable. Yet we cannot ask of it a precision incompatible with both its nature as a principle and with the imprecision of the science that supports it. What can be done instead, is to define what might be appropriate, globally, within the parameters of today's knowledge.

The first step remains the designation of different areas globally and regionally, within which different forms of integrity would be appropriate, that is, I_a and I_b. The second step entails a consideration of the possible reach of the principle in interhuman ethics and in the designation of social goals. Without commanding a specific ideology or interhuman moral doctrine, PI was shown to be compatible with noncontractarian and nonutilitarian approaches in morality, and with any approach to social issues and public policy within which it could retain its primacy. Hence the principle would impose limits not only on individual rights and freedoms, but also on those of groups and nations. The next step entailed a dialogue with moral doctrine beyond our species. Many of the arguments of animal ethicists are clearly individualistic, because they are based on (individual) feelings or (individual) rights, hence they need to be reexamined in the light of PI. The proposed "reconciliation" of the previous section may not appeal to animal ethicists any more than other (human) consequences appeal to defenders of ideologies intended as defense of dominated or oppressed individuals or aggregates. Nevertheless, the urgency of the task before us was recently indicated by Henry Kendall, representing the Union of Concerned Scientists, who suggested a maximum of ten years' lead-time to turn around the present ecological crisis.[67] The "Warning to Humanity" issued by the same group, also lists as their number-one priority, under the heading of "What We Must Do," the following: "We must bring environmentally damaging activities under control *to restore and protect the integrity* of the earth's systems we depend on" (my emphasis). This mandate continues with some examples of what we must do but does not attempt any definition of "integrity." The same document adds, "A new ethic is required, a new attitude toward discharging our responsibility for caring for ourselves and for the earth."

This work has suggested another way of formulating this "new ethic" and of making its primary recommendation (that is, the restoration and protection of the integrity of the earth) operational. As we noted, in order to achieve operationality, we need to understand what is meant by "integrity," but that is not sufficient. It is also necessary to specify the *scale* of integrity that is required globally, to meet the Concerned Scientists' criteria. Their own work speaks of the earth, as a whole. In that case, it is probably implicitly understood that integrity encompasses both I_a and I_b, in our sense, and that even the areas that are entirely under the sway of "culture" and that are "artifacts," rather than retaining a "natural" component, will also need to operate in a way that does not conflict with I_a and I_b.

2. Buffer Zones and Areas in "Culture"

The scale of all three areas and their relative proportions are vitally important, but unfortunately that is precisely where scientific support fails us, because no global or even national studies exist that can be used for guidance. Perhaps a "case" taken from the business world might be the best indication of the correct way to proceed and therefore of the practical value of the principle of integrity as it stands, even without the precise scientific data we would prefer.

The "case" appears in the "Business Section" of Canada's *Globe and Mail* newspaper, March 1, 1993, under the heading "Brazil's joke is thriving." Although there is no scientific confirmation of the data provided, let us assume, for the sake of argument, that the facts are exactly as they are provided. Jari, the corporation involved in the "case," is probably the world's largest forestry project. Conceived in 1967 and intended to supply a perceived market need for pulp and paper, the project lasted through twenty-five years of false starts and failures and expenses totaling $1 billion before it finally started showing a profit. Originally the brain child of billionaire Daniel Ludwig, the project was taken over by a consortium of twenty-three Brazilian companies in 1982 for $300 million, after a financial crisis in the Ludwig empire, which forced the sale. Project president Eduardo Barreto could finally say, in 1992, "we were as competitive as the best world pulp operation." At the same time, he added, "we are protecting biodiversity and proving that it is possible to create an environmentally friendly and economically sound business enterprise in the Amazon Rainforest." The most important point is that, eventually, their guideline was that "the prevailing forces are Mother Nature and the market," where the former runs a clear first. The eventual achievements came after many attempts at exploitation, involving unsustainable practices and non-native species introduction.

What is even more noteworthy is that *now* the "exploited" areas account "for less than 10% of the company-owned land. . . ." This in turn indicates that the adoption of the principle of integrity at the outset would have saved an enormous amount of time and resources, the latter probably beyond recall. What was "discovered" in the end is precisely what should have been mandated at the start. PI would have recommended first of all that the meaning of "integrity" for *that* ecosystem and that area should have been understood through all the conditions for its presence (see Chapter Two).

Second, studies should have been required at the outset, to specify (a) the necessary size of the "integrity zone," to include both I_1 and I_2 (or I_a); (b) the size required for the buffer zone (I_b), or area where respectful, careful, low-input agroforestry could be practiced; and (c) the maximum area that could be used for housing, medical, teaching, commercial facilities, and the like. Because the "trial and error" method was adopted in place of the principle of integrity, both economic and biodiversity losses were generated. What is even more noteworthy is that, in stark contrast with our efforts to date, to establish the "minimum safe" area to be kept free of human interference and as "wild" as possible, the right approach is the opposite one.

The correct question to ask ourselves is, "How much urban culture is the minimum we can live with and, at the same time, the maximum the Earth can tolerate?" It is only when the answer to this question had been found, and only then, that sustainability and an integrated, harmonious system was in place in Brazil.

Once humankind understands itself as one of the species constituting the Earth's biota, the *first* question to be asked is the one that can be answered, at least in principle, according to PI and of I_a and I_b in relation to it. Another example can be used to show PI's reach, taken from the application of the Clean Water Act (1972), which was our original starting point for the concept of "integrity." Perhaps it is no coincidence that the closest effort to look at buffer zones in some detail is to be found in the EPA's regulations concerning wetlands.

A recent paper by Robert Pierce discusses wetland regulations and proposes the division of areas into "three basic categories of lands" without however specifying percentages of scale relative to different landscapes. These are:

1. Areas that should be preserved for future generations;
2. Areas which are suitable for some activities but not others and need to be regulated carefully; and
3. Areas which generally are suitable for consumptive use with only minimal regulation when best management practices are implemented.[68]

Category 3 in this list is clearly ambiguous, and its intent is different from the one defended here, according to PI, there is *no* area which is "suitable" for consumptive use with only minimal regulation," because the requirements of harmony and compatibility with I_a and I_b persist everywhere on Earth. Nevertheless, at least categories 1 and 2 demonstrate a clear awareness of the sort of problems and issues this work has addressed.

Pierce's work also show the pitfalls of setting forth legislation and guidelines that are left undefined and that take into consideration only *one* aspect of the problem (e.g., just "wetlands"), and only a specific area. After describing the waste of time, money, effort, and litigation which followed upon George Bush's "Budget Message" (February 2, 1989), when he said, "I believe this should be our national goal, no net loss of wetlands . . ." followed by the EPA Federal Manual (1989) aimed at that goal, Pierce says:

> The years of arguments, criticisms and frustrations could have been avoided had we as a society recognized that no program, no matter how good, which concentrates on one element of the natural systems can ever satisfy all interests.[69]

He contrasts this approach with the *holistic* one he favors in land use planning. That approach, he believes, should even transcend "state boundaries." Examples could be multiplied, but the main point has been made clear: both sustainable, nonhazardous human activity and the environment itself benefit more from the application of PI than of other moral doctrines. Other "deep ecology" positions are too vague, although their goals are not too different from ours. Ecofeminism provides a powerful explanation of the roots of environmental exploitation and degradation, but if asked to provide clear guidelines and priorities, its main thrust to individual and social rights disqualifies it from attaining a fully holistic position granting primacy to the Earth. Other positions that attempt to extend purely human moral doctrines do not fare as well, because if their first concern remains with human rights and/or happiness (especially when the latter is understood as the satisfaction of preferences), then it is very hard to factor in environmental imperatives. Certain levels of education, understanding of the issues, and the availability of choices should be present before "preferences" and democratic votes might reflect truly sustainable options and the commitment to long-term "goods."

The principle of integrity supports the primacy of environmental issues but will still continue to make high demands on science, legislation, and governments for global issues, and to require much thought and care for decisions concerning detailed, smaller issues. It will also demand continued interaction with science, in order to ensure that possible revisions of the concept and definition of integrity are kept current, particularly in regard to scale, area percentages, and so on; that will remain an ongoing project because the lack of detailed research indicates that the last word has not been said. Moreover, as the definition is used by scientists and professionals in real projects, problems may come to light that go beyond the present discussion.

There is a final issue that should be briefly addressed, and that is the question of world hunger, thus of agricultural sustainability. The previous example taken from forestry deals with that problem and suggests answers. Still, there are further questions involved in present-day agricultural practices that need to be addressed too, in addition to what has been said. These will be discussed in the next (and last) section of this chapter.

3. Global Ecology and Sustainable Agriculture

The problem of world hunger can perhaps be used as the best "case" to demonstrate the unique usefulness of the principle of integrity. In fact, the somewhat clearer and more established goal of "sustainable development" helps to clarify the reach and meaning of the goal of integrity in the global sense.

Now the former is a morally defensible goal only in the *global* context, that is, only when related to less developed countries. There it means, in essence, an attempt to develop an area where the terror of disease and famine is no longer the constant companion of those who live there. It is desirable development since the goal is the satisfaction of *needs* not, as it would be in the case of industrialized Western countries, development in order to continue to sustain uncritically accepted "preferences" well beyond needs and often even comfort. As far as the latter is concerned, the goal of "restoring integrity" and the quest for a changed "mind-set" stems from the recognition that the present rate of consumption and the lifestyle of Western industrialized countries are neither sustainable in themselves, nor just, in the face of the squalor and hunger prevalent in less developed countries, which do not receive their fair share of the benefits and resources available.

International agencies concerned with sustainable development are intent upon fostering policies and practices that will feed the world's starving people on a continuing basis, globally. They are also concerned with altering the present mind-set that dictates practices, policies, and regulations that are divisive, and economics with a profit orientation that is limited in scope as well as geographically. *Food 2000* (Report of the World Commission on Environment Development) states categorically:

> A reorientation of agricultural research and development strategies so as to promote a steady improvement in the productivity, stability and profitability and sustainability of major farming systems is necessary.[70]

Their primary concern is with human suffering and hunger, not with instilling respect for nonhuman entities. Yet, even if "this new analysis starts with the poor," and if it is a given that "their well-being is a moral imperative," still environmental concern is driven to the forefront by the recognition that the two goals are not in conflict, in fact, they are "mutually supporting" and, "the integrating concept . . . is sustainable livelihood security."

Thus, even starting from an explicitly anthropocentric position, that of concern for the hunger of the poor, the compatibility and interdependence of sustainable agriculture and ecological integrity are recognized. Unfortunately, even openly admitting their inescapable connection is not sufficient to bring about the results clearly desired, by all sectors, with the possible exception of some purely commercial enterprises,

> The effort needed to increase production in pace with an unprecedented increase in demand, while retaining the essential ecological integrity of food systems, is colossal both in magnitude and complexity. Given the obstacles to be overcome, most of them man-made, it can fail more easily than it can succeed.[71]

A footnote following the discussion culminating in the passage just cited, adds, "ecological integrity refers to the imperatives to conform to principles of sustainable development." Now "integrity," as emerging from our discussion, is at least that, but it also carries connotations which far exceed this narrow definition. "Integrity" denotes both an ideal and a practical goal. The ideal remains the point of reference, the standard our actions aspire to, while we admit, at the practical level, that it is unattainable as such over the whole Earth, as our discussion of I_a and I_b indicates.

Hence a true understanding of ecosystem integrity is absolutely necessary before the task of defining sustainability can even be approached.

Agricultural examples abound. Studies concerning chemically based agriculture show the dangers of reliance on short-term "solutions." There is a wealth of literature pointing out the *human* risks and dangers of chemical products from "cradle to grave," so to speak, that is, in their manufacture, distribution, use, and eventual disposal, as well as through possible ingestion by humans (e.g., fruits and vegetables), and other grave problems exist as well.[72]

The manufacturing of these products is unsafe, as Elaine Draper, for instance, amply proves in *Risky Business*.[73] It is so fraught with perils that in order to avoid the increasing financial burden of precautionary measures and workers' compensation and litigation, the chemical industry has been introducing programs to impose genetic testing on its employees, in order to attempt to "blame" faulty genetic makeup of individuals (and sometimes of whole ethnic groups), for "susceptibility" to chemicals, rather than accept the blame for hazardous conditions in the workplace.

When the product is marketed and put to use, as a pesticide or fertilizer in agriculture, the problems multiply. Agricultural laborers often have no understanding of the hazards they are exposed to as they spray pesticides or even mix the products. Such recent works as Angus Lindsay Wright's *The Death of Ramon Gonzales* point to the disastrous results of North American so-called "developed" countries' greed and disrespect for Third World persons, whose own poverty and helplessness conspire to turn them into easy victims.

Further, south of the U.S. border, it is not only the *campesinos* who have work (a doubtful benefit, given the extreme hazards accompanying their activity), but also those who are not so "lucky," whose life is severely affected by "agribusiness." The requirement for blemish-free fruit and vegetables requires capital outlays well beyond the capacity of small independent farmers in less developed countries. In a recent trip to Brazil, for instance, in the city of São Paulo, I was dismayed to see whole families with small children lying and sitting on the sidewalks around public buildings, trying to keep dry in the rain, and trying to cook and heat themselves with a small open fire. Older children were begging, stealing, and depending on prostitution in order to contribute to the family's support.

When I inquired about the reasons for such horrors, I was told they were *nordestinos*, displaced farmers. Without training or education other than their traditional farming, there were no ways of absorbing them into an already strained economy. The government, I was told, could only hire so many street cleaners and other unskilled laborers. In an attempt to alleviate a small fraction of their problems, they were studying a way of funding free hot lunches for children who could then be coaxed away from the streets and back into schools.

Cosmetic preferences and exorbitant production requirements, in essence, forced those who could not compete to lose their livelihood. The recent introduction of costly biotechnologies only exacerbates the problem. Nor are these simply necessary casualties in the quest for a "better way" of feeding the world's hungry. The hazardous pesticides and improperly tested and largely untried transgenics (the latter, at least not sufficiently tested in the fields, outside controlled conditions), impose known and unknown risks to those who consume these products, most of which are altered in various ways for *marketing* improvements, not for nutritional or health reasons.[74]

The follow-up book to the *Limits of Growth* came out in 1992, entitled *Beyond the Limits*.[75] Through computer modeling prepared in the Netherlands (RIVM Institute, Bilthoven), and largely through the work of Dr. Bert de Vries, the volume shows clearly how multiple stresses on ecosystems might cause collapse, although each separate stress might have been "handled" in some fashion by the affected ecosystem. Global stresses, if they continue unchecked, might cause global collapse, and this problem must be faced directly, so that saner options might be sought, while there might be still time to respond and correct specific problems.

Pesticides protect economic interests and may seem to ease hunger in the short term. But as they eliminate unwanted species, they also eliminate countless other species which are necessary to preserve ecosystem health and sustainability in agriculture. David Pimentel says,

> Furthermore, both high agricultural productivity and human health depend on the activity of a diverse natural biota composed of an estimated 10 million (range 2–80 million) species of plants and animals that inhabit the world.[76]

He adds,

> As many as 1 million species of plants and animals will be exterminated worldwide during the next 50-year period. This high rate of extinction is alarming because these organisms may be vital to the functioning of ecological systems that sustain our planet.[77]

In essence, we have no idea just how vast is the damage we inflict when we interfere with the natural functioning of an ecosystem for the purpose of exploitation. We *do* know that soil erosion, desertification, decreasing productivity, lack of nutrients in the agricultural products, and the need for higher and higher pesticide applications to counteract more and more resistant species of pests are part and parcel of these intensive, petrochemically based agricultural practices.[78]

A country with almost no naturally evolving ecosystems (or "integrity") left because of its small size and the intensive agricultural and animal husbandry practices commonly used there, the Netherlands, has enacted draconian laws to reverse the trend, by cutting pesticide use in half already (this represents a Canadian goal as well), and by giving its ministries veto powers over projects which are not ecologically defensible. If a people as tolerant and freedom-loving as the Dutch see the urgent need for such a step, perhaps it is time that all of us start to rethink our priorities. Not only wasteful lifestyles and choices, but also insistence on too many individual rights, without either consideration or respect for our commonality as human animals in an acutely stressed biosphere *must* be rethought.

The forestry example in the previous section showed how the adoption of the principle of integrity goes well beyond other common sense or "business" approaches and would serve to achieve the goal of sustainability while preserving integrity at the same time. The additional problems introduced by biotechnologies and transgenics in agriculture are even harder to address without an all-encompassing principle such as PI. The latter permits us to bring into the argument, for instance, small invertebrates and all small creatures that otherwise slip "through the cracks" of animal ethics perspectives.

As integral parts and members of ecosystems without which, as we indicated, agricultural sustainability is not possible, they now regain importance, respect and moral considerability from the holistic position that PI supports, in a way they could never achieve from even the most sincere and concerned animal ethicist. I am not claiming that aphids, worms, or dung beetles should be accorded respect *equal* to all other forms of life, including humankind, indiscriminately. But the principle of integrity makes respect for the whole, *and all within it*, primary. It is within that primacy that all natural entities gain considerability, at least prima facie, although the acknowledged necessity for areas such as agricultural or forestry zones (I_b) provides less stringent criteria than I_a zones. Only PI restores prima facie moral considerability without speciesism, whereas animal ethicists limit their concern to mammals, birds, or, at most, fish communities and individuals. This is easily proven: most of Regan's and Singer's arguments, for instance, remain speciesist. For them some species are morally considerable, most are not, (and are not even mentioned in their writings).

One may object that both Taylor and Schweitzer admit the moral considerability of all life, as was shown in Chapter Three; but their morality could not be lived, because no second-order principles were provided beyond the all-encompassing ones, which could not be adopted without self-contradiction. It is perhaps ironic that a "fascist," holistic approach can be used finally to readmit *all* biota to moral considerability. As far as sustainability is concerned, it is precisely this "readmission" that is a vital cornerstone to the rebuilding of that goal. When, as Wes Jackson, for instance, puts it, no one "listens to the land," or as it has been claimed here, no one understands the meaning, scope, and role of ecosystem integrity, and is prepared to adopt the imperatives that follow upon the acceptance of the principle, then sustainability in agriculture and with it the elimination of world hunger will remain a mirage, rather than a goal.

In regard to the environment, we are not billionaires like Daniel Ludwig (in the Jari case described in the previous section), and the Earth's resources are not inexhaustible. Moreover, we do not have another twenty-five years to continue our present try-and-fail methods. We have done our "worst," often without evil intent, simply through ignorance and carelessness. At this time, no matter how hard and demanding it might be for some extended period, we *must* now attempt to do our "best" instead, hoping, without any assurances, that it might be enough.

Notes

1. L. Westra, "A Transgenic Dinner? Ethical and Social Issues in Biotechnology and Agriculture," *The Journal of Social Philosophy* 24 (no. 3, Winter 1993): 215–32; c.f. Noss, op. cit., Ch. 5, fn. 58.

2. Monte Hummel, *Endangered Spaces* (Toronto: Key Porter Books, 1989), 36–45.

3. For Ontario, the information comes from personal communication: Dr. Henry Regier, Director, Institute for Environmental Studies; for Costa Rica, I am indebted to Dr. Tom Lacher, Humboldt Agricultural Institute, Clemson University, Clemson, S.C.; see also Monte Hummel, *Endangered Spaces* (Toronto: Key Porter Books, 1989), 36-45.

4. F. H. Allen and T. W. Hoekstra, *Toward a Unified Ecology* (New York: Columbia University Press, 1992), 238–55. Discusses in detail the "Biome and Biosphere Criteria."

5. David Pimentel, personal communication, spring 1993; the information arises from a manuscript and research presently being compiled.

6. D. VandeVeer argues in this manner in his article on "Interspecific Justice" in *People, Penguins, and Plastic Trees*, 51–66, in his introduction to the problem of animal ethics and in his proposed solution to the difficulties engendered by Tom Regan's and Peter Singer's treatment. Similar discussions of the inclusion of increasing ranges of "right-bearers" can be found in R. Nash, *The Rights of Nature* (Madison: University of Wisconsin Press, 1989), especially 4–8. Mary Midgley, "Duties Concerning Islands," in *People, Penguins, and Plastic Trees,* 156–64.

7. L. Westra, et al., "Agricultural Practices, 60–77.

8. Charles Beitz, *Political Theory and International Relations* (Princeton, N.J.: Princeton University Press, 1979), 104.

9. Ibid., 106: cp. W. Ivor Jennings, *The Approach to Self-Government* (Cambridge, U.K.: Cambridge University Press, 1956), 56.

10. L. Westra, "Normative Statement," as part of the recommendations to the Working Conference on "Toxic Chemicals in the Great Lakes Basin Ecosystem," Great Lakes Institute, State University of New York—Buffalo, 1989.

11. World Commission on Environment Development, *Food 2000, Global Policies for Sustainable Agriculture* (London: Zed Books, 1987).

12. Eugene C. Hargrove, *Foundations of Environmental Ethics* (Englewood Cliffs, N.J.: Prentice-Hall, 1989), 206.

13. Ibid., 207.

14. Ibid., 208.

15. Ibid., 209.

16. Ibid.

17. K. Shrader-Frechette, *Nuclear Power and Public Policy* (Dordrecht, The Netherlands: D. Reidel, 1982).

18. Ibid., 154–49.

19. Beitz, 55; cp. Hans J. Morgenthau, *Politics Among Nations,* 5th ed. (New York: Alfred A. Knopf, 1973), 10.

20. Beitz, 55.

21. Ibid., 71; cp. Hugo Grotius, *De jure belli ac paces libri tres* (1625), II, XXV, sec. vi, p. 582.

22. Beitz, 73.

23. Ibid., 78.

24. Ibid., 79.

25. Ibid., 81.

26. S. I. Benn and R. S. Peters, *The Principles of Political Thought* (New York: Free Press, 1959), 431.

27. Ibid., 430.

28. Ibid., 438.

29. Beitz, 87; cp. Wolfgang Friedmann, "Intervention, Civil War and the Role of International Law," in Richard A. Falk, ed., *The Vietnam War and International Law*, vol. 1 (Princeton, N.J.: Princeton University Press, 1968), 158.

30. The term "ecosabotage" is here used as "deliberate interference with the environment, harming life-support systems" rather than in the sense the term has acquired in recent literature. For instance, M. Martin in "Ecosabotage and Civil Disobedience," *EE* 12, no. 4 (Winter 1990): 291—310. Martin uses the term to indicate environmentalists' acts of civil disobedience, monkey wrenching and such, performed with the protection of the environment in mind.

31. Beitz, 140–41; cp. J. Rawls, *A Theory of Justice*, 284–93.

32. Beitz, 143.

33. Ibid.

34. Ibid., 145.

35. Ibid., 147; cp. K. J. Holsti, "A New International Politics?," *International Organization* 32, no. 2 (Spring 1978): 523–30.

36. Kai Nielsen, "Global Justice, Capitalism and the Third World," *Journal of Applied Philosophy* 1, no. 2 (1984). Reprinted in *Justice and Economic Distribution*, 2nd ed., J. Arthur and W. Shaw, eds. (Englewood Cliffs, N.J.: Prentice-Hall, 1991).

37. Nielsen, 239.

38. *Earthkeeping, A Quarterly on Faith and Agriculture*, published by the Christian Farmers Federation of Ontario, normally takes this position. Both readers and contributors are of either Mennonite or Dutch Reformed Christian background. For instance, vol. 6, no. 3, March 1991 devotes the whole issue to the topic of "Caring for Creation: Is Stewardship Enough?" Their Summer 1991 issue comprises a central "take-out" section on biblical quotations and discussions in regard to the "Earth," including suggestions for church services.

39. In fact, Nielsen also suggests that Africa's food production would somehow magically improve under a new ideology. This does not take into consideration ecological problems such as chemical "addiction," fostered by well-meaning more developed countries, in both the East and West; also problems of desertification and soil erosion connected with poor agricultural practices and many other factors.

40. Shrader-Frechette, *Nuclear Power and Public Policy*, 49–72.

41. Shrader-Frechette, *Risk and Rationality*, especially Chapters 2, 3, and 4.

42. Beitz, 176; a shorter version of my argument in the last two sections has appeared in *Environmental Values* 2, no. 2 (Summer 1993): 125–36.

43. Taylor, *Respect for Nature*, 286. A longer version of the argument presented in this chapter has appeared in *Environmental Ethics*, as L. Westra, "Ecology and Animals: Is There a Joint Ethic of Respect?" 11 (1989): 215–30.

44. Callicott, "Animal Liberation and Environmental Ethics," 165–66. John A. Fischer also argues for sympathy as an appropriate tool for animal ethics in "Taking Sympathy Seriously," *Environmental Ethics* 9(1987): 197–215. The problem with his interesting proposal is—to my mind—twofold. First, it is *necessarily* anthropocentric because the sympathy it is based upon seeks out admirable humanlike qualities in animals and then allows these preferred specimens to color our consideration of the ecosystem as well. Second, it is entirely dependent, even for whole ecosystems, on our knowledge/perception of qualities/properties we might find admirable. Both aspects of this grounding of sympathy are therefore open to the objections Peter Singer, for instance, raises, as well as those I cite throughout this chapter.

45. Callicott, "Animal Liberation and Environmental Ethics," 165.

46. Rolston, *Environmental Ethics*, 79.

47. Aldo Leopold, "The Land Ethic," 238.

48. J. Baird Callicott, "Animal Liberation: A Triangular Affair," *Environmental Ethics* 2 (1980): 333.

49. Rolston, *Environmental Ethics*, 79.

50. Philip Wheelwright, ed., *The Presocratics* (New York: Odyssey Press, 1966), 71 (DK80).

51. Rolston, *Environmental Ethics*, 103.

52. Ibid., 126.

53. Thomas Nagel, "War and Massacre," in eds., H. Cohen, T. Nagel, and T. Scanlon, *War and Moral Responsibility* (Princeton, N.J.: Princeton University Press, 1974), 3–24: R. M. Hare, "Rules of War and Moral Reasoning," 46–61.

54. Nagel, "War and Massacre," 21.

55. Ibid., 19.

56. I have argued for intrinsic value in "Shrader-Frechette, Risk Assessment, and the 'Is-Ought Fallacy,'" *Agrarian*, Clemson University, 1987; for the value of "integrity" in Chapter Two, and for the "principle" based on "integrity", and *commanding* respect, in Chapter Three.

57. Callicott, "Animal Liberation: A Triangular Affair," p. 335. He notes that the shift to vegetarianism "represents an increase in the efficiency of the conversion of solar energy from plant to human biomass, and thus, by bypassing animal intermediates, increases food resources for human beings." He sees this possibility as a mixed blessing at best, as it would permit increases in numbers of humans whose "life requirements" would further tax other natural resources.

58. Rolston, *Environmental Ethics*, 225.

59. Ibid., 73.

60. Ibid., 80.

61. Ibid., 79.

62. Tom Regan, *The Case for Animal Rights* (Berkeley: University of California Press, 1983), 342-43.

63. Callicott, "Animal Liberation: A Triangular Affair," 335.

64. Ibid., 336.

65. I am indebted to my husband, Peter Westra, for this example.

66. Rolston, *Environmental Ethics*, 79.

67. Henry Kendall, MIT physicist, spoke at the American Association for the Advancement of Science (AAAS) meeting in Boston, Mass., February 15, 1993, representing the Union of Concerned Scientists, and reemphasizing their urgent message.

68. R. J. Pierce, "Wetland Delineation: Science and Politics Collide with Private Property Rights," paper presented at the annual AAAS meeting, Boston, Mass., February 14, 1993; cp. Reed F. Noss and David L. Cooperrider, *Healing Turtle Island: A National Strategy for Biodiversity* (Washington, D.C.: Island Press, forthcoming 1994)

69. Ibid.

70. *Food 2000,* 1987, op. cit.

71. Ibid.

72. L. Westra, "Corporate Responsibility and Hazardous Products," forthcoming in *Business Ethics Quarterly*, as review article on E. Draper's *Risky Business* (Cambridge: Cambridge University Press, 1991).

73. Ibid.

74. Westra, "A Transgenic Dinner?"

75. D. Meadows, et al., *Beyond the Limits.*

76. D. Pimentel, et al., "Conserving Biological Diversity in Agricultural/ Forestry Systems," in *Bioscience* 42 no. 5 (1992): 354–62; cp. E. O. Wilson, 1988.

77. Pimentel, ibid; cp. D. Pimentel, et al., "The Relationship between 'Cosmetic Standards' for Food and Pesticide Use," in D. Pimentel and H. Lehman, eds. *The Pesticide Question: Environment Economics and Ethics* (New York: Chapman and Hall, 1993), 85–105.

78. D. Pimental, et al., "Assessment of Environmental and Economic Impacts of Pesticide Use," in D. Pimental, et al., eds., *The Pesticide Question*, 47–84; cp. Meadows et al., *Beyond the Limits.* In regard to agriculture and "buffer zones," cp. also J. L. Fail, et al., "Riparian Forest Communities and Their Role in Nutrient Conservation in an Agricultural Watershed," *American Journal of Alternative Agriculture* 2 no. 3 (1987): 114–21; "Economic Impact of Proposed Oregon Forest Practices Rules on Industrial Forest Lands in the Oregon Coast Range: A Case Study," Oregon State University Forest Research Laboratory, *Research Bulletin* 61 (1987); N. J. Payne, et al., "Estimating Buffer Zone Widths for Pesticide Applications," *Canadian Forestry Service Forestry Pest Management Institute*; *Pesticide Science* 24 no. 2(1988): 147–61. See also additional references in Chapter Five, fn. 58.

Index

Agazzi, Evandro, 116
Agriculture (agribusiness), 161, 165, 171, 185, 186, 192, 201, 202, 215, 217, 219–26, 228
Aiken, William, 125, 126, 132, 133, 146, 147
Allen, F. H., 225
Animals, nonhuman, 10, 31, 81–86, 89, 93–95, 97, 98, 101, 107, 121, 129, 131, 132, 143, 186, 189, 202, 204, 205–15, 223, 224
Anthropocentrism and nonanthropocentricism, xvii, 5, 6, 14, 62–64, 69, 82, 88, 111, 135, 144, 211
Aquinas, Thomas, 61, 159
Aristotle, xix, 45–48, 53, 60, 61, 69, 91, 99, 109, 110, 114, 116, 119, 121, 128, 134–42, 147
Attig, Thomas, 180
Ayer, A.J., 101

Baier, Annette, 182
Bambrough, Renford, 160, 181
Bartolommei, Sergio, 127, 147
Behe, Bridget, 182, 225
Being, 8, 9, 61–63, 82, 86, 87, 97, 134, 207, 210
Beitz, Charles, 198–200, 205, 225, 226
Benjamin, Martin, 155, 156, 159, 172, 173, 180, 181
Benn, S.I., 199, 226
Biocentrism, 54, 80–85, 101, 105, 121, 123, 174, 211; biocentric holism, 91, 123–34, 137, 138, 141, 153, 174
Biodiversity, 5, 25, 39, 70, 182, 188, 217
Biological, 35, 51, 54, 66, 127, 154, 156–59, 170, 172, 176, 177, 182, 186, 187, 203, 224
Biome, 38
Biosphere, 95
Biotechnology. *See* Transgenics
Bowen, Kira, xx, 182, 225
Boyer, Barry, 32–34, 73
Bramwell, Anna, 175, 182
Breslow, Lester, 72
Brittain, Jere A., xx
Brown, Donald, 118
Brown-Weiss, Edith, 13, 19
Buber, Martin, 128
Burns, Noel M., 77

Caldwell, Lynton K., 31, 33, 73
Callicott, J. Baird, 8, 14, 18, 19, 35, 40, 73, 80, 86, 88, 89, 116–18, 124–26, 131, 146, 147, 189, 205–8, 214, 227
Cancer environmental morbidity, 23, 26, 143, 145
Caring, 12, 14, 169
Categorical imperative, 11, 91, 94, 95, 97, 102, 124, 155, 176, 190, 200, 203, 205, 212, 220
Charter of Rights and Freedoms (Canada), 191

About the Author

Laura Westra received her Ph.D. in philosophy from the University of Toronto in 1983. She is associate professor of philosophy at the University of Windsor, where she teaches ancient philosophy, environmental philosophy, bioethics, and business ethics. She is the author of *Freedom in Plotinus* and many articles on environmental ethics.

Dr. Westra is secretary of the International Society for Environmental Ethics, and has served as a consultant to the Canadian Consulate General to prepare an *Environment Services Resource Guide*. She is the recipient of a Social Sciences and Humanities Research Council of Canada Thematic Grant for 1993–1995 which will allow her to continue work on the "Integrity Project."